Andreas Wombacher

Decentralized Establishment of Consistent, Multilateral Collaborations

Andreas Wombacher

Decentralized Establishment of Consistent, Multilateral Collaborations

A formal model and its application in the Web Service domain

Südwestdeutscher Verlag für Hochschulschriften

Impressum/Imprint (nur für Deutschland/ only for Germany)
Bibliografische Information der Deutschen Nationalbibliothek: Die Deutsche Nationalbibliothek verzeichnet diese Publikation in der Deutschen Nationalbibliografie; detaillierte bibliografische Daten sind im Internet über http://dnb.d-nb.de abrufbar.

Verlag: Südwestdeutscher Verlag für Hochschulschriften Aktiengesellschaft & Co. KG
Dudweiler Landstr. 99, 66123 Saarbrücken, Deutschland
Telefon +49 681 37 20 271-1, Telefax +49 681 37 20 271-0, Email: info@svh-verlag.de
Zugl.: Darmstadt, Technical University, Diss, 2006

Herstellung in Deutschland:
Schaltungsdienst Lange o.H.G., Berlin
Books on Demand GmbH, Norderstedt
Reha GmbH, Saarbrücken
Amazon Distribution GmbH, Leipzig
ISBN: 978-3-8381-0056-2

Imprint (only for USA, GB)
Bibliographic information published by the Deutsche Nationalbibliothek: The Deutsche Nationalbibliothek lists this publication in the Deutsche Nationalbibliografie; detailed bibliographic data are available in the Internet at http://dnb.d-nb.de.

Publisher:
Südwestdeutscher Verlag für Hochschulschriften Aktiengesellschaft & Co. KG
Dudweiler Landstr. 99, 66123 Saarbrücken, Germany
Phone +49 681 37 20 271-1, Fax +49 681 37 20 271-0, Email: info@svh-verlag.de

Printed in the U.S.A.
Printed in the U.K. by (see last page)
ISBN: 978-3-8381-0056-2

Abstract

Multi-lateral collaborations are based on the interaction of several parties. In particular, each party contributes different tasks to the execution of the collaboration. The coordination of these different tasks, that is, the handling of the dependencies between the different tasks, is known as a workflow. When this coordination ensures a successful interaction between the different parties the workflow is called consistent, guaranteeing deadlock-freeness. Currently, a multi-lateral collaboration is set up by people meeting and discussing the collaboration, specifying the workflow (also called the global workflow) and checking its consistency. Afterwards the global workflow is split into parts (also called local workflows) performed by the individual parties. Following this top-down approach, the combination of the local workflow guarantees consistency of the global workflow. Applying a bottom up approach, that is, deriving global properties from local ones is known to be hard in distributed systems. Thus, the issue is to provide an approach which can determine global consistency based on local consistency decisions.

Recent technologies such as Service Oriented Architecture (SOA) support decentralized and loosely coupled applications. In particular, parties make the provided functionality available as a service, which is maintained and controlled completely independent of a centralized coordinator. Further, the loose coupling supports the late binding of services, that is, a service requestor may decide at run-time which service provider to use for that particular collaboration. As a consequence of these decentralized decisions and the lack of a centralized coordinator, the top-down approach is not applicable to SOA, but requires a bottom up approach.

Deciding consistency of a global workflow in a decentralized way requires additional local information which is provided by the method proposed in this thesis. In particular, information on parameter constraints and execution sequences between local workflows has to be exchanged and propagated through the collaboration to gather sufficient information. It is shown that this propagated information suffices to determine global workflow consistency in a decentralized way. Further, Web Services are used as a concrete technology supporting the SOA paradigm and the theoretical results are applied to this technology as a proof of concept to illustrate the applicability of the approach presented.

The approach can be applied to synchronous or asynchronous communication models. While there already exist approaches for asynchronous communication models, there are none available for the synchronous case. Therefore, a formal model for synchronous communication is introduced which is called annotated Finite State Automata. This model extends standard Finite State Automata by annotating states with logical expressions to differentiate between mandatory and optional automata transitions. An optional transition can be illustrated by a party providing the option to receive one of two messages, where the interacting party may use one of the options. Optional transitions represent standard automata semantics. However, a mandatory transition can be illustrated by a party sending either one of two messages, where the receiving party is required to support both options, because supporting only a single option results in a deadlock if the sender selects the other option. This formal model is introduced and discussed in detail for bilateral and multi-lateral collaborations. In particular, the propagation of parameter constraints and execution sequences are defined based on this model and the construction of the corresponding global workflow is introduced.

For the asynchronous communication model, Workflow Nets are used as a formal model based on an existing approach to constructing the corresponding global workflow. However, since the computational complexity of Workflow Nets prevents satisfactory application of the propagation definitions, the execution sequences of the Workflow Nets involved are represented as annotated Finite State Automata and thus allow handling of the synchronous and asynchronous communication model based on a single formal model, that is, annotated Finite State Automata.

Based on the common formal model, it can be shown that the propagation of parameter constraints and execution sequence constraints result in a fixed point, where further propagation will not change the local workflow any further. Based on this fixed point, it can be shown that if all parties decide locally that the workflow is consistent then the global workflow is also consistent. Therefore, the final consistency decision is based on the consensus of the parties' local consistency decisions.

The approach is implemented within the Web Services framework. In particular, a partial mapping of the Web Service process specification language (Business Process Execution Language for Web Services (BPEL)) to annotated Finite State Automata is provided. Based on this mapping an extension of standard service discovery, considering process descriptions in terms of BPEL, is implemented. Further, the relevant operations for annotated Finite State Automata are implemented. Finally, in order to be able to apply the approach presented, a decentralized collaboration establishment approach is introduced.

Contents

Chapter 1

Introduction

A multi-lateral collaboration is the act of several parties working jointly [Wor04]. Several forms of collaboration exist covering almost all areas of people's life like for example at work, where people are employed by a company involved in creating a product. In this example, the employees have the same goal of producing something. However, there exist collaborations where each party has its own goal that can only be achieved by interacting with other people, for example, people going shopping to a market or companies developing joint ventures.

These two generic types of collaborations also exist in Information Technology. The execution of such a collaboration usually involves several parties, each contributing different tasks. That is, a task is a "logical unit of work that is carried out as a single whole by one party" [AH02]. A collaboration can be characterized by a set of tasks that have to be performed and the causal and temporal dependencies between the different tasks. A model describing the coordination of tasks, that is, managing dependencies between these tasks [MC94], dependencies between activities within a collaboration is known as a workflow.

Workflows have been studied in the last few years. Initially, workflows have been carried out entirely by humans manipulating physical objects [GHS95]. Later, with the introduction of Information Technology, these processes have been partially or totally automated by information systems, which control the execution of tasks and the performance of the tasks themselves. Thus, the main goal of workflow management systems is not the complete automation of workflows but the separation of control logic and logic contained in the tasks, where a task is either performed by an information system or by a human. Based on this separation, reuse of tasks in different workflows will be supported [Moh98]. Electronic data interchange (EDI) over the Internet and the Extensible Markup Language (XML) standard family are key factors for the emergence of Web-based workflows. Due to these improved and simplified communication and coordination mechanisms, inter-organizational cooperations and virtual organization structures are evolving, where the interaction and work performed by several parties forming a multi-lateral collaboration have to be coordinated and controlled. Establishing such a multi-lateral collaboration is a major challenge, which increases with the number of parties that have to agree on three aspects:

1. the connectivity, that is, the supported communication protocols (like for example FTP, HTTP, SMTP,...) as well as the communication languages, which are message formats in the case of electronic data interchange (EDI).

2. the tasks to be used within the collaboration, that is, the combination of tasks taken from different parties forming a successful collaboration.

3. the coordination of the selected tasks, that is, the order in which the different tasks have to be executed to guarantee a successful collaboration.

To achieve connectivity the transformation of protocols and messages may be required. An automated transformation of messages requires an "understanding" of the meaning of a message's content, which is expressed in terms of an ontology and is developed by the Semantic Web community. The second and third aspect, that is, deriving the set of tasks to be used and the coordination of those tasks represents a building of a commonly agreed workflow specification. This thesis focuses on those workflow aspects required to establish a multi-lateral collaboration.

1.1 Centralized Establishment of Multi-lateral Collaborations

Nowadays, multi-lateral collaborations are usually set up by a group of people representing the different parties involved in the collaboration. In particular, these people meet, discuss the different options, and finally decide on the definition of a multi-lateral collaboration: which communication protocols and messages are going to be used, and what are the workflow options that have to be supported by a collaboration.[1] The agreement on the multi-lateral collaboration derived by this group specifies a multi-lateral collaboration from a global point of view. Based on this specification a multi-lateral collaboration can be checked for consistency, that is deadlock-freeness: A consistent multi-lateral collaboration has to ensure that all potential execution sequences of the collaboration reach a final state for all involved parties.

The global view specification of a multi-lateral collaboration can be used to derive a specification of the collaboration from a local point of view, that is, the view of an individual party. Approaches exist which allow the derivation of the local point of view from the global one, ensuring that the interaction of the local views implements the global view of a multi-lateral collaboration [Aal99]. Further, it can be guaranteed that the interaction of the local views is consistent if the global specification of a multi-lateral collaboration is consistent.

The global view approach described above is also known as the top-down approach to establishing a collaboration. This approach is quite expensive, because people have to meet to come to an agreement and the implementation of the local views of a collaboration afterwards requires a considerable implementation effort. Further, changes to the collaboration require the parties to

[1] As a basis for this discussion, the different parties try to ensure that the integration effort needed to adapt the local infrastructure and processes to the multi-lateral collaboration is minimized.

go through the whole process again making changes also very expensive. As a consequence, the top-down approach to collaboration establishment works fine for well established and quite static multi-lateral collaborations. However, current development in IT technology supports more flexible structures like for example Service Oriented Architectures (SOA), which are used to realize loosely coupled systems inherently providing a high potential for establishing collaborations between parties in a quite flexible and dynamic way. This kind of collaboration establishment is also known as the bottom-up approach. However, the bottom-up establishment of the collaboration is based on local workflows which hide workflow information for often well justified business reasons contained in the complete workflow model implemented by a certain party. In particular, mission critical information as well as internal structures for handling certain business cases are not made transparent to trading partners.

1.2 Web Services

A Service Oriented Architecture (SOA) is defined as "a set of components which can be invoked, and whose interface descriptions can be published and discovered" [HB04]. A component is a "software object interacting with other components, encapsulating certain functionality or a set of functionalities" [FK04] and maintaining an internal state [Fie00]. Thus, a SOA consists of components accessible as services, where each service provides a certain functionality, an internal state, and an interface to publish the provided functionality to potential service requesters. In contrast to component based architectures, where components are combined during the development phase, in SOAs services are combined after the deployment of services, that is, at run-time [Kay03]. This change can be characterized as a step from supply-driven collaborations to demand-driven ones [Bus03].

A concrete technology implementing the SOA is Web Services. In particular, the World Wide Web Consortium (W3C) Web Service Architecture Working Group defines a Web Service as "a software system designed to support interoperable machine-to-machine interaction over a network. It has an interface described in a machine-processable format (specifically Web Service Description Language (WSDL)). Other systems interact with the Web service in a manner prescribed by its description using SOAP-messages, typically conveyed using HyperText Transfer Protocol (HTTP) with an eXtensible Markup Language (XML) serialization in conjunction with other Web-related standards." [HB04]

The following properties can be derived from the definition of SOA: i) the services are distributed, since each service can be provided by a different party, and ii) the services are autonomous, because state changes within a service are independent of other service's states. As a consequence, a stateless service represents a certain functionality and is comparable to a single task within a workflow. A stateful service represents contains an implicit definition of a local workflow, that is, representing dependencies between different tasks. The interaction of several services results in a multi-lateral collaboration being constructed from a set of pre-existing local workflows provided by services, resulting in a global workflow. This describes the bottom-up approach.

1.3 Decentralized Establishment of Multi-lateral Collaborations

Establishing multi-lateral collaborations should always result in a consistent collaboration, that is, a consistent global workflow. As a consequence, the bottom-up approach has to guarantee that the resulting global workflow is consistent. Because the global workflow is never instantiated explicitly, the decision on the consistency of the global workflow has to be made by local decisions of the involved parties. Consistency of a multi-lateral collaboration can be decided locally by a single party in case of a hierarchical structure of services, where a single service requester centrally coordinates the services, which interact only with the service requester and are provided by the remaining parties of the multi-lateral collaboration. Due to the limitation of services to interact with the service requester only, a single party knowing all complete local workflows exists, which is able to derive the global workflow of the multi-lateral collaboration and to decide on the global workflow consistency [WMR03].

In contrast to this special case, in all other cases no party knows the global workflow, thus, the decision on consistency of the global workflow has to be made in a decentralized way based on partial knowledge of the global workflow. From decentralized system research it is known that this kind of decision cannot be derived directly from local decisions based only on bilateral comparisons [Lyn96].

The thesis addresses this issue and presents an approach to determining consistency of a multi-lateral collaboration in a decentralized way, that is, without instantiating the corresponding global workflow. The decision then can be made in a decentralized way by deriving additional consistency properties of the workflows.

1.4 Contributions of the Dissertation

The main contribution of the thesis is the decentralized establishment of consistent, multi-lateral collaborations. This requires solutions to several subproblems:

- Modeling consistency based on a synchronous communication model namely annotated Finite State Automata.
  Multi-lateral collaborations may rely on different communication infrastructures that can be generally classified as synchronous, that is, a message sent by a party must be received by the recipient immediately, and asynchronous, that is, a message sent by a party has to be received by a party afterwards, but at the latest before completion of the local workflow. It will be demonstrated that approaches exist for modeling consistent multi-lateral collaborations

based on an asynchronous communication model, while the synchronous case has not been addressed so far. Thus, the first aspect of this thesis' contribution is the proposal of a workflow modeling approach based on a Annotated Finite State Automata (aFSA) that supports consistency in a synchronous communication model.

- Mapping WF-Net consistency representing an asynchronous communication model to Annotated Finite State Automata.
  Workflow modeling methods for an asynchronous communication model are already available, among them, Workflow Nets were selected for this thesis. The evaluation of properties of a Workflow Net are defined on the derived occurrence graph, which has the same expressiveness as aFSA. Thus, the second aspect of the contribution is a mapping from Workflow Nets to aFSA, which represents a homomorphism with regard to multi-lateral consistency, that is, it guarantees a successful business transaction. As a consequence, the continuing discussion of decentralized consistency checking can be focused on the notion of aFSA, only.

- Decentralized consistency checking of multi-lateral collaborations based on Annotated Finite State Automata.
  Decentralized consistency checking of a multi-lateral collaboration as a major aspect of the contribution of this thesis is defined as a fixed point of constraint propagation on acyclic local workflows forming the collaboration. In particular, algorithms and specifications are provided for generating acyclic workflow models and propagating constraints locally as well as to trading partners. Finally, the equivalence of multi-lateral consistency and the local consistency of a party in a fixed point representation of multi-lateral collaborations is shown.

- Implementation of the proposed approach and evaluation in the domain of Web Services.
  Combining the three methodological contributions, decentralized multi-lateral collaborations can be realized by decentrally forming a multi-lateral collaboration, next applying decentralized consistency checking to it, and finally determining whether a fixed point has already been reached in order to make the final decision on the consistency of the collaboration. This last aspect of the contribution of this thesis is the realization of this proposal in the domain of Web Services and its successful application on workflows constructed from the Internet Open Trading Protocol specification.

1.5 Outline of the Dissertation

The thesis starts with an analysis of requirements for multi-lateral collaboration establishment in Chapter 2 and an overview of the approach presented in this thesis. In particular, different cases are discussed and relevant properties of potential workflow models are identified. Based on these requirements a solution is outlined illustrating the overall approach presented in detail in Chapters 4 and 5.

Based on the overall approach and the requirements identified, related work is discussed. The discussion addresses different workflow models and their corresponding definition of consistency. Besides classical workflow models, workflows realized by web based Electronic Data Interchange are also discussed. Finally, work related to bilateral and multi-lateral consistency is investigated in more detail.

A detailed discussion of the relevant definitions follows in Chapter 4. In particular, a common model for modeling parameters within workflow models is discussed, which is afterwards applied to Workflow Nets as the workflow model used for asynchronous communication and to the proposed workflow model called annotated Finite State Automata (aFSA) used for synchronous communication. The operations outlined in the previous chapter are now specified for aFSA.

Based on these formal definitions, a mapping from Workflow Nets to aFSA can be provided and the equivalence of the notion of multi-lateral consistency is shown. As a consequence, the further discussion can be limited to prove that the aFSA definitions for decentralized consistency checking are equivalent to the definition of multi-lateral consistency. This formal discussion is provided in Chapter 5.

The application of these theoretical results to the domain of Web Services is described in Chapter 6. In particular, the implementation of the approach is described and the expressiveness of the proposed aFSA workflow model is investigated by applying it to model all workflows derivable from the Internet Open Trading Protocol. The implementation is based on a mapping from the Business Process Execution Language for Web Services to the aFSA workflow model and an application of this mapping to bilateral consistency checking (also known as service discovery in the Web Service domain). Finally, the whole approach is summarized and a protocol for finding potential multi-lateral collaborations based on bilateral consistency is outlined.

The thesis concludes with Chapter 7, where the contributions of this thesis are summarized and further application domains from the technical and the conceptual point of view are discussed. The chapter concludes with a discussion of further research topics.

Chapter 2

Requirements and Overall Approach

In this chapter requirements for decentralized establishment of consistent multi-lateral collaborations are discussed, which are derived from process descriptions illustrated by means of example scenarios.

As a necessary condition to achieve consistent collaborations it must be ensured that the trading partners have consistent bilateral collaborations resulting in an initial set of requirements. In the case of multi-lateral collaborations, additional requirements can be observed forming a sufficient set of requirements for a decentralized collaboration establishment.

2.1 Bilateral Consistency

Bilateral collaborations involve message exchanges. To visualize message exchanges, an edge between two nodes represents a concrete message exchange, where a node represents a state of a message exchange sequence. Final states are identified by a circle with a solid line. Edges are labeled with messages denoted as *s#r#msg*, where *s* represents the message sender, *r* represents the message recipient, and *msg* is the name of the message. This notation is taken from finite state automata [HMU01] which are a well known formalism used for representing message sequences.

2.1.1 Example

The example scenario involves two trading parties: a vendor *V* and a customer *C*. In particular, Figure 2.1(a) shows the message sequences supported by the vendor, where the vendor expects to receive a purchase order (*C#V#PO*) message, followed by a credit card payment (*C#V#ccPay*) and finally sends back a delivery (*V#C#delivery*) message providing parcel tracking information to the respective customer. The message sequences supported by the customer depicted in Figure 2.1(b) also initiates the process with a purchase order request (*C#V#PO*). But then it insists on delivery (*V#C#delivery*) before payment by credit card (*C#V#ccPay*) or by invoice (*C#V#invoicePay*).

At the level of individual messages these two parties are able to interact, because they share

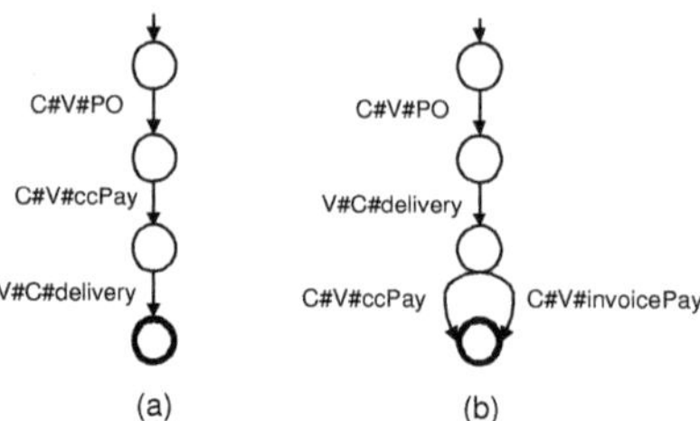

Figure 2.1: (a) Vendor Message Sequence. (b) Customer Message Sequence.

several messages. However, because they require a different ordering of payment and delivery, they are incompatible, that is, they cannot have successful business transactions. In order to guarantee successful transactions message sequences rather than individual messages need to be taken into account. Based on this criterion, the two process descriptions are not consistent, since they do not have a single message sequence in common.

Figure 2.2(a) shows the message sequences supported by another vendor. The process starts with a purchase order (*C#V#PO*) message, followed by a delivery (*V#C#delivery*) message, and either a credit card payment (*C#V#ccPay*) or an invoice payment (*C#V#invoicePay*) message. In case the ordered product is not in stock, the vendor may reject a purchase order by sending a no stock available (*V#C#noStock*) message. The vendor process can decide by itself to accept or decline the purchase order by sending the *V#C#noStock* or the *V#C#delivery* message, and thus can make an active choice. To guarantee consistency the receiving party must support both of these messages, thus, both messages are considered to be mandatory. On the other hand, the vendor message sequences support two payment options as genuine alternatives, since it is not the sender but the receiver of these messages. To guarantee consistency the trading partner has to support at least one of these messages to ensure at least a single common message sequence, thus, these messages are considered to be optional.

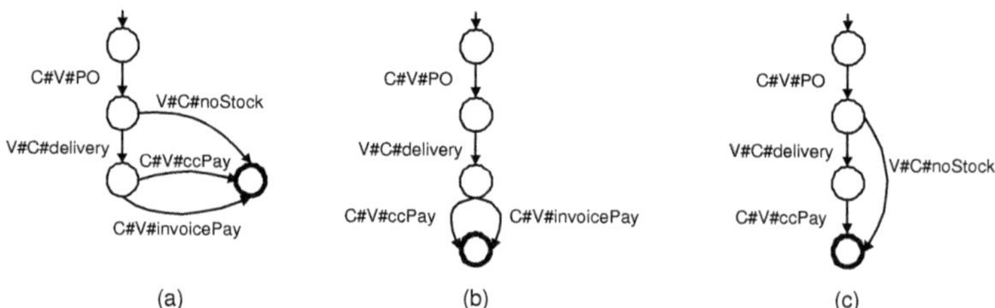

Figure 2.2: (a) Vendor Message Sequences Insisting on *V#C#noStock* and *V#C#delivery* Messages. (b) Customer Message Sequences. (c) Customer Message Sequences with Optional *V#C#noStock* Message.

Figure 2.2(b)[1] depicts message sequences supported by a customer. While customer and vendor have a message sequence in common with respect to the delivery payment order, the customer does not support a message sequence handling the mandatory *V#C#noStock* message. Therefore, the two parties have no common message sequence, if an ordered product is not in stock, thus, they are not consistent.

Conversely, the customer message sequences depicted in Figure 2.2(c) support *V#C#noStock* and *V#C#delivery* messages, whereas it supports only one payment option. This customer now satisfies all mandatory and optional messages of the vendor. Thus, the vendor and the customer message sequences are consistent.

2.1.2 Requirements

As a summary the following requirements have been identified so far:

1. The decision making for a consistent collaboration must be performed in a decentralized way. This is part of the overall problem statement and thus also a requirement for the modeling approach.

2. Deciding consistency must be based on observable message exchanges under specific consideration of message sequencing. In particular, the trading partners need to share at least a common message sequence.

3. The modeling of message sequences must differentiate between mandatory and optional messages. In particular, all messages that may be selected by their sender at a particular state must be supported by the trading partner resulting in a final state.

4. The comparison of message sequences is based on a notion of message equivalence defined as equivalence of syntactic structure as well as intended semantics. This equivalence definition allows to focus on the workflow aspects of the collaboration establishment problem by leaving the issues of schema subsumption and semantic equivalence to the specific communities.

5. The comparison of message sequences requires a matchmaking definition, where two parties match if the corresponding bilateral collaboration is consistent.

2.2 Bilateral Consistency Approach

Bilateral consistency means that the bilateral collaboration is consistent, that is, fulfilling the requirements stated in the previous section. A well established approach supporting these requirements is based on Workflow Nets (WF-Nets) [AH02], which are used to represent the workflow of

[1]This message sequence is equivalent to the one depicted in Figure 2.1(b) and described above.

a single party, called local workflow. In particular, a WF-Net based approach called interorganizational workflow [Aal99] exists, which characterizes the guarantee for consistency as a WF-Net property called soundness. Due to this property WF-Nets have been selected for further discussion. Other notations like for example, Petri Nets [Pet81, Jen92], flowcharts [GAHL00, KWA99], or statecharts [Har87, HN96, Per95] could also have been used. However, WF-Nets provide better computational complexity because they do not allow recursion.

A Workflow Net (WF-Net) consists of places (circles) representing business tasks and transitions (rectangles) connecting places representing a message exchange. Again, transitions are labeled with *s#r#msg* representing sender *s* and recipient *r* of the message as well as its message name *msg*. Messages may in addition contain parameters annotated in brackets. WF-Nets contain a single final place represented by a circle with a solid line within the graph.

The execution of a workflow is realized by pushing tokens through the WF-Net, which are depicted as a dot within a place. A transition is enabled if all input places of a transition contain a token. If a transition is enabled, it may fire, which removes tokens from incoming places and inserts new tokens to all outgoing places of the transition. The current distribution of tokens over the places represents the state of the workflow and is called marking. The firing of a transition can be further constrained by a logical formula on the parameters of the message, which is annotated in square brackets.[2]

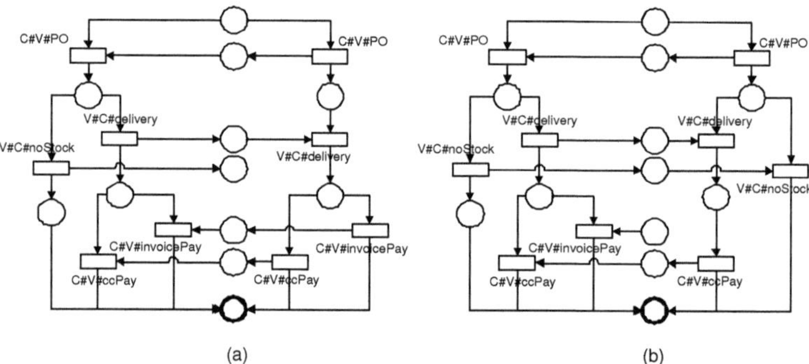

Figure 2.3: (a) Vendor and Customer WF-Net from Figure 2.2(a) and (b). (b) Vendor and Customer WF-Net from Figure 2.2(a) and (c).

Bilateral consistency or the interorganizational soundness of two WF-Nets is decided on behalf of a WF-Net constructed by combining the two WF-Nets. In particular, two transitions with the same message and a matching sender and recipient pair are related via an asynchronous channel. Each channel is represented by an additional place connected by an incoming arc with the "sending"

[2]This extension of the WF-Net model by parameters and constraints is also known as color extension (see e.g. [Jen92]) and is not contained in the original WF-Net definition.

transition of a message and an outgoing arc to the "receiving" transition. A token located in a newly introduced place can be interpreted as a message contained in the channel waiting for being received by the corresponding party. Finally, new initial and final places are connected by new transitions t_{start} and t_{final} to the local initial and final places. The constructed interorganizational WF-Net representing the interaction of the vendor message sequences and the customer message sequences contained in Figure 2.2(a)+(c) and (a)+(b) respectively are shown in Figure 2.3(a) and (b).

Such a bilateral workflow can be analyzed for bilateral consistency by constructing a so called occurrence graph. The vertices of the occurrence graph represent all possible markings of a WF-Net, and the directed edges represent the transitions leading from one marking to the next. The WF-Net is consistent, if all vertices in its occurrence graph have either at least one outgoing transition or are a final marking [Aal99]. On this basis, it can be shown that the bilateral workflow depicted in Figure 2.2(a) is not consistent, since the vendor sending a *V#C#noStock* message will never be removed from the channel place. However, the bilateral workflow depicted in Figure 2.2(a) is consistent, that is, is deadlock free. Based on this interpretation, all messages sent by a party are considered to be mandatory, that is, they cause inconsistency if not supported by the corresponding party, while messages received by a party are considered to be optional since the lack of a corresponding sending transition does not cause inconsistency.

2.3 Multi-lateral Consistency

Consistency of multi-lateral collaborations requires the underlying bilateral collaborations to be consistent, that is, fulfilling the requirements stated in Section 2.1.2. A well established approach for bilateral consistency has been introduced in the previous section, which can be extended to the multi-lateral case as explained with an example in the following sections.

2.3.1 Example

The example scenario used for further discussion is a simple procurement workflow within a virtual enterprise incorporating a buyer, an accounting department, and a logistics department.

The accounting department checks orders (*order* message) of buyers and forwards them to the logistics department (*deliver* message) to deliver the requested goods. The logistics department confirms the receipt (*deliver_conf* message), which is forwarded by the accounting department to the buyer (*delivery* message). Further, the buyer may perform parcel tracking (*get_status* and *status* messages) as sometimes offered by logistics companies, where in some cases an additional authentication (*auth* message) is required prior to parcel tracking. The overall scenario is shown in Figure 2.4 representing the global relationships, but not the local workflows of the parties involved.

The local workflows of the parties involved are shown in Figure 2.5 forming the global workflow described above and being consistent. The process is started by the buyer *B* sending a *B#A#order*

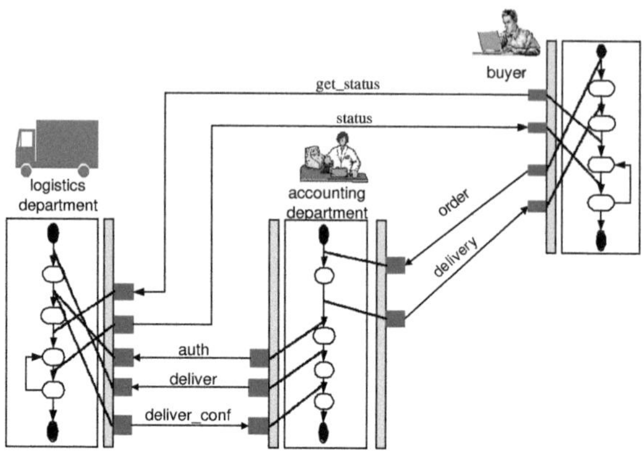

Figure 2.4: Global Procurement Scenario

message to the accounting department *A* with the parameters item number *it*, price *p*, and amount *a*, which is restricted to being below 100. The accounting department *A* informs the logistics department *L* via a *A#L#deliver* message to deliver the ordered goods without forwarding the price parameter *p* of the order. The logistics department *L* accepts this request from the accounting department *A* if the amount *a* is below 100, and confirms it with a *L#A#deliver_conf* message providing an additional tracking number (*tn* parameter). The accounting department *A* forwards the delivery details of the order (*A#B#delivery* message) to the buyer *B*. Afterwards, the buyer *B* can track parcels directly with the logistics department *L* by sending a *B#L#get_status* message containing a tracking number parameter *tn* answered by a *L#B#status* message with an additional status parameter *st*. While the buyer *B* must have sent the *A#B#delivery* message before tracking parcels the logistics department *L* allows parcel tracking at any time after receiving an authentication message from the accounting department *A* (*A#L#auth* message). Finally, the buyer *B* terminates the buyer and logistics department process by sending a *B#L#terminate* message.

2.3.2 Centralized Collaboration Establishment

The global workflow for these local workflows can be constructed as described in Section 2.2 in accordance to [Aal99] by forming an interorganizational WF-Net now based on more than two workflows being involved. Applying this approach to the example workflow in Figure 2.5 leads to the global workflow in Figure 2.6. Note that one parcel tracking option of the logistics department has been discarded because no corresponding sender transition labeled *A#L#auth* exists at the accounting workflow, thus it is never used.

Such a global workflow can be analyzed for consistency based on the occurrence graph again and it can be shown that this global workflow is consistent, that is, fulfills all local constraints

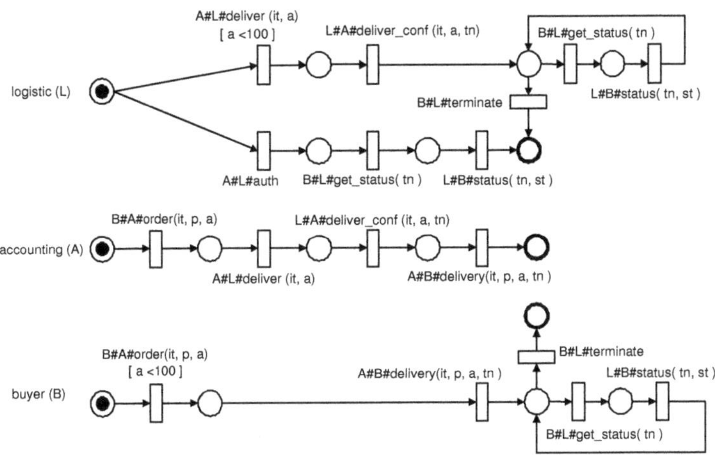

Figure 2.5: Local WF-Net Models

on parameters and is deadlock free. However, the decision on the consistency of the multi-lateral collaboration is centralized based on the constructed global workflow. As a consequence, at least one party needs to know the local workflows of all parties involved.

2.3.3 Decentralized Collaboration Establishment

In contrast to the centralized consistency checking based on a global workflow,decentralized consistency checking must be entirely based on each party's local knowledge: its own local workflow and the bilateral communication of the party with its partners. For example the buyer should only need to know about their own local workflow and individual interaction with logistics and accounting departments, but not about the entire local workflows of logistics and accounting departments and not about their possible interaction.

As a consequence, bilateral WF-Nets extend the local workflow by the relevant parts of a trading party's local workflow, which can be derived by neglecting those parts of the trading party's workflow not being part of this particular bilateral interaction. In particular, those transitions are omitted, which doe not represent a message exchange with the trading partner. A transition is omitted by relabeling with a silent message τ subscribed by an index to differentiate different τs, that is the WF-Net equivalent to ε-transitions in finite state automata. Thus, a silent message represents an internal state change not resulting in a message exchange between the trading partners. In [Aal02, Aal00, BA99] such a definition on WF-Nets is provided known as abstraction. Applying this abstraction definition to a trading partner interaction results in the party's view on a trading partner's local workflow. Combining this view and the party's local workflow results in a bilateral

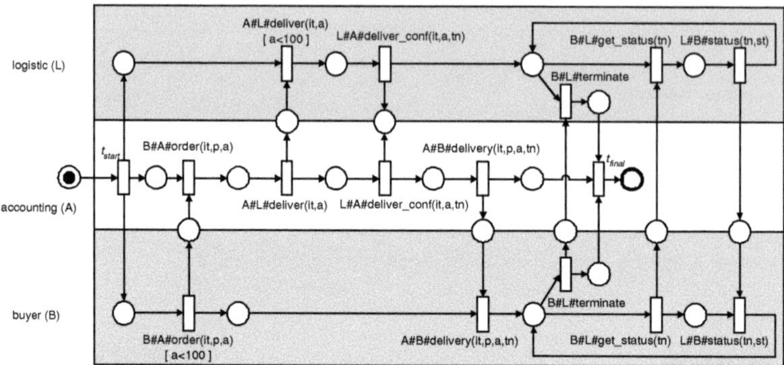

Figure 2.6: Global WF-Net Model

WF-Net, which is used by the party to decide consistency of the global workflow in a decentralized way. Figure 2.7 depicts an example bilateral WF-Net of accounting department and buyer.

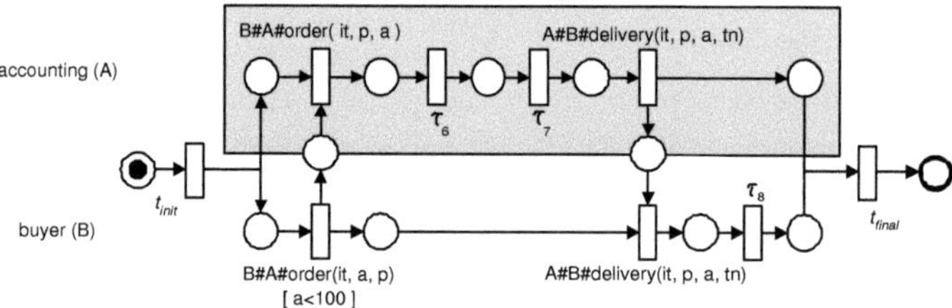

Figure 2.7: Bilateral WF-Net of Buyer and Accounting Department

Unfortunately, this intuitive approach does not work due to the information loss introduced by the abstraction. In the following, two scenarios are described illustrating two categories of information loss during abstraction, which need to be considered for deciding consistency of multi-lateral collaborations in a decentralized fashion.

2.3.4 Occurrence Graph Constraints

The bilateral WF-Net of logistics department and buyer results in a deadlock, although the example global workflow is consistent. Figure 2.8 depicts the bilateral WF-Net, where the logistics department workflow (grey box) interacts with the view of the buyer workflow (above the grey box)[3].

The bilateral WF-Net can result in the following execution sequence: *B#L#get_status L#B#status* This sequence results in a marking where no other transition is enabled and the final place is not

[3]The bilateral WF-Net is constructed from the local workflows depicted in Figure 2.5.

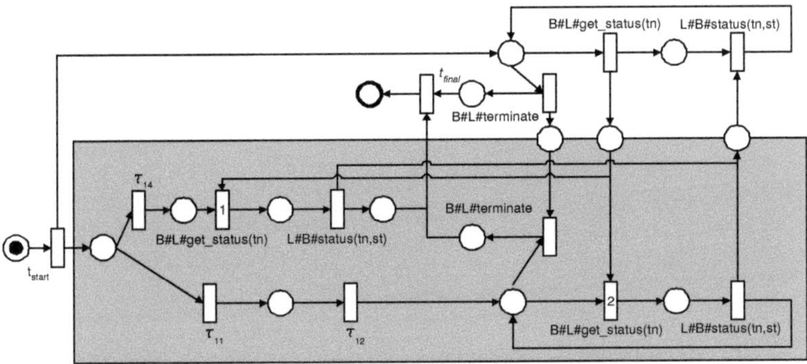

Figure 2.8: Bilateral WF-Net of Logistics Department and Buyer

marked and thus is deadlocked. The detected deadlock in the bilateral WF-Net indicates the virtual global workflow as not consistent, although it is consistent.

The reason for the detected deadlock is the loss of information introduced by the abstraction of the buyer workflow. In particular, the local workflow of the accounting department ensures that the transition τ_{14} (representing the *A#L#auth* message) preceding the *B#L#get_status* message is never sent, thus, the occurrence graph of the logistics department does not contain the branch causing the deadlock in the bilateral WF-Net of logistics department and buyer. As a consequence the occurrence graph of a party is transitive to all occurrence graphs of bilateral interactions.

2.3.5 Parameter Constraints

Another type of information loss is related to parameter values within messages, which are constrained by conditions assigned to transitions. This case can be observed in the bilateral WF-Net of the logistics and accounting department in Figure 2.9, where the logistics department workflow (grey box) is combined with the view of the accounting department workflow (below the grey box)[4].

The bilateral WF-Net is not consistent, because all message sequences starting with a *A#L#deliver(it,a)* message, where the amount a is greater than 100 result in a deadlock like, e.g., *A#L#deliver(120)*. The deadlock is due to the limitation of the logistics department workflow to accept order amounts below 100 only. Again, the deadlock in the constructed workflow indicates that the virtual global workflow may not be consistent, although this is not the case.

Similarly to the previous case, the inherent parameter value constraint of the buyer workflow, which has been omitted by the abstraction, causes this deadlock on the bilateral WF-Net. The observation here is that again neglecting these constraints results in irrelevant options not applicable to the global workflow, but causing a deadlock in the bilateral WF-Net.

[4]The bilateral WF-Net is constructed from the local workflows depicted in Figure 2.5.

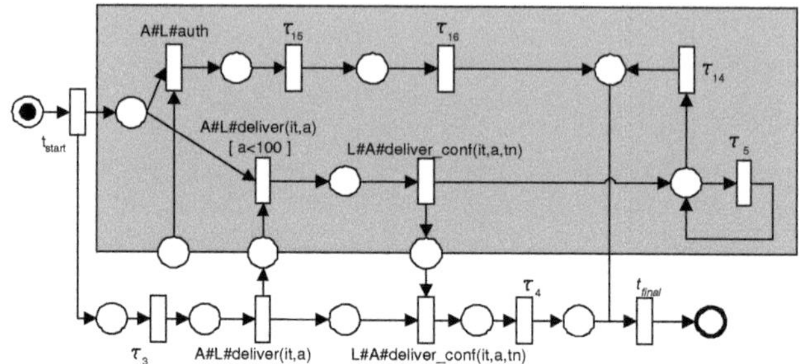

Figure 2.9: Bilateral WF-Net of Logistics and Accounting Department

2.3.6 Requirements

The approach used in the previous subsections does not guarantees that only consistent global workflows will be accepted. Thus, the requirement is to derive a decentralized approach for deciding consistency of a multi-lateral collaboration, which considers exactly those multi-lateral collaborations to be consistent, which are consistent based on the centralized approach. In the previous example it was shown that the decision whether the three local workflows guarantee successful business interaction cannot be made correctly using only bilateral WF-Nets for the following reasons:

- The parameter value constraint of the *B#A#order* and the *A#L#deliver* message fit each other, because it is guaranteed by the local workflows that the accounting will never be able to send an order with an amount higher than 100. This transitivity of parameter constraints can not be derived by bilateral WF-Nets.

- The occurrence graph constraint that the *B#L#get_status* message will never be received before the *L#A#deliver_conf* message has been sent by the logistics department is guaranteed by the local workflows. This transitivity of occurrence graphs cannot be derived by bilateral WF-Nets.

Based on these requirements, a valid approach for decentralized decision making on consistent multi-lateral collaborations should extend the above outlined approach by propagating the constraints to enable their local usage. In particular, the transitivity property of these constraints needs to be exploited.

2.4 Decentralized Consistency Checking Approach

A Workflow Net (WF-Net) as introduced in Section 2.2 provides a definition of interorganizational soundness, which fulfills the bilateral consistency definition discussed in Section 2.1. Due to the loss of information, decentralized consistency checking requires use of transitivity properties on parameter and occurrence graph constraints, where an occurrence graph represents all possible markings derivable from a WF-Net (see Section 2.2).

Deciding consistency of a multi-lateral collaboration in a decentralized way proceeds in four steps:

1. Resolving Cycles:
   Local workflow models of the parties are made acyclic by representing cycles as iterations of at most *N* steps.

2. Propagation:
   Parameter constraints and occurrence graph constraints on previous transitions are made available to all parties involved in the multi-lateral collaboration. This comprises:

   (a) Propagation of parameter constraints within the local workflows, as well as between the bilateral interactions until a fixed point has been reached.

   (b) Propagation of occurrence graph constraints within the local workflows, as well as between the bilateral interactions until a fixed point has been reached.

3. Decentralized Consistency Checking:
   Each party checks consistency of its bilateral interactions and the local workflow. If they are all consistent, then the party considers the multi-lateral collaboration to be consistent until any other party proves this decision wrong by considering the multi-lateral collaboration to be inconsistent.

4. Consensus Making
   A protocol is required to decentrally check whether all parties consider their bilateral interactions and local workflows as consistent, and to inform all parties about the final consensus. This kind of problem is known in distributed systems as a consensus making problem [Lyn96].

A decentralized decision requires use of the transitivity properties of parameter and occurrence graph constraints, which requires the underlying workflow model to support parameter constraint transitivity. Since cyclic graph structures are not transitive, workflow models used have to be acyclic. As a consequence, cycles have to be resolved in step 1. With regard to the example, this affects the buyer and the logistics department WF-Nets representing the local workflow respectively.

Step 2 is required because the bilateral WF-Nets hide all parameter and occurrence graph constraints that are not immediately seen by the two involved parties. Without propagating this information two of the bilateral WF-Nets in the example would be inconsistent:

As discussed in Section 2.3.5 the bilateral WF-Net for the logistics and accounting department (Figure 2.9) is inconsistent, because a message *A#L#deliver(it,a)* with an amount *a* greater than 100 violates the constraint of the "receiving" transition *A#L#deliver*. However, the guarantee of this constraint is only provided by the bilateral WF-Net for accounting department and buyer, which is not seen by the bilateral WF-Net for logistics department and buyer.

The bilateral WF-Net for buyer and logistics department (Figure 2.8) is inconsistent (see also Section 2.3.4), because the sequence *B#L#get_status - L#B#status* results in a deadlock. The two "receiving" transitions *B#L#get_status*(1,2) are both enabled after the corresponding "sending" transition in the buyer's workflow has been fired. Since the selection of the enabled transition is non-deterministic, both options must be considered for consistency checking. Taking transition (1) for direct parcel tracking leads to a deadlock since the *B#L#terminate* transition cannot be fired afterwards, thus, the final place cannot be reached. Thus, the WF-Net is considered to be inconsistent although it is guaranteed by the accounting workflow that the transition (1) that causes the deadlock will never be fired, because no transition *A#L#auth* will be sent.

Since the global WF-Net is consistent, the decentralized consistency checking without propagation of constraints derives wrong results. Next, the resolution of cycles is introduced followed by a description of constraint propagation, and a brief discussion of consensus making.

2.4.1 Resolving Cycles

The approach does not support cyclic local workflows, because parameter constraints of a particular transition may vary within different steps of a cycle, thus, each step has to be represented explicitly. In the following an approach is described where cyclic workflows are transformed into different non-cyclic workflows. Cycles may be loops as contained in the buyer and logistics department workflows depicted in Figure 2.5 or recursions. Next, loops are discussed in detail, while the approach can similarly be applied to recursions. A loop can be transformed by simulating it as a sequence of at most N repetitions of a loop step:

- The transitions forming the loop are replaced by two subsequent silent transitions labeled $\tau_{loop}(1)$ and $\tau_{loop'}(N+1)$, where the first transition initiates the loop and the second one represents the end of the loop.

- Transitions in a loop step are encapsulated by silent transitions $\tau_{loop'}(i)$ and $\tau_{loop}(i+1)$ representing the start and end of the i-th step of the loop. To execute the loop not all N steps have to be performed, thus an additional silent transition τ is added to shortcut a single step.

- Parameters of transitions within a loop step i are made unique by adding the suffix i to each parameter.

- The output places of transition $\tau_{loop}(i)$ and the input places of transition $\tau_{loop'}(i)$ share a single state.

Applying this transformation to the buyer workflow results in the acyclic WF-Net in Figure 2.10. All steps of the parcel tracking loop are represented by equivalent WF-Subnets except for

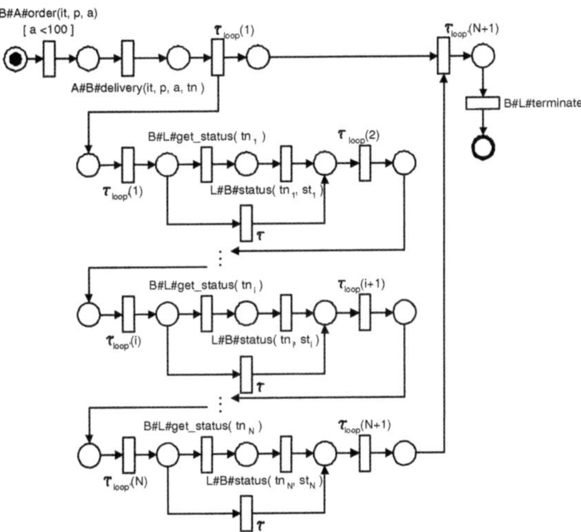

Figure 2.10: Acyclic Buyer WF-Net

the varying parameter indicating the number of the step. To reduce the complexity of this WF-Net a shorthand notation of the repetition is introduced, where only a single step is contained and the maximum number of iterations N is annotated (Figure 2.11). Obviously, the transformed representation is different from the original local workflow. However, in literature it has been accepted that research can focus on non-cyclic workflows, because in real business applications the number of repetitions a party is accepting is usually constrained anyway and non party will accept infinite loops.

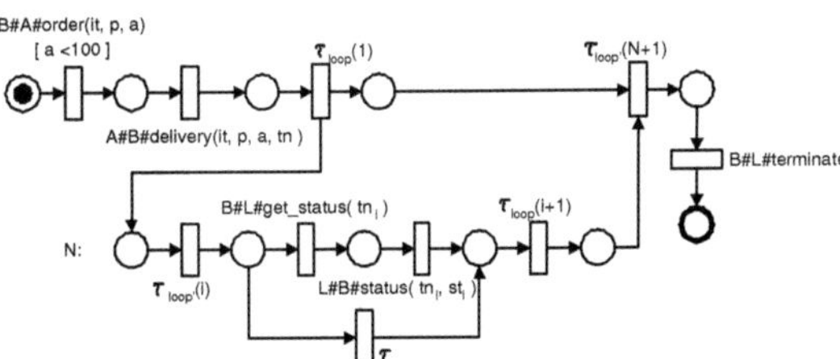

Figure 2.11: Shorthand Notation of the Acyclic Buyer WF-Net (see Figure 2.10)

The loop in the logistics department workflow can be simulated in a similar way. Based on the constructed acyclic local workflows of the buyer and the logistics department the bilateral WF-Net depicted in Figure 2.12 can be constructed.

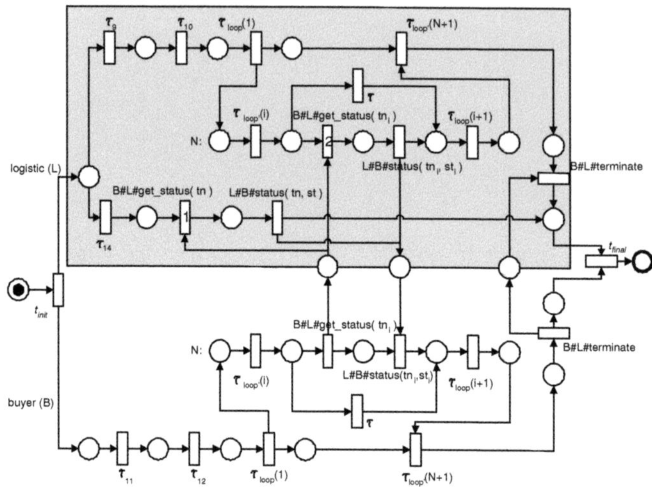

Figure 2.12: Shorthand Notation of the Bilateral WF-Net for Buyer and Logistics Department

2.4.2 Propagation of Parameter Constraints

The goal of parameter constraint propagation is to make sure that all parameter constraints can be met, even though they may not immediately be visible in a bilateral WF-Net. The parameters of transitions are assumed to be immutable, that is, after they have been set initially they cannot be changed. As a consequence, a parameter constraint holds for all transitions following the transition for which it has been specified. On these grounds parameter constraints can be propagated to all following transitions within a workflow as well as to the workflow of the partner.

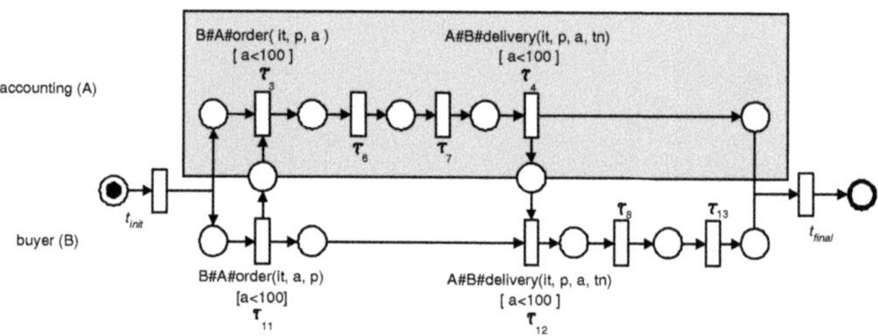

Figure 2.13: Extended Bilateral WF-Net Model for Buyer and Accounting Department

The result of propagating the constraint on amount *a* annotated to the transition labeled *B#A#order(it,p,a)* within the bilateral WF-Net for buyer and accounting department (Figure 2.7) is depicted in Figure 2.13. The result of propagating this constraint to the accounting department

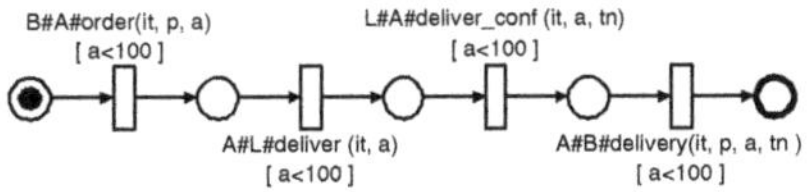

Figure 2.14: Extended Accounting Department WF-Net

local workflow (Figure 2.5) is depicted in Figure 2.14. By further propagation the constraint on the bilateral WF-Net for logistics and accounting department (Figure 2.9) results in Figure 2.15.

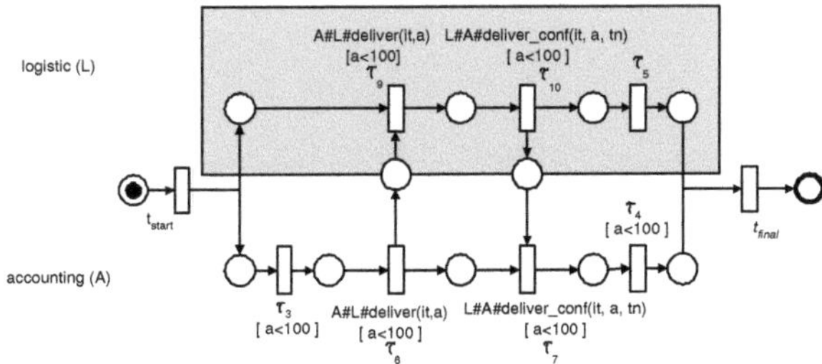

Figure 2.15: Extended Bilateral WF-Net Model for Logistics and Accounting Department

Due to the propagation of the parameter constraints the deadlock discussed in Section 2.4 can no longer occur. As a consequence the bilateral WF-Net is consistent.

2.4.3 Propagation of Occurrence Graph Constraints

The goal of propagating occurrence graph constraints is to discard all those transitions which cause a deadlock in a bilateral WF-Net but will never fire due to constraints imposed by the invisible part of the global workflow. An example for such a transition is the *B#L#get_status* transition (1) in the bilateral WF-Net between logistics department and buyer in Figure 2.12.

When the global workflow is known, such spurious transitions can be discarded by analyzing the occurrence graph of the global WF-Net. A transition can be discarded, if it does not occur in the occurrence graph.

In the following it is described how the occurrence graph can be constructed only on the basis of the bilateral workflows without explicating the entire global workflow. The approach consists of two steps. In the first step for each bilateral WF-Net occurrence graphs are constructed and used to discard spurious transitions. In the second step these transitions are also discarded in the other bilateral WF-Nets. As a consequence, the occurrence graph constraints of one bilateral WF-Net are propagated to the other bilateral WF-Nets. These two steps are repeated until a fixed point is reached, that is, no further transition can be discarded.

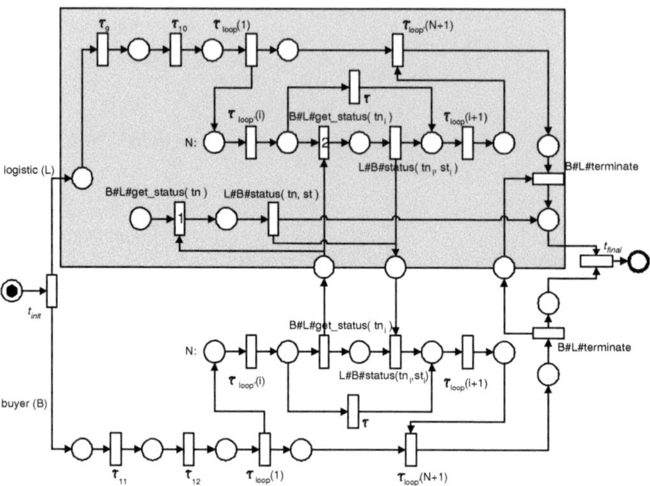

Figure 2.16: Shorthand Notion of the Bilateral WF-Net for Buyer and Logistics Department after Discarding Transition *A#L#auth*

In the example, the "receiving" transition *A#L#auth* within the bilateral WF-Net for accounting and logistics department (Figure 2.9) does not appear in the occurrence graph, since the corresponding "sending" transition does not exist. Thus, the transition can be discarded (Figure 2.15). Further, the same transition occurring in the bilateral WF-Net for logistics department and buyer (Figure 2.12) labeled τ_{14} can also be discarded resulting in Figure 2.16. Next, the occurrence graphs of the modified bilateral WF-Nets involving logistics department have to be recalculated. Analyzing the occurrence graph of the modified bilateral WF-Net between buyer and logistics department reveals that the transition *B#L#get_status* (1) and the subsequent transition *L#B#status* of the logistics department local workflow will never be fired, thus it can be discarded resulting in the final bilateral WF-Net for buyer and logistics department shown in Figure 2.17. The resulting bilateral WF-Nets (Figures 2.13, 2.15, and 2.17) represent a fixed point.

The removal of the *A#L#auth* transition of the bilateral WF-Net for logistics and accounting department has been propagated to the bilateral WF-Net for logistics department and buyer by removing the corresponding transition labeled τ_{14}. Due to the propagation of the occurrence graph constraints the deadlock discussed in Section 2.4 can no longer occur. As a consequence the bilateral WF-Net is consistent.

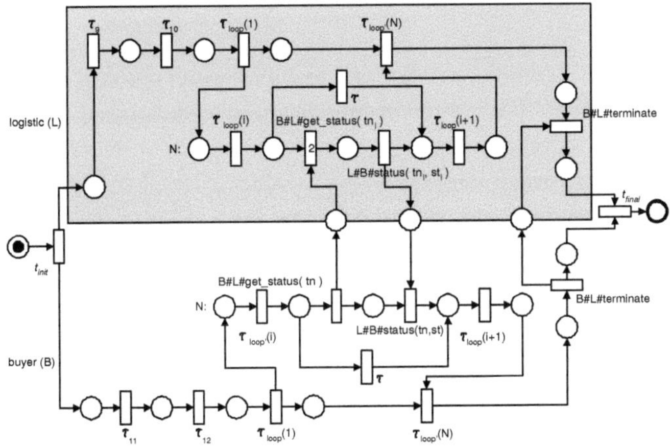

Figure 2.17: Extended Bilateral WF-Net for Buyer and Logistics Department

2.4.4 Consensus Making

Consensus making aims to make an agreement between a set of parties having reached a fixed point with regard to parameter and occurrence graph constraint propagation, and forming a multi-lateral collaboration. Since no party knows all parties involved in the collaboration none can act as a coordinator of the collaboration. In particular, the following tasks must be performed:

- collect the local consistency decision of each party,
- check whether all parties consider the collaboration to be consistent, and finally
- inform all parties being involved of the final decision.

This generic consensus making problem is addressed by the distributed systems and algorithms community (see for example [Lyn96]). However, due to the fact that a fixed point on constraint propagation of constraints is required anyway, the aim is to define multi-lateral consistency as a kind of propagation to overcome the consensus making problem. The underlying idea is to reflect mandatory and optional messages as structural workflow model aspects effecting the occurrence graph, thus, being propagated via the corresponding propagation mechanism as discussed above. However, the modification of the occurrence graph with respect to mandatory and optional messages has to be performed via an explicit operation. As a consequence, a fixed point can be reached, where either none or all local workflows of the collaboration are consistent.

2.5 Summary

In this chapter example scenarios have been used to discuss issues observed during decentralized collaboration establishment. As a basis for multi-lateral consistency, bilateral consistency checking relies on a comparison of message sequences under the assumption of structural subsumption and semantic equivalence of equally named messages. Further, bilateral consistency checking must differentiate between mandatory and optional messages, that is, all messages sent by a party must be supported by a recipient party and thus are called mandatory messages, while messages received by a party are called optional messages, because they are not necessarily sent by another party. An approach based on Workflow Nets (WF-Nets) has been outlined realizing the bilateral consistency for asynchronous communication.

Deciding multi-lateral consistency based on bilateral consistency decisions turned out to be incorrect, because of information loss introduced by having only a partial view on the multi-lateral collaboration. Especially, information loss has been observed for message parameter constraints, that is, parameter values are considered which have been excluded by other parts of the global workflow already, and occurrence graph constraints, that is, message sequences are considered although the execution of a message contained in this message sequence has been excluded already by another part of the global workflow. Again, an approach based on WF-Nets has been outlined, which provides the same notion of consistency as provided by the centralized approach. The formal specification and discussion of the equivalence relation follows in the next sections.

Chapter 3

Related Work

Based on the requirements derived and the approach outlined in the previous chapter the state of the art is discussed starting with local consistency of workflow modeling. In accordance to [GHS95] workflow models are differentiated by task based and communication based models. In addition to scientific workflow models, several industrial standards have emerged on the Internet providing specific use cases being an alternative to flexible distributed workflows. Starting with local consistency, a discussion of bilateral consistency and multi-lateral collaborations follows.

3.1 Task Based Workflow Model

A task based workflow model consists of tasks as basic building blocks representing basic units of work, which can exemplary be performed by humans, agents, computers, or sensors. A task might be called *primitive*, that is, can be performed in a single step, or *complex*, that is, can be decomposed into simpler tasks [Mar02]. In particular, the critical principle in the study of workflow has been identified by Winograd and Flores [WF86] as coordination in general within organizations. Malone and Crowston [MC94] defined "coordination as managing dependencies between tasks" and examined all sorts of scientific domains like social, psychological, economical and computer science to identify relevant *tasks* and their *dependencies*.

In case of a direct, automated coordination of tasks exemplary workflow models are Finite State Automata (FSA) [HMU01], Place/Transition Nets (P/T-Nets) [Pet62, Pet81, Gen87], Coloured Place/Transition Nets (CP/T-Nets) [Jen92], Workflow Nets (WF-Nets) [AH02], message sequence charts [Uni99], statecharts [Har87, HN96], or flowcharts [GAHL00, KWA99]. However, these models mainly represent a single workflow model processed at a single party, while the coordination of tasks within a multi-lateral collaboration, which can also be described as a distributed workflow model involving several parties requires additional communication [PL01]. Besides generic event based publish/subscribe protocols like for example deployed in [CD01, EP99] or Internet communication protocols like for example Web Services [1], specialized communication methods for coor-

[1] See also Section 3.3.

dinating workflow systems have been proposed [HPS+00]. The Workflow Management Coalition [WfM04b] provides a Workflow Interoperability Interface within their reference workflow model [Fis04, WfM04a] supporting direct interaction of workflow systems based on Wf-XML [Coa01]), while the OMG Workflow Management Facility [OMG04] proposed jointFlow [OMG97]. Independent of the used protocols, different kinds of coordination can be implemented [Coa99] such as subsequent execution of partial processes, nested processes, loosely coupled processes, or processes coordinated by a centralized workflow system as discussed in Section 3.5. In particular, the interface provides the mechanism to exchange data between workflow systems, while the realization and coordination of the different kinds of processes is not addressed.

As opposed to approaches based on message exchanges there exist approaches based on shared data spaces. A specific data oriented approach to coordination, which is based on a general indirect, anonymous, undirected and asynchronous communication model, provides operations to insert, read and withdrawn data from a shared multi-set. The so called tuple space is the basis for coordination languages like for example Linda [Gel85] describing coordination models by rules specified on a tuple space. Different extensions of the tuple space exist, like for example allowing several potentially distributed tuple spaces (PeerSpace [BMMZ03]), or supporting structured data (XMLSpaces [TG01, XML04]).

Coordination theory has been applied on different layers of a generic communication stack: protocol layer (e.g. especially considering multi-cast [DGLA00]), the message layer (e.g. discussing different exchange patterns [SSOH95]), and the application layer. Further, these methods have been applied in different application domains like Computer Supported Cooperative Work (CSCW) for coordinating objects shared by users [SS96], agent systems (e.g. [PSG02]) realized by coordinating documents containing data, representation, and modeling of behavior [CTZ02], and workflow coordination [Tol00a].

The workflow coordination is data-driven in contrast to control-driven task based workflow models [Tol00a]. The WorkSpace approach proposed by Tolksdorf [Tol00b] is based on a notion of steps representing a transformation of one or several documents. There exist automatic steps doing direct data manipulation, external steps invoking external functionality, user steps enabling direct user interaction, coordination steps like JOIN and SPLIT known from workflow modeling, and meta steps modifying the workflow structure itself. Another similar approach addressing workflow coordination is [Ban96]. However, the shared data space always are based on a centralized component maintaining the shared data. Hence, such a component does not exist in a multi-lateral collaboration, thus, these approaches are not applicable. Although for the different workflow models a definition of local consistency of a single workflow based on a notion of execution sequences can be provided.

3.2 Communication Based Workflow Model

A communication based workflow model provides a description of the effects of receiving messages on an internal state as well as the potential ordering of messages exchanged with communication partners. The theoretical foundation of these approaches is Speech Act Theory (SAT) [Aus65, BH79], which characterizes the communication between parties by means of the intention of the speaker, the effect on the listener, and the physical manifestations of an utterance [Mar02]. One application domain of SAT is a theoretical modeling of interaction between machines, which is also known as agent communication languages (ACL) [FIP04]. In ACL an internal context/ state of a party is maintained locally, that is, in a decentralized fashion. The Knowledge Query and Manipulation Language (KQML) [FFMM94] has been one approach addressing ACL [FLM97]. KQML is data centric representing states in terms of data values, while state changes are represented by performatives, that is, actions on content exchanged via a message being constraint by pre-conditions. This approach has been applied to an office communication environment resulting in a language called "Formal Language for Business Communication" (FLBC) [KM97, KH95, Moo00, WvdH98, Kim98]. In particular, the approach is based on flexible bilateral interactions causing a single party to deal with a high amount of potential message sequences causing high control flow complexity. Based on FLBC Hasselbring and Weigand proposed a business communication language XLBC [HW01, WH01], which extends FLBC by introducing ontologies and a notion of aggregated communication patterns being a hierarchy extension.

An alternative approach represents the semantics of ACL by a logical model, which extends standard predicate logic with concepts to capture dynamics of processes (dynamic logic), modalities, like for example obligation (deontic logic) [MWD98, LF94], and intention (illocutionary logic) [WVD96]. Dynamic deontic logic [DW95, Mey88, MWD98] is such a model representing illocutionary acts. In this approach a transition named *action* represents a change from one propositional *world* to another. In addition, deontic operations express permission, prohibition, and obligation of actions, that is, corresponding transitions. In particular, dynamic deontic logic has been applied on modeling integrity constraints in business processes [WMW89] as well as representing temporal constraints [DWV96].

Another logic based approach is Courteous Logic Programs [GLC$^+$95] being a non-monotonic logic, that is, allowing changes of predicate truth assignments. An implementation of this concept is the Business Rules Markup Language (BRML) [GLC99, GL00, com04, BRM04]. Alternatively, also linear logic has been used for modeling workflows [Sin03] providing a distributed enactment.

All these different approaches focus on particular properties of workflow modeling like communication aspects, deontic aspects, or logical and time constraints. However, all these approaches can be used to represent local workflows and a definition and an evaluation of local consistency based on message sequences can be realized. Further, consistency of multi-lateral collaborations can be decided if all local specifications are merged, while a decentralized notion of consistency has not been presented so far.

3.3 Web based Electronic Data Interchange

Contrary to the before mentioned generic workflow models Web based Electronic Data Interchange (EDI) standards exist, which focus on a specific domain and specify quite detailed the involved parties as well as the particular local workflows forming the multi-lateral collaboration. Examples are

- the Micropayment Markup language [Mic99, HY97], which specifies a pay-per-view business model including micropayments to access digital content via the Internet
- the Information and Content Exchange (ICE) Protocol [WOH+98, ICE04], which allows the distribution of digital content on a publish-subscribe pattern
- the Netbill [Tyg98, CTS95] protocol, which supports fair delivery and payment of digital information atomically. Similar protocols have been proposed supporting anonymity of the payer [CHTY96] or providing an optimistic approach [ASW98] requiring a third-party for conflict resolution.
- the Internet Open Trading Protocol (IOTP) [Bur00], which specifies a fixed set of business cases based on a fixed role model of parties being involved.

All these approaches have in common that local workflows adhering to one of these specifications can interact with each other without any risk of inconsistency, thus, a successful execution of the multi-lateral collaboration is guaranteed. Obviously, these protocols are specified by a consortium and thus are established in a centralized way. Further, they do not provide much flexibility on modeling workflows.

However, less restrictive Web based EDI standards evolved like for example ebXML [ebX04], RosettaNet [Ros04], or the Open Travel Alliance (OTA) [OTA04], just to name a few. These standards are based on predefined, semantically agreed, and static message structures as well as basic building blocks (sub-processes) for constructing application and domain specific local workflows. Dependent on the standard or the used communication paradigm, concrete language proposals exists for constructing local workflows, which are mainly based on the formal workflow models introduced above. Examples are the process specification language BPSS [Tea01] within the ebXML framework or the Business Process Execution Language for Web Services (BPEL) [ACD+03] related to Web Services Infrastructure. Unfortunately, these languages are not necessarrily based on a formal model [Aal03], although mappings from a subset of a language to a formal model are provided as for example for a subset of BPEL to CP/T-Nets by Yi and Kochut [YK04] or to Message Sequence Charts (MSC) [Uni99] by Foster et.al. [FUMK03].

Contrary to the initially presented Web based EDI standards, successful execution of a multi-lateral collaboration can not be guaranteed, but has to be checked explicitly. However, the flexibility in modeling workflows is much higher. Since the outlined approaches are strongly related to classical workflow models as introduced in Section 3.1 the same holds for these standards: Local consistency can be defined for a single workflow based on a notion of message sequences. Further, consistency of a multi-lateral collaboration can be derived if a mapping of the multi-lateral collaboration to a single workflow model can be provided as outlined in Section 2.3.2 for Workflow-Nets. A decentralized approach for deciding consistency has not been addressed so far.

The same applies to the generic workflow models introduced in the previous two sections.

3.4 Bilateral Consistency

An extension of local consistency to two parties being involved is bilateral consistency as discussed in Section 2.1. Bilateral consistency is an essential part of establishing a multi-lateral collaboration, since it can be used for example to find potential trading partners to form a multi-lateral collaboration, also known as service discovery.

An approach of bilateral consistency based on Workflow Nets for an asynchronous communication model has been outlined in Section 2.2. Similar approaches exist, like for example by Molina-Jimenez et.al. [MJSSW03] where bilateral consistency is defined as intersection of execution sequences in terms of Finite State Machines, that is, a kind of Place/Transition Nets without support for parallel execution. Another similar approach has been proposed by Mecella et.al. [MPC01] also providing concrete algorithms. However, models supporting the synchronous communication model like for example based on Finite State Automata do not provide means to distinguish between mandatory and optional messages. In particular, it turned out, that there exist no appropriate notion of bilateral consistency for the synchronous communication model. However, in the next chapter such a model is introduced as an extension of Finite State Automata.

In contrast to the theoretical workflow models a technology oriented proposal is for example the matchmaking tool developed in the openXchange project [php04], which matches two collaboration protocol profiles belonging to different business partners and creates an agreement (collaboration protocol agreement) [FK03, Kru03] under the ebXML framework. However, this approach does not distinguish between mandatory and optional messages and, thus, does not meet the bilateral consistency requirements.

3.4.1 Web Services

In the following the discussion focuses on concrete Web Service related technologies. The W3C Web Service architecture working group note [W3C04a] states service discovery as an essential part of the architecture, which can be implemented as a registry like UDDI [IMH+02], an index like Web Service Inspection Language (WSIL) [BBM+01], or a peer-to-peer system like Meteor-S WSDI [VSS+04, ESAA04]. However, the underlying matchmaking approach is orthogonal to the storage and query infrastructure, thus, the further discussion focuses on the matchmaking itself.

Overhage and Thomas [OT02] propose a framework, named WS-specification, which categorizes Web Services into white, yellow, blue, and green pages. The terms, white, yellow, blue, and green pages are adopted from UDDI, but extended and sometimes redefined in WS-specification. White pages for example contain information about general and technological (architecture specification, performance, security) information about services. Yellow pages contain classification information (like in UDDI), blue pages contain conceptual information (process-related, semantics), and green pages contain interface information. Among the observations made in [OT02] is the deficiency of UDDI specification for not describing process-related information of services. Process-related information is thus provided for in the blue pages of WS-specification. They propose BPEL as a possible formal definition language for business process descriptions, but they do not give any hint on how querying of Web Services based on process information can be realized.

Alternatively, Ali et.al. [ARAAW03] proposed UDDIe as an extension to UDDI as an open source implementation [udd03]. UDDIe extends UDDI in three main ways: (i) service leasing support, (ii) introducing properties for describing services and the ability to search on these properties and (iii) extending the UDDI *find* API with the ability to support numeric and logical AND/OR operators. This extension provides a more expressive way to describe and query services than originally provided by UDDI. Further, Field et.al. [FH03, FFH+03] extended the classical UDDI search capabilities by allowing a scripting option to express the queries.However, again the representation of workflows is not covered by these approaches.

A concrete consideration of workflow aspects has been addressed by different language proposals like for example Web Service Conversation Language (WSCL) [BBB+02], Conversation Policy XML (cpXML) [HNL02, Han], Web Service Choreography Interface (WSCI) [W3C02], or Web Services Choreography Description Language (WS-CDL) [W3C04b]. However, these different language proposals allow to specify bilateral collaborations syntactically, but they do not provide an algorithm for the calculation of a bilateral collaboration on behalf of two local workflows nor a consistency criterion.

3.4.2 Semantic Web

Semantic [BLHL01, MSZ01] approaches have also been applied on matchmaking based on local workflows. In particular, OWL-S [Coa04] (formerly DAML-S [ABH+02]) provides a semantic markup for Web Services. A Web Service is characterized by the following dimensions [Coa04]:

- What the service does: a description of the input and output of the service as well as its preconditions and effects denoted in the *service profile*
- How the service works: a description of the composition of the service by other services denoted in the *service model*
- How to access it: a specification of the communication protocols, message formats, and other service specific details denoted in the *service grounding*

As a consequence, semantic matchmaking can be based on *service profiles* and *service models*. Up to now, semantic service discovery focuses on the service profiles as for example done by Srinivasan et.al. [SPS04, PKPS02] where an advertised service profile matches a requested service profile, if "all outputs of the request are matched by the outputs of the advertisement, and all inputs of the advertisement are matched by the inputs of the request." [PKPS02]. Since this approach extends a UDDI registry, again the application to P2P infrastructures has been proposed as for example by Paolucci et.al. [PSNS03]. A detailed analysis of potential matchmaking definitions based on OWL-S is provided by Li and Horrocks in [LH03]. In particular, the different definitions represent kinds of similarities ranging from exact match, subsumption, and intersection up to disjointness, that is, no match at all. However, no matchmaking definition has been applied to service models so far, which somehow needs exact match on control structures, while less restrictive matches for the different tasks are required.

A much simpler semantic approach has been proposed by Bernstein et.al. [BK02, KB01] being based on a process ontology, where each potential workflow model is represented by a concept in the ontology. Thus, querying can be realized as a key word based search. The main draw back of semantic annotation is the necessity of a common ontology used for annotating and querying services. However, this kind of approach requires a very detailed and specific ontology of processes to achieve the required precision, which makes the ontology quite complex and potentially unusable.

Other kinds of logic based approaches addressing service discovery are Web Service Request Language (WSRL) and Product Lifecycle Management PLM_{flow}. WSRL [PAPY02, $APY^{+}02$] addresses planning of an orchestration and composition of services to fulfill user requirements. While WSRL performs service discovery on behalf of temporal and linear constraints, PLM_{flow} [ZFCJ02] is based on rule inferencing using the specified business rules rather than a fixed workflow. Thus, PLM_{flow} is characterized as a rule-based non-deterministic workflow engine aiming to establish cooperation based on local decidability of the trading partners involvement. These approaches are based on the fact that local workflow models are provided to trading partners without hiding business critical information, which makes the approach less applicable to real world scenarios.

3.5 Multi-lateral Collaboration Consistency

A multi-lateral collaboration representing a distributed workflow, is based on communication between several parties each providing its own local workflow. However, several interaction structures of distributed workflows can be differentiated. In accordance to v.d.Aalst [Aal99] in the further discussion capacity sharing, chained execution, subcontracting, and loosely coupled interactions are distinguished. The additionally proposed case transfer interaction is neglected, because it represents a kind of workload balancing rather than a distributed execution.

3.5.1 Capacity Sharing

Capacity sharing means the centralized coordination of a workflow, while the execution of tasks is distributed.

One such approach is OSIRIS, which has been proposed by Schuler et.al.[SWSS04]. The workflow management system requires a centralized deployment of the coordinating global workflow, which is split into several *distributed execution units* each assigned an execution party at run-time. The control of the workflow execution, however, is not done by a centralized workflow engine but by the local parties themselves. That is, after completion of an execution unit, the local party derives another party to continue the execution and forwards the process state to this party. The persistent maintenance of the state is based on a distributed higher order database called *hyperdatabase* [SBG+00, SSSW02].

An agent based approach has been presented by Zeng et.al. [ZBNN01, ZNBO01], where the different tasks are implemented by agents, supervised by monitor agents. The centralized coordination has been slightly weakened to avoid single point of failure.

Due to the existence of a global workflow at initialization time of a workflow, consistency can easily be checked in advance. Thus, there is no need and hence no solution to decentralized establishment of consistent multi-lateral collaborations.

3.5.2 Chained Execution

Chained execution means the global workflow is split into several disjoint sub-processes which are executed by different parties in a sequential order. One such approach is based on a container including a specification of the global workflow and an assignment of a single sub-process for each task of the global workflow. The approach called DigiBox [SBW95] proposed by Intertrust [Int04] addresses the superdistribution [Cox96] of digital content. Since the application domain of this proposal has been limited to trading digital goods, the supported workflow models are focused on digital right management processes [GWW01].

A more flexible approach similar to the DigiBox approach is the XML contracting containers introduced by Greunz et.al. [SGH00]. Their container maintains information flow representing a workflow, legally relevant information, interface specification of the services to be incorporated, and security specifications. In addition, the container maintains the execution state of the process, thus, the container is subsequently passed from one service to another each executing the corresponding local workflow.

Since the different local workflows represent a chained execution, consistency is guaranteed if and only if all local workflows are consistent. The first party of the chained execution can be used as a coordinator for consistency checking in accordance to the linear 2-Phase-Commit protocol [ÖV99]. Thus, no decentralized consistency checking is required.

3.5.3 Subcontracting

Subcontracting means that there exists a coordinator of a multi-lateral collaboration, who delegates execution and coordination of complex tasks to other parties. However, the execution dependencies are hierarchical, thus, representing a tree rather than a graph. In particular, based on a specification of the sub-process, potential partners have to be found, a particular one has to be selected, and the execution/enactment can be started.

One example of such an architecture has been proposed by Merz et.al. [MGT+98], where sub-processes are characterized by parameters and maintained in a hierarchical structure of specialization and generalization, called *service types*. Sub-processes can be combined by so called *service type templates* to model application specific composite services involving several services. These templates are used for bilateral consistency checking to find service providers, which finally can be executed.

Casati et.al. [CIJ+00b, CIJ+00a] proposed the eFlow approach as a very dynamic hierarchically organized composition of simple or composite services, thus, representing a nested workflow execution. Due to the late binding of a service to a concrete service instance either at process initialization time or at process run-time the service instances need to be stateless to guarantee successful business interactions.

In the CrossFlow project [GAHL00, Cro04] sub-processes are specified in terms of Quality of Service, price of the service, other attributive constraints, and a set of tasks that can be outsourced. Thus, the matching of sub-processes drills down to matching of parameters and finding adequate sub-processes on a level of tasks [KWA99]. Bilateral consistency of workflows requires a complete match of the requested tasks that is known as the exact set cover problem [GJ79, Bea87] meaning to find a set of sub-processes, where each task is assigned exactly one sub-process. Due to the complexity of the service description, templates are used since application specific workflows provide quite flexible interfaces to trading partners [HLGA01].

Georgakopoulos et.al. [GSCB99] used a notion of conversation, that is, explicating only exchanged coordination activities to potential trading partners rather than the complete local workflow. By hiding business critical information from trading partners this approach is applicable to real world scenarios, although the loss of information may result in failing business transactions. Another approach to derive a conversation has been proposed by Martens [Mar04], where the original workflow model is Coloured Place/Transition Nets.

Due to the tree-based dependency structure of a collaboration, consistency can be guaranteed if and only if all local workflows are consistent. Consistency checking can be realized by a classical 2-Phase Commit protocol [ÖV99], where the top-level node of the dependency tree is the coordinator of the protocol. Thus, a decentralized consistency checking is not required.

3.5.4 Loosely Coupled

Loosely coupled execution of a global workflow is based on several parties where each party is coordinating its own local workflow, while the combination of the local workflows results in a global workflow. Since consistency of a workflow model can usually be defined based an the set of potential execution sequences, a straight forward approach is to check consistency on a centralized global workflow model, which has to be split afterwards into several local ones forming the multi-lateral collaboration. This approach has been applied to several workflow models, like for example by v.d.Aalst and Weske [AW01a] to Workflow Nets (WF-Nets), by Fu et.al. to guarded Finite State Automata [FBS04], by Yi and Kochut [YK04] to Coloured Place/Transition Nets, or by Wodtke and Weikum [WW97] to statecharts. However, this represents the top-down approach based on a centralized consistency checking, which is not addressed in this thesis.

The bottom-up approach of constructing the global workflow based on several local workflows has been investigated to a lesser extend. An approach based on WF-Nets has been proposed by v.d.Aalst [Aal02, Aal99] as informally introduced in Section 2.3.2 and formally specified later on in Section 4.2.4. However, the proposed approach is based on deciding consistency of a multi-lateral collaboration based on the constructed global workflow, which requires a single party knowing the local workflows of all parties involved, thus, being a centralized consistency checking.

An alternative approach has been proposed by Kindler, Martens, and Reisig in [KMR00]. In particular, local consistency criteria are specified to decide global consistency based on an asynchronous communication model. However, local consistency is decidable only with regard to a globally defined "specification", where a specification is a set of execution sequences. Thus, the approach allows to locally check consistency of several local workflows with a predefined abstract global workflow, which represents all exchanged message sequences. It is another approach of abstracting local workflows opposed to the inheritance proposed by v.d.Aalst. This work has also been applied to calculate abstract representations of local workflows as presented by Martens in [Mar04].

The approach proposed by Fu et.al. [FBS04, Fu04] is based on FSA with an unbounded FIFO queue to store incoming messages based on a reliable communication infrastructure (no loss of messages). Consistency of a multi-lateral collaboration is based on a globally defined "conversation protocol", that is, the set of potentially exchanged message sequences in the multi-lateral collaboration, and a set of conditions to ensure consistency called *realizablity* of the conversation protocol. To represent message parameters, FSA are extended by guards, which are used to limit parameters as well as to assign values to parameters, called Guarded Automata. The proposed set of conditions is quite restrictive since for example parallel execution of tasks can not be represented by serialization of execution sequences.

However, the approaches [Aal99, KMR00, FBS04] require a centralized decision making and are not constructive, that is, they only specify criteria for various notions of consistency but do not provide an approach to adapt local workflows to make the collaboration consistent. In addition, neither of the approaches addresses the synchronous communication model, nor allows for decentralized consistency checking.

3.5.5 Conclusion

Based on these observations, different consistency definitions have been investigated. The discussion starts with local consistency of different workflow models, continues with multi-lateral consistency definitions under specific consideration of the decentralization aspect, and concludes with bilateral consistency definitions. It turns out, that local consistency can be defined on every workflow model in terms of execution sequences of a workflow. However, multi-lateral consistency is based on a centralized aspect, that is, either the decision making is centralized or a global specification of the message exchanges within the multi-lateral collaboration has to be provided. Thus, a proposal of a decentralized multi-lateral consistency checking has not been found.

Due to the decentralization aspect multi-lateral consistency checking has to rely on bilateral consistency checking of parties being involved in the multi-lateral collaboration. The discussion of bilateral consistency definitions can be summarized as follows: Most bilateral consistency definitions are based on asynchronous communication models supporting mandatory and optional messages. A potential approach realizing bilateral consistency on a synchronous communication model is based on standard Finite State Automata not supporting mandatory and optional messages. As a consequence, decentralized multi-lateral consistency based on a synchronous communication model requires a definition of a sufficient bilateral consistency definition, while sufficient definitions for an asynchronous communication model are already available.

Chapter 4

Local Consistency Checking

The WF-Net approach presented so far supports an asynchronous communication model as illustrated in the example depicted in Figure 4.1. The example involves party A and party B, where party A is sending two messages (*A#B#msg2* before *A#B#msg1*), which are received by party B in reverse order. However, the bilateral WF-Net is consistent, since after sending *A#B#msg2* to the channel the second message can be sent to another channel. Party B picks up the messages from the channels, while message *A#B#msg1* is picked up first, followed by message *A#B#msg2*. As a consequence no deadlock can occur, thus, the WF-Net is consistent. The communication is asynchronous due to placing messages on channels without knowing when the receiving party will pick them up. As a consequence the order of receiving messages might be different from the initial sending of messages, which is not possible within synchronous communication models, since a sent message has to be received immediately.

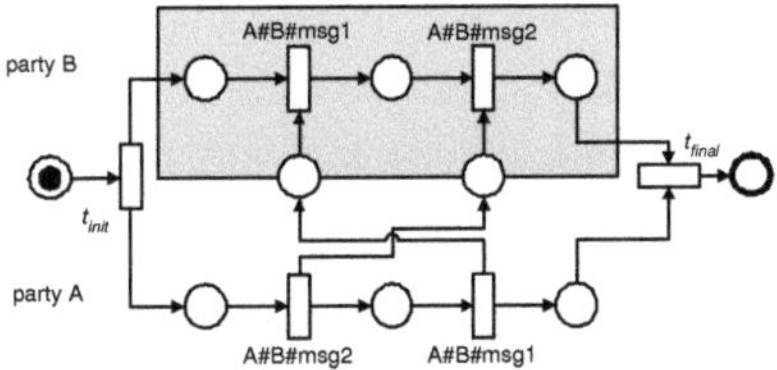

Figure 4.1: Asynchronous WF-Net Example

Service Oriented Architectures may be asynchronous or synchronous dependent on the underlying communication protocol like for example SMTP or HTTP respectively. To prove the correctness of the presented approach for decentralized collaboration establishment, a formal specification of the underlying workflow model is required. For asynchronous communication WF-Nets have been studied extensively, thus, further discussion focuses on recalling existing results. However, synchronous communication is not adequately covered by WF-Nets and no adequate formal model exists. Thus, annotated finite state automata are introduced and discussed in detail.

Independent of the underlying communication model, a formal model of parameter constraints is needed, which supports reasoning on the satisfiability and subsumption of parameter constraints. In particular, parameters may be of different types like, for example, integer or string, and individual constraints can be used to construct more complex logical expressions which are used afterwards in the formal workflow models to decide local consistency.

4.1 Parameter Constraint Model

Modeling of parameter constraints within a less restrictive form of WF-Nets known as Place/ Transition Nets (P/T-Nets) is well known from Predicate/Transition Nets [Gen87] or colored Place/ Transition Nets [Jen92], where arcs connecting transitions and places are labeled with colors, that is, assigning a finite data type. At execution time of a colored P/T-Net tokens are associated with concrete values in accordance with the data type assigned to the arc a token moves along. The value assigned to a token is further used to constrain the enabling of transitions during the execution of the net, where the constraints are related to transitions via a so called guard function. In particular, a guard function associates a transition with a guarded expression, that is, a conjunction of constraints on values assigned to tokens expressed by comparison operations corresponding to the data type of the token value.

Obviously, the color extension is evaluated at execution time of a net. Further, the color extension is a shorthand notation of a more complex classical P/T-Net, where all combinations of parameters and their satisfaction of constraints is modeled explicitly. In particular, it can be shown that for every non-hierarchical colored P/T-Net an equivalent P/T-Net can be constructed, which ensures that equivalent markings are reachable by both nets [Jen92].

The modeling of parameter constraints for decentralized collaboration establishment requires reasoning capabilities on the satisfiability of guard expressions. Due to the equivalence of colored P/T-Nets to classical P/T-Nets token values and guard expressions are translated into a structural representation, which can be analyzed by consistency checking. Since the approach is applicable only to finite domains and the complexity of the equivalent P/T-Net can be quite great, this approach is not feasible.

Alternatively, guard expressions are modeled by means of description logic [BCM+03], where a complex decidable reasoner on satisfiability of parameter constraints exists which is dependent on the data types used. Description logic is based on a terminology representing an application domain representing the "world" and the representation of properties of the terminology representing the description of the "world". A terminology called TBox is based on concepts representing the vocabulary of the terminology and on roles representing relations between concepts to create a classification of concepts. While concepts and roles are relevant at specification time of a model and thus relevant to the collaboration establishment phase, the description of the "world" in terms of concrete assertions on concepts and roles called ABox is related to the execution time of a multi-lateral collaboration. In the following basic definitions and explanations to Description Logic are provided as far as they are relevant to this thesis. An overview of the different definitions and their interdependencies is depicted in Figure 4.2, where arcs have the semantics "is based on".

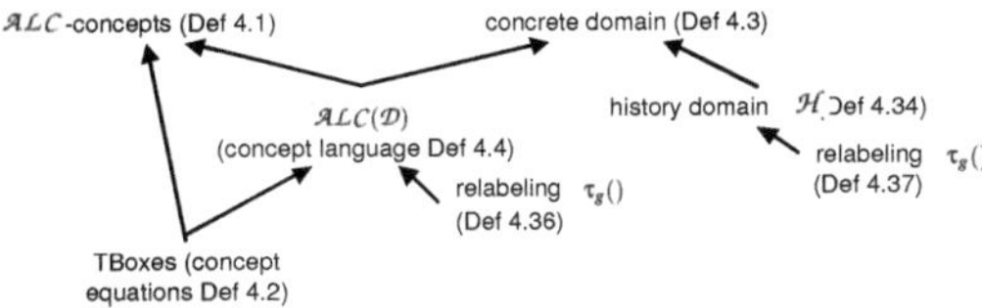

Figure 4.2: Map of Description Logic Definitions

The set of definitions is based on an Attributive Language including Complement $\mathcal{ALC}$ (Definition 4.1), which is the basis for expressing static (so called TBox (Definition 4.2)) and dynamic (so called ABox) constraints. Since the consistency checking of collaborations is based on the workflow specifications as opposed to the workflow execution, TBoxes representing the concepts are used instead of ABoxes instantiating the concepts at execution time. Thus, ABoxes are not used in the course of this thesis and therefore are not formally introduced. A formal definition of ABoxes can be found in [BCM$^+$03]. Since $\mathcal{ALC}$ does not provide the possibility to consider domain specific constraints, concrete domains $\mathcal{D}$ (Definition 4.3) are introduced being comparable to abstract data types providing constraint predicates, which are introduced as a generic extension of $\mathcal{ALC}$ resulting in the concept language $\mathcal{ALC}(\mathcal{D})$ (Definition 4.4). Later on in this thesis, these basic definitions are extended by a relabeling operation $\tau_g()$ (Definitions 4.36 and 4.37), which are defined on the concept language $\mathcal{ALC}(\mathcal{D})$ and therefore must also be defined on concrete domains $\mathcal{D}$ themselves. Further, a specific concrete domain, the history domain (H) (Definition 4.34), is introduced later on to overcome the problem of cyclic interdependencies.

Next, detailed definitions are given. In particular, a language used to define concepts is introduced and a formal definition of TBoxes is provided based on [Lut02, BCM$^+$03].

To describe TBoxes and ABoxes the attributive language including complement $\mathcal{ALC}$ is used to specify concepts and is formally defined as follows [Lut02]:

Definition 4.1
Let N_C and N_R be disjoint and countably infinite sets of concept names and role names. The set of $\mathcal{ALC}$-concepts is the smallest set such that

- every concept name $A \in N_C$ is an $\mathcal{ALC}$-concept and
- if C and D are $\mathcal{ALC}$-concepts and $R \in N_R$ a role name, then $\neg C, C \sqcap D, C \sqcup D, \exists R.C$, and $\forall R.C$ are $\mathcal{ALC}$-concepts.

The following abbreviations are used for some fixed propositional tautologies such as $\top$ for $A \sqcup \neg A$, $\bot$ for $\neg\top$, $C \rightarrow D$ for $\neg C \sqcup D$, and $C \leftrightarrow D$ for $(C \rightarrow D) \sqcap (D \rightarrow C)$.

Based on this language the terminology of description logic known as TBox can be formally defined [Lut02].

Definition 4.2
An expression of the form $C \doteq D$, where C and D are concepts, is called a *concept equation*. A finite set $\mathcal{T}$ of concept equations is called general *TBox* (or TBox for short).

An example of such a concept equation is the classical definition of the concept "Mother" as a person having at least one child, which can formally expressed as

$$Mother \doteq Person \sqcap \exists hasChild.Person$$

The reasoning performed on a TBox is checking subsumption and satisfiability of the concepts, that is, are the concept equations non-contradictory. In either case well established algorithms exist [BCM+03].

So far, concepts and relations between these concepts have been introduced. With regard to representing parameter constraints within description logic, a potential approach is to model data types explicitly in a TBox. This approach turned out to be impractical due to the large number of order relations that have to be modeled explicitly. An alternative approach is to extend the $\mathcal{ALC}$-language by a data type such as, for example, non-negative integer values $\mathbb{N}$ and functional roles, that is, relations associating concepts with a data type. Based on this extension, the concept language is extended by a data type and the predicates provided by it. Exemplary data types and related predicates are numerical data types providing predicates like "less-than" or "greater-than", while a lexical data type provides predicates like "starts-with" or "contains". This extension of description logic is known as description logic with concrete domains [BH91, BCM+03]. A concrete domain $\mathcal{D}$ representing a data type consists of a set of symbols and a set of predicates defined as follows [Lut02]:

Definition 4.3
A concrete domain $\mathcal{D}$ is a pair $(\Delta_{\mathcal{D}}, \Phi_{\mathcal{D}})$, where $\Delta_{\mathcal{D}}$ is a set and $(\Delta_{\mathcal{D}}, \Phi_{\mathcal{D}})$ is a set of predicate names. Each predicate name $P \in \Phi_{\mathcal{D}}$ is associated with an arity n and an n-ary predicate $P_{\mathcal{D}} \subseteq \Delta^n_{\mathcal{D}}$.

An example of a concrete domain is the set of all non-negative integers $\mathbb{N}$ supporting the binary predicates $<, \leq, \geq, >$ to compare two numerical values, as well as the unary predicates $<_n, \leq_n, \geq_n$ $, >_n$, where n represents the numerical value of the right hand side of the comparison predicate with $n \in \mathbb{N}$ [Lut03]. An additional example is the domain of strings $\mathbb{S}$, where predicates like "contains" and "substring-of" are relevant [HS01, PH02].

To be able to extend the reasoning algorithms of description logic to concrete domains, the concrete domains must be closed under negation, since the reasoning algorithms are based on a normal form of concepts requiring negation operation. In addition, finite conjunctions of predicates have to be evaluated on their satisfiability, that is, deciding whether there exists at least a single value in the domain fulfilling the logical expression. Thus, the concrete domain requires the satisfiability of finite conjunctions of predicates to be decidable. It can be shown that the set of real numbers is a concrete domain, although the set of rational numbers is not [BCM$^+$03].

Definition 4.4
The concept language $\mathcal{ALC}(\mathcal{D})$ with a concrete domain $\mathcal{D}$ is constructed by extending Definition 4.1 of $\mathcal{ALC}$ by

- adding a disjoint set of functional roles N_{fR} to the set N_R of roles, where the right hand side of a functional role belongs to the domain $\mathcal{D}$ and
- adding the following production rule $C, D \longrightarrow \exists(u_1, \ldots, u_n).P$, where C and D are concepts, $u_1, \ldots, u_n$ functional roles, and P be an n-ary predicate within the domain $\mathcal{D}$.

With regard to the example (see Section 2.3.1), the data types used within the example are $\mathbb{N}$, representing positive integers and $\mathbb{S}$, representing the concrete domain of strings. In particular, parameters used within the different messages are considered to be semantically equivalent if they are named equally. This simplification rules out mappings of parameter names without limiting the general approach. As a consequence, only a single base concept is needed called "self" meaning the transition itself, while binary functional roles are used to relate a message parameter with the concrete domain of a single numerical or lexical parameter. Thus, the single concept used is *self*, while the functional roles are: $has\_a, has\_it, has\_p, has\_tn, has\_st$. Thus, for example the deliver confirmation message (see Section 2.3.1) *deliver_conf(it,a,tn)* has the parameters item number *it*, amount *a*, and tracking number *tn*. Representing the constraint of the amount *a* being below 100 can be expressed as

$$\exists has_a. < 100$$

where the predicate $<$ is the unary predicate in the concrete domain of natural numbers meaning that the value following the predicate is bigger than the one derived from the binary functional role.

These concept and functional roles can be used to construct a TBox representing a single constraint, which is assigned by the guard function to a particular transition. For example, the constraint of the amount being below 100 assigned to the transition labeled *B#A#order* at the buyer workflow is represented in $\mathcal{ALC}(\mathbb{N})$ by the TBox containing the single line $\exists(has\_a). \leq_{100}$. In general, a parameter constraint has the form of an existential quantification on the functional role referencing the parameter followed by a predicate on the parameter value. Additional parameter constraints can be added using conjunction or disjunction. In contrast to the current example, the combination of several concrete domains representing different data types is possible as shown by [BH91],for example.

The reasoning on the satisfiability of a TBox is provided by standard algorithms, which are often based on the tableau algorithm [BCM$^+$03]. The computational complexity of the reasoning strongly depends on the used concrete domains and the complexity of the TBoxes. A general computational complexity result is that satisfiability of general $\mathcal{ALC}$-concepts with regard to general TBoxes is EXPTIME-complete[1] [Lut02]. Extending $\mathcal{ALC}$ by concrete domains increases complexity. In particular, Lutz showed that satisfiability of general $\mathcal{ALC}(\mathcal{D})$-concepts with regard to general TBoxes is undecidable. However, the $\mathcal{ALC}(\mathcal{D})$-concept satisfiability with regard to acyclic TBoxes for a concrete domain deciding satisfiability of conjunctions in polynomial time is NEXPTIME-hard[1][Lut02]. Thus, the general modeling approach has quite high computational complexity, however, the subsumption problem in description logic with concrete domains is decidable. Due to the fact that companies do not provide many details about internal decisions and constraints, the complexity of the workflows provided by them as a basis for decentralized consistency checking is not complex. Thus, an approach based on description logic with concrete domains is applicable.

Based on this representation of parameter constraints, the formal models for asynchronous and synchronous communication can be introduced.

4.2 Asynchronous Model

The formal model to represent asynchronous communication is based on Workflow Nets (WF-Nets), while description logic as introduced in the previous section is used to specify parameter constraints. The following definitions, which are based on [Mar02, Pet81, Jen92, Aal99], are required to provide a clear semantics of the extensions of WF-Nets and the effects on the corresponding operations. Then, an overview of the definitions and their interdependencies is provided without explaining the different concepts in detail but referencing them. Afterwards, basic definitions for WF-Nets are

[1]The used relations between the different complexity classes are
$P \subseteq NP \subseteq PSPACE \subseteq EXPTIME \subseteq NEXPTIME \subseteq EXPSPACE$.

introduced as far as needed later on for the definition of constraint propagation and consistency. In particular, WF-Nets are a specific form of Place/Transition Nets (P/T-Nets) introduced previously.

4.2.1 Overview of Definitions

In the following an overview of the different definitions and their interdependencies is given and summarized in Figure 4.3 containing a graphical representation including definition numbers, where arcs have the semantics of "is based on". Local consistency based on an asynchronous communication model is based on labeled Place/Transition Nets (labeled P/T-Nets) (Definition 4.5) representing a workflow model and its execution model called marked labeled P/T-Nets (Definition 4.6). The marking of a labeled P/T-Net represents the current "execution state" of a P/T-Net. Relevant properties on marked labeled P/T-Nets are (i) the enabling (Definition 4.7) of a transition within a P/T-Net, that is, when a transition can be performed, and (ii) the reachable markings (Definition 4.8) being a set of transition sequences which can be derived from a particular marking of a labeled P/T-Net. An alternative graph based representation of the reachable markings derived from an initial marking of a labeled P/T-Net is the so called occurrence graph (Definition 4.10), where the vertices represent a specific marking of a marked labeled P/T-Net and an arc represents performing a single transition.

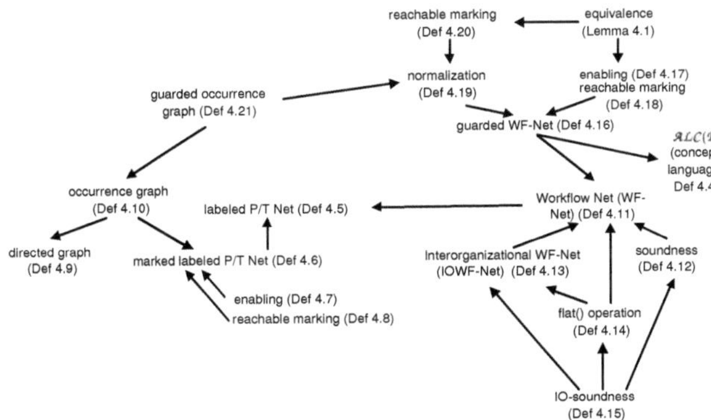

Figure 4.3: Map of Definitions for the Asynchronous Model

Based on these basic definitions of P/T-Nets, the restirctions to Workflow Nets (WF-Nets) (Definition 4.11) are introduced in Section 4.2.3. In particular, a WF-Net is a P/T-Net restricted by having a single start and final place, and containing only transitions which are contained in at least one transition sequence within the reachable markings. Since WF-Nets are a restriction of P/T-Nets, the properties of P/T-Nets remain valid, while an additional property is soundness (Definition 4.12), which means that the workflow does not contain any recursion and is deadlock free. Extending WF-Nets to multi-lateral collaborations results in an interorganizational WF-Net (IOWF-Net) (Definition 4.13) (see Section 4.2.4), where asynchronous channels between the different local workflows represented each by a WF-Net are introduced. In particular, such an IOWF-Net can be transformed into a WF-Net by the *flat()* operation (Definition 4.14). Further, an IO-soundness property (Definition 4.15) can be defined on IOWF-Net which is based on soundness of the local WF-Nets contained in the IOWF-Net and soundness on the WF-Net derived by the *flat()* operation.

In the next step (see Section 4.2.5) guarded WF-Nets (Definition 4.16) are introduced, which allow the modeling of parameters and constraints on executing transitions. These constraints are based on a conceptual language with concrete domains $\mathcal{ALC}(\mathcal{D})$ (Definition 4.4) as introduced in Section 4.1. Since the additional constraints affect the enabling of transitions due to the constraints, the definitions of enabling (Definition 4.17) and reachable marking (Definition 4.18) as known from P/T-Nets have to be adapted. However, the modified enabling definition requires an evaluation of constraints, thus, an analysis based on structural properties does not suffice. Therefore, a normalization of guarded WF-Nets (Definition 4.19) is introduced in Section 4.2.6, where the reachable marking of the normalized guarded WF-Net is equivalent to the reachable marking of the original guarded WF-Net. As a consequence, a guarded occurrence graph (Definition 4.21) based on normalized guarded WF-Nets is defined in accordance with the structural reachable marking definition.

4.2.2 Place/Transition Net

A Place/Transition Net consists of places and transitions and connections between them, where transitions are labeled with message names. The formal definition is as follows [Mar02]:

Definition 4.5

Let U be a universe of identifiers and L a set of labels. A labeled Place/Transition Net (P/T-Net) is a tuple $N = (P, T, F, \ell)$ such that:

- $P \subseteq U$ is a finite set of places,
- $T \subseteq U$ is a finite set of transitions,
- $F \subseteq (P \times T) \cup (T \times P)$ is a set of directed arcs, called flow relations, and
- $\ell : T \rightarrow L \cup \{\tau\}$ is a labeling function, where τ represents a silent transition and all other labels are of the form *s#r#msg* with sender s sending message *msg* to recipient r.

A P/T-Net specifies the structure of a workflow, while an execution requires an additional notion of state. States are known as *markings* in P/T-Nets. A marking is a distribution of tokens on the set of places. In particular, a marking is formally represented as a bag of places, that is, a multiset of symbols (here places) and therefore represents a function from the set of symbols (here places P) to the set of natural numbers indicating the number of symbol occurrences [Mar02]. The set of all bags over a set A is denoted as $\mathcal{B}(A)$. The bag of places from which input tokens are removed by a transition t is noted as $\bullet t$, while $t\bullet$ represents the bag of places where output tokens are added.

Additional operations available on bags are $+$ and $-$, that is, adding and removing tokens from a bag [Mar02].

Definition 4.6
A marked, labeled P/T-Net is a pair *(N,s)*, where $N = (P,T,F,\ell)$ is a labeled P/T-Net and where $s \in \mathcal{B}(P)$ is a bag over places P denoting the marking (also called state) of the net.

Based on the marking the enabling of transitions can be defined as follows [Aal00]:

Definition 4.7
Let *(N,s)* be a marked, labeled P/T-Net, where $N = (P,T,F,\ell)$ is a labeled P/T-Net and s a marking. A transition $t \in T$ is enabled, denoted $(N,s)[t\rangle$, if and only if each of its input places p contains a token. That is, $(N,s)[t\rangle \Leftrightarrow \bullet t \leq s$.

If a transition is enabled, it can be fired, that is, the marking is changed in the sense that tokens of the input places of the transition are removed and tokens are added to the output places of the transition. Formally, the firing of a transition is expressed for a label a of a transition t by $(N,s)[a\rangle(N,s')$ with $s' = s - \bullet t + t\bullet$.

Due to the fact that equivalence of P/T-Nets is undecidable [Hac76], similarity of P/T-Nets is analyzed with regard to the sequence of fired transitions supported by a P/T-Net, called firing sequences. Two P/T-Nets are considered to be similar, if they have the same set of firing sequences, which are represented via an occurrence graph. To formally introduce occurrence graphs, the set of all states that may occur during the execution of the P/T-Net has to be defined as the set of reachable markings [Aal00].

Definition 4.8
The set of reachable markings of a marked, labeled P/T-Net (N,s) with $N = (P,T,F,\ell)$, denoted $[N,s\rangle$, is defined as the set $\{s' \in \mathcal{B}(P) \mid \exists \sigma \in T^*.(N,s)[\sigma\rangle(N,s')\}$.

An occurrence graph is a directed graph, where markings are represented as vertices and arcs connect vertices via a node function representing transition labels. A directed graph is formally defined by [Jen92] as follows:

Definition 4.9
A directed graph is a tuple $DG = (V,A,Node)$ such that V is a set of vertices, A is a disjoint set of arcs ($V \cup A = \emptyset$), and $Node$ is a node function assigning an arc the source and target vertices.

The relation of a P/T-Net and the directed graph is formalized by the following definition [Jen92]:

Definition 4.10
An occurrence graph of a labeled P/T-Net $N = (P,T,F,\ell)$ derived from an initial marking s_0 is a directed graph $OG = (V,A,Node)$, where

- the set of vertices V is $V = (N,s_0\rangle$,
- the set of arcs A is $A = \{(s_1,t,s_2) \in V \times T \times V \mid s_1[t\rangle s_2\}$,
- and the node function $Node$ is defined by $\forall a = (s_1,t,s_2) \in A.Node(a) = (s_1,s_2)$,

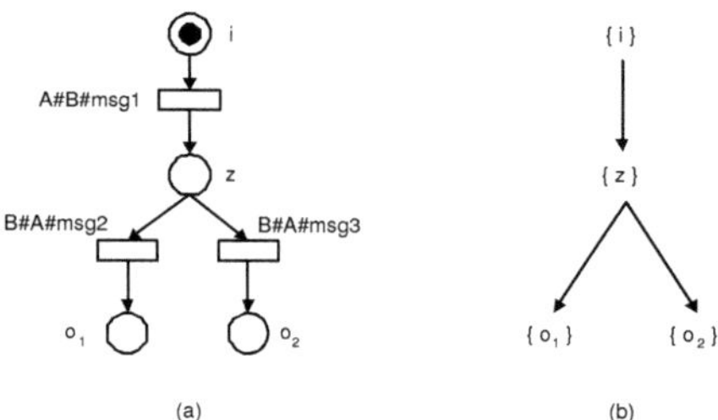

Figure 4.4: Example P/T-Net: (a) P/T-Net (b) corresponding Occurrence Graph

To illustrate the above definitions, Figure 4.4(a) depicts a simple P/T-Net representing two potential execution sequences *A#B#msg1 - B#A#msg2* and *A#B#msg1 - B#A#msg3*. The corresponding occurrence graph derived from this P/T-Net is depicted in Figure 4.4(b) where each marking is a vertex and the transitions between the markings are arcs.

4.2.3 Workflow Net

Based on the definition of P/T-Net, the actions of a Workflow Net (WF-Net) of having a single start place, a single final place, and the requirement of having no transitions, which cannot be fired in any reachable marking, can be introduced formally [AH02].

Definition 4.11
Let $N = (P,T,F,\ell)$ be a labeled P/T-Net. Net N is a Workflow Net (WF-Net) if and only if the following conditions are satisfied:

1. instance creation: P contains an input (source) place $i \in U$ such that this input place i is not an output place of any transition, that is, $\forall t \in T.i \notin t\bullet$,
2. instance completion: P contains an output (sink) place $o \in U$ such that this output place i is not an input place of any transition, that is, $\forall t \in T.o \notin \bullet t$,

3. connectedness: every node $x \in P \cup T$ is on a path from i to o.

Based on this WF-Net definition consistency as informally introduced in Section 2 can be defined formally equivalently to soundness in WF-Nets. In particular, a WF-Net is consistent, if no deadlock can occur, that is, there exists no firing sequence resulting in a marking not being a final marking and no further transition is enabled. The formal definition is as follows, where $[i]$ and $[o]$ represent a marking where a single token resides in source and sink place respectively [Aal00]:

Definition 4.12
A WF-Net N with $source(N) = i$ and $sink(N) = o$ is said to be weakly sound if and only if the following conditions are satisfied:

1. safeness: $(N, [i])$ is safe, if and only if, for any reachable marking $s' \in [N, [i]\rangle$ and any place $p \in P$, the place p within the reachable marking s' contains at most one token[2], that is, $s'(p) \leq 1$,

2. proper completion: for any reachable marking $s \in (N, [i]\rangle$, $o \in s$ implies $s = [o]$, and

3. completion option: for any reachable marking $s \in (N, [i]\rangle$, $[o] \in [N, s\rangle$.

N is said to be strongly sound, or *simply* sound, if and only if, in addition there are no dead transitions, that is, $(N, [i])$ contains no dead transitions.

It can be shown that each weakly sound WF-Net can be transformed into a sound WF-Net by removing dead transitions [Aal99].

4.2.4 Interorganizational Workflow Net

Interorganizational Workflow Nets (IOWF-Nets) represent the interaction of several WF-Nets within a single WF-Net via asynchronous communication. In particular, a single communication channel per message transmitted between different WF-Nets is introduced, which are connected with sending transitions by an incoming arc and with receiving transitions by an outgoing arc. In case of several equally labeled receiving transitions the selection of a transition is non-deterministic. An Interorganizational Workflow Net represents the global workflow, that is, the global view of a multilateral collaboration as discussed in Section 2.3.2. The formal definition is as follows [Aal00]:

[2]This property excludes recursion to be modeled in WF-Nets although it can be modeled in P/T-Nets.

Definition 4.13
An Interorganizational Workflow Net (IOWF-Net) is a tuple $(C, F_C, n, N_0, N_1, \ldots, N_{n-1})$ where:

- $C \subseteq U$ is a finite set of channels,
- $N_0, N_1, \ldots, N_{n-1}$ are n WF-Nets such that:
  - each defined by a set of places, a set of transitions, a flow relation, and a labeling function, that is, $\forall 0 \leq k < n. N_k = (P_k, T_k, F_k, \ell_k)$,
  - where the sets of places and transitions of all WF-Nets are pairwise disjoint, that is, $\forall 0 \leq k < l < n. (P_k \cup T_k) \cap (P_l \cup T_l) = \emptyset$, and
  - where the set of places and tranisitions of all WF-Nets are disjoint to the used channels, the input and output places, and the transitions t_i and t_o, that is, $\forall 0 \leq k < n. (P_k \cup T_k) \cap (C \cup \{i, o, t_i, t_o\}) = \emptyset$,
- $F_C \subseteq (C \times (\bigcup_{0 \leq k < n} T_k)) \cup ((\bigcup_{0 \leq k < n} T_k) \times C)$ is a set of directed arcs, called the channel flow relation.

In the above definition it is assumed that the WF-Nets being involved in the IOWF-Net have pairwise disjoint places and transitions and non of them contains the IOWF-Net source place i and sink place o. Further, the transitions t_i and t_o connecting the source and sink places of all WF-Nets with i and o respectively are not used by the WF-Nets already. The WF-Net representation of the IOWF-Net can be constructed by applying the *flat* operation [Aal00].

Definition 4.14
Let $Q = (C, F_C, n, N_0, N_1, \ldots, N_{n-1})$ be an IOWF-Net with $\forall 0 \leq k < n. N_k = (P_k, T_k, F_k, \ell_k)$. The WF-Net $N = (P, T, F, \ell)$ can be derived by $N = flat(Q)$ by taking the union of the WF-Nets contained in the IOWF-Net and combining it with the additional constructs needed such as new input and output place. Thus,

- the set of places P is $P = C \cup \{i, o\} \cup (\bigcup_{0 \leq k < n} P_k)$,
- the set of transitions T is $T = \{t_i, t_o\} \cup \bigcup_{0 \leq k < n} T_k$,
- the labeling function ℓ is $\ell = \{(t_i, \tau), (t_o, \tau)\} \cup \bigcup_{0 \leq k < n} \ell_k$, and
- the flow relation F is
  $$F = F_C \cup (\bigcup_{0 \leq k < n} F_k) \cup \{(i, t_i), (t_o, o)\} \cup \{(t_i, source(N_k)) \mid 0 \leq k < n\} \cup \cup \{(sink(N_k), t_o) \mid 0 \leq k < n\}$$

Since the *flat* operation transforms an IOWF-Net to a WF-Net, soundness of an IOWF-Net, called IO-soundness, is defined as soundness of each WF-Net being involved and soundness of the flattened IOWF-Net [Aal00].

Definition 4.15

An IOWF-Net $Q = (C, F_C, n, N_0, N_1, \ldots, N_{n-1})$ is IO-sound, if and only if it is locally and globally sound. IOWF-Net is locally sound, if and only if each of its local Workflow Nets N_k with $0 \leq k < n$ is sound. IOWF-Net is globally sound, if and only if *flat(Q)* is sound.

Based on this definition, global consistency of a multi-lateral collaboration can be expressed as IO-soundness of the corresponding IOWF-Net. With regard to the example in Section 2.3.1 the IOWF-Net as depicted in Figure 2.6 is IO-sound, that is, consistent. In addition, the construction of IOWF-Nets can be used to check consistency of a bilateral collaboration by forming an IOWF-Net with two parties involved and checking IO-soundness. An example of such a bilateral WF-Net with regard to the example in Section 2.3.1 again, is the bilateral WF-Net of buyer and accounting department depicted in Figure 4.5 [3].

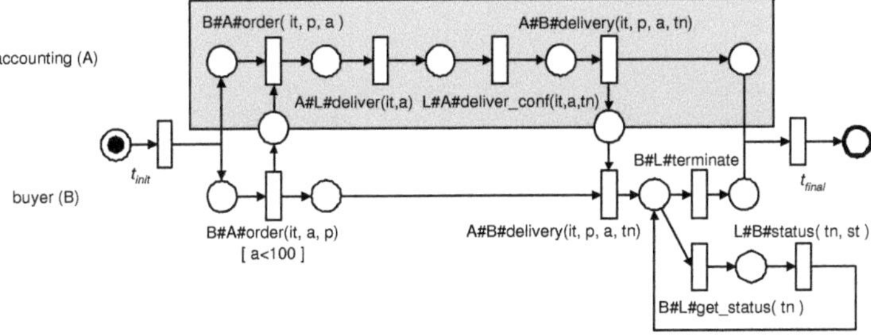

Figure 4.5: Bilateral WF-Net of Buyer and Accounting Department without Abstraction

Based on this interpretation, the requirements for bilateral consistency stated in Section 2.1.2 with regard to deciding consistency under specific consideration of message exchange sequences and differentiating mandatory and optional messages are fulfilled. By introducing channels and relating transitions to the channel places, a final marking can be reached, if and only if all messages sent by one party are received by the corresponding party. As a consequence, message exchange sequences supported by the two trading parties are taken into account. In particular, sending a message inserts a token into a channel, where the lack of a receiving party makes the WF-Net inconsistent. As a consequence, sending messages represent mandatory messages, while receiving messages are optional messages, because receiving of a message enables the receiving transition only if the corresponding message has been sent before, thus, has no influence on the consistency of the WF-Net.

Next, the expressiveness of WF-Nets with regard to handling parameter constraints is extended.

[3]This figure represents the same bilateral WF-Net as depicted in Figure 2.7 without abstraction and cycle resolution. However, this bilateral WF-Net is sound if and only if the abstracted WF-Net used in Section 2.3.3 and depicted in Figure 2.7 is sound.

4.2.5 Parameter Constraints

Parameter constraints are introduced to WF-Nets via a guard function similar to colored P/T-Nets, where logical guard expressions assigned to transitions are provided in terms of description logic as introduced in Section 4.1. The original color extension assigns each place a single color as opposed to tuples of colors in the following definition.

Definition 4.16
A guarded WF-Net $N = (P,T,F,\ell,C,G,E)$ is based on a WF-Net (P,T,F,ℓ), a color function $C : P \rightarrow \mathcal{D}_{i_1} \times \ldots \times \mathcal{D}_{i_m}$ assigning a tuple of concrete domains to a place, a guard function $G : T \rightarrow \mathcal{ALC}(\mathcal{D}_0,\ldots,\mathcal{D}_{n-1})$ for a set of concrete domains $\mathcal{D}_0,\ldots\mathcal{D}_{n-1}$, and a flow relation function $E : F \rightarrow \mathcal{D}_{i_1} \times \ldots \times \mathcal{D}_{i_m}$ assigning each flow relation a variable related to a tuple of concrete data types with $0 \leq i_1 < \ldots < i_m < n$.

All guard expressions, that is, the description logic TBox representing constraints, have to be bounded, that is, the variables used in the expression are either quantified within the guard expression or bound by the incoming or outgoing flow relation of the transition.

As a consequence of the data types introduced, the standard semantics of colored P/T-Nets adapts the definition of marking by associating data types with tokens called token elements. In particular, a token element is a tuple of a token and a value of the data type related to a place. In accordance, the enabling of transitions must be redefined using binding elements, that is, a pair of a transition and a binding, where a binding is a function providing possible values for tokens fulfilling the guard expression of the transition [Jen92].

Definition 4.17
Let $N = (P,T,F,\ell,C,G,E)$ be a guarded WF-Net, then

- a binding b is a function assigning all variables $\{v_0,\ldots,v_{m-1}\} = Var(G(t))$ contained in a guard expression $G(t)$ related to a transition t a concrete value c_i of the corresponding data type $\mathcal{D}$ where the concrete values fulfill the guard expression $G(t)$, thus, a binding is a set of variable assignments $b := \{v_0 = c_0,\ldots,v_{m-1} = c_{m-1}\}$;
- $B(t)$ denotes the set of all bindings for a transition t;
- a binding element is a pair (t,b) of a transition t and a corresponding binding b;
- a token element is a pair (p,c) of a place p and a concrete value c of a domain $\mathcal{D}$ or a variable;
- a marking is a bag over token elements.

As a consequence of this extension, a transition t is enabled for a binding element $b = \{v_0 = c_0,\ldots,v_{m-1} = c_{m-1}\} \in B(t)$ denoted as $(N,s)[b\rangle$, if the bag of token elements

$\{(p_0,c'_0),\ldots,(p_{n-1},c'_{n-1})\}$ evaluated from the binding element b of transition t is contained in the current marking s, that is, $\bigcup_{0\leq i<n}(p_i,c'_i)[b] \leq s$, where

$$(p_i,c'_i)[b] := \begin{cases} c_j & if\ c'_i = v_j \wedge (v_j = c_j) \in b \\ c'_i & otherwise \end{cases}$$

The guard function has to be checked for satisfiability to determine the binding elements, which is supported by description logic algorithms, as described in Section 4.1. In accordance to P/T-Nets using the definition of an enabled transition, reachable markings can be defined as follows:

Definition 4.18
The set of reachable markings of a guarded WF-Net (N,s) denoted $[N,s\rangle$, is defined as the set $\{s' \in \mathcal{B}(P\times\mathcal{D}) \mid (\exists\sigma \in B(T)^*.(N,s)[\sigma\rangle(N,s'))\}$.

In case of cyclic guarded WF-Nets or usage of infinite domains, this semantics based on binding elements results in an infinite set of markings, which causes the soundness check to be undecidable. However, the restrictions on acyclic guarded WF-Nets allows a declarative modeling of bindings within a marking resulting in a finite and less complex set of reachable markings.

4.2.6 Constraint Propagation

Since the approach presented in Section 2.4 is based on acyclic WF-Nets, the following discussion focuses on acyclic guarded WF-Nets. The introduced markings are based on representing the distribution of tokens and the constraints collected along the path to reach the marking. This requires to exclude alternatives by introducing a normalized form of guarded WF-Nets, that is, WF-Nets with guard expressions consisting of conjunctions only. This can be achieved by transforming guard expressions in disjunctive normal form and replicating the corresponding transition once per conjunction in the disjunctive normal form of the guard expression.

Definition 4.19
An acyclic guarded WF-Net $N = (P,T,F,\ell,C,G,E)$ can be represented as a normalized acyclic guarded WF-Net $N' = (P,\bigcup_{t\in T}T'_t,\bigcup_{t\in T}F'_t,\bigcup_{t\in T}\ell'_t,C,\bigcup_{t\in T}G'_t,\bigcup_{t\in T}E'_t)$, where for a transition $t\in T$, the corresponding guard expression $e = G(t)$, and the disjunctive normal form of e given as $e' := e_1 \vee \ldots \vee e_n$, the following definitions hold:

- $T'_t := \{t_1,\ldots,t_n\}$ being unique new transitions each representing one disjunction of the guard expression of transition t,
- $F'_t := \bigcup_{t_i\in T'_t}\{(p,t_i) \mid p \in \bullet t\} \cup \bigcup_{t_i\in T'_t}\{(t_i,p) \mid p \in t\bullet\}$ is the new flow relation ensuring that the newly introduced transitions in T'_t have the same input and output places as transition t,

- $\forall t_i \in T_t'.\ell'(t_i) = \ell(t)$ is the new labeling function ensuring that the newly introduced transitions in T_t' have the same labels as transition t ,

- $\forall t_i \in T_t'.G'(t_i) = e_i$ is the new guard function assigning each newly introduced transition in T_t' a conjunctive guard expression taking from the disjunctive normal form e' of transitions t's guard expression e,

- $\forall t_i \in T_t', p \in \bullet t.E'(p,t_i) = E(p,t)$ and $\forall t_i \in T_t', p \in t \bullet .E'(t_i,p) = E(t,p)$ is the new flow relation function ensuring that the newly introduced transitions in T_t' have the same variable assignment at the arcs as transition t.

The above definition is illustrated in Figure 4.6(a) by a WF-Net with a guard expression $e_1(x,y,z) \vee e_2(x,y,z)$, where $e_i(x,y,z)$ are conjunctions of predicates, and a similar normalized WF-Net depicted in Figure 4.6(b). The transition is replicated and the conjunctions of the guard expression are assigned as new guard expressions.

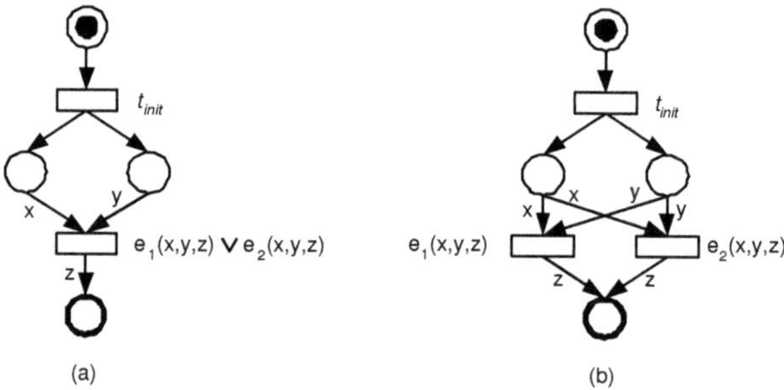

Figure 4.6: (a) WF-Net with Guard Function in Disjunctive Normal Form (b) Normalized WF-Net Equivalent to (a).

Based on this definition, a marking is defined as a marking of a P/T-Net in combination with a conjunction of all guard expressions along the path of transitions resulting in a marking. Further, in case of two transitions contained in the firing sequence, which are equally labeled representing the sending and receiving of a message within a single firing sequence, the guard expression of the transition performed first (representing a sending transition) must be subsumed by the guard expression of the later transition (representing the receiving transition). This additional constraint has to be added to the definition to ensure that no markings are accepted, which are causing deadlocks during the execution of the WF-Net. The initial marking is denoted as $([i], \top)$, where $\top$ is the tautology within description logic (see also Definition 4.1).

Definition 4.20
The set of reachable markings of a normalized acyclic guarded WF-Net (N,s) denoted $[N,s\rangle$, is defined as the set

$$\{(s',e') \in \mathcal{B}(P) \times \mathcal{ALC}(\mathcal{D}) \mid \exists \sigma \in T^*.(N,s)[\sigma\rangle(N,s') \wedge e' = \sqcap_{t\in\sigma} G(t) \wedge e' \text{ is satisfiable} \wedge \forall t',t \in \sigma.t' < t \wedge (\ell(t) \neq \ell(t') \vee (\ell(t) = \ell(t') \wedge G(t) \sqsubseteq G(t')))\}$$

This definition of marking on normalized acyclic guarded WF-Nets is equivalent to the one based on binding elements with regard to soundness of the WF-Net. The following Lemma formalizes this equivalence.

Lemma 4.1 A normalized acyclic guarded WF-Net is sound, based on the declarative marking defined in Definition 4.20, if and only if it is sound based on the marking defined in Definition 4.18.

Proof: Soundness as defined in Definition 4.12 is based on safeness, proper completion and a completion option. Since the first two properties are related to the structure of the WF-Net they are independent of the introduced notion of constraints. The proper completion may further restrict the structural firing sequences, thus the introduction of constraints has an impact.

It has to be shown that the effects of both notions of markings are equivalent. Based on the notion of binding elements, the guard function of a transition fires, if the input places contain token elements which fulfill the guard function. In particular, token elements are omitted which do not fulfill the guard function and therefore are not available for the further processing of the firing sequence. As a consequence, within a marking of a firing sequence, only those token elements are contained, which fulfill all guard functions along the transitions of the guard function. That's exactly the construction of the second marking representation, thus, they are equivalent. In particular, the normalization is needed to have a strict conjunction along a firing sequence. □

Standard algorithms for deciding soundness of WF-Nets can no longer be used, since they rely on a special cyclic extension of a WF-Net, which does not work on the above definitions because of the guard expressions. As a consequence, soundness has to be decided on behalf of the occurrence graph derived from the corresponding WF-Net.

Based on the notion of reachable markings introduced in Definition 4.20, the finite occurrence graph can be constructed and soundness can be decided by traversing all paths of the occurrence graph. Since the WF-Net is acyclic, the occurrence graph is also acyclic, thus, the number of paths is finite. Therefore the computational complexity of deriving the occurrence graph is similar to tree traversal algorithms while the computational complexity of deciding the satisfiability of the leaf nodes of the occurrence graph depends on the concrete domains used as discussed in Section 4.1. The observations made so far apply also to a IOWF-Net and its soundness definition, since it can be represented as a WF-Net.

The relation of a normalized acyclic guarded WF-Net and the directed graph is formalized as follows:

Definition 4.21
A guarded occurrence graph of a normalized acyclic guarded WF-Net $N = (P,T,F,\ell,C,G,E)$ is a directed graph $OG = (V,A,Node,Guard)$, where

- the set of vertices V is $V = (N,([i],\top)\rangle$,
- the set of arcs A is $A = \{(s_1,t,s_2) \in V \times T \times V \mid s_1[t\rangle s_2\}$,
- the node function $Node$ is $\forall a = (s_1,t,s_2) \in A.Node(a) = (s_1,s_2)$, and
- the guard function $Guard$ is $\forall (s_1,t,s_2) \in A.Guard((s_1,t,s_2)) := G(t)$.

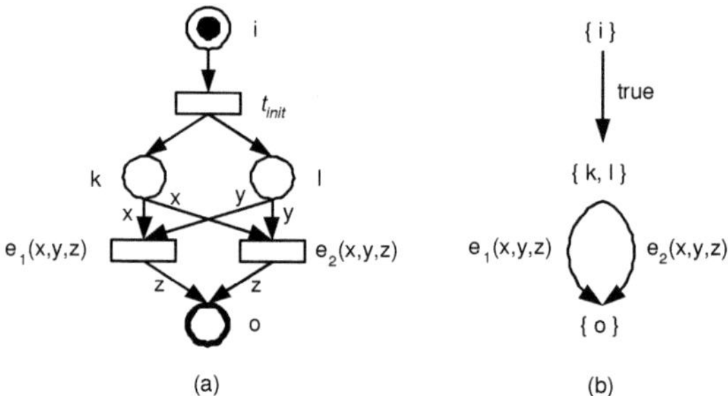

Figure 4.7: (a) Normalized WF-Net (b) Guarded Occurrence Graph of (a).

To illustrate the above definitions, the example discussed in Figure 4.6(b) is reused, which is depicted in Figure 4.7 representing a normalized WF-Net. The occurrence graph constructed from that WF-Net is depicted in Figure 4.7(b) where the vertices are the reachable markings and the guard expressions are assigned to the arcs representing the conjunction of the guard expressions resulting in that particular marking.

Since subsumption and satisfiability of description logic with concrete domains is decidable, the occurrence graph defined above can be constructed. Further, due to the restrictions on acyclic WF-Nets, the occurrence graph is finite. As a consequence, an acyclic guarded WF-Net is sound (in accordance to Definition 4.12), if all path of the finite occurrence graph result in a marking $([o],p)$, where p is a satisfiable predicate, and each marking contains at most one token per place. In addition, the calculation of the occurrence graph provides the propagation of parameter constraints within a normalized acyclic guarded WF-Net.

Due to the undecidability of equivalence in P/T-Nets, they are lacking a minimization theory. As a consequence, modifications performed on the occurrence graph as a consequence of propagation of parameter or occurrence graph constraints cannot be fed back to changes in the WF-Net structure. Thus, after the initial specification of the workflows in terms of guarded WF-Nets, the propagation of constraints and the decentralized decision making on multi-lateral collaboration consistency has to be performed on an occurrence graph representation.

These propagation operations and the corresponding definition of consistency are quite similar to the ones of the synchronous communication model introduced next. In particular, the model is based on finite state automata. This mapping is possible, because occurrence graphs have the same expressiveness as finite state automata. The discussion of the concrete mapping is provided in Section 5.1.

4.3 Synchronous Model

In the previous section a model based on Workflow Nets (WF-Nets) was introduced and extended by parameter constraints called guarded WF-Nets. Further, interorganizational WF-Nets (IOWF-Nets) have been introduced to model multi-lateral collaborations. In particular, the soundness property of WF-Nets has been introduced, which has been extended to IOWF-Nets as a notion of local consistency of a multi-lateral collaboration. Since guarded WF-Nets require an evaluation of constraints during soundness checking, a normalization has been proposed, where the normalized WF-Net can be evaluated with regard to soundness based on structural properties only. This kind of evaluation can be performed based on an occurrence graph representing all executable transition sequences represented in a WF-Net. So far, parameter constraint propagation has been addressed, while resolution of cycles and propagation of occurrence graph constraints (as the remaining conceptual steps of the approach presented in Section 2.4) are not addressed. They will be addressed in the next chapter after the asynchronous model, namely the occurrence graph representation, has been mapped to the formal model for synchronous communication introduced in this section.

As a starting point for a synchronous communication model Finite State Automata [HMU01] are considered to be suitable for modeling multi-lateral collaborations. They can represent (possibly infinite) sets of message sequences without considering branching conditions and parallel execution capabilities as provided by more expressive approaches such as Place/Transition Nets (P/T-Nets). While P/T-Nets are also closed under intersection [Pet81], they require a much higher computational and space complexity compared to Finite State Automata. In particular, P/T-Nets allowing concurrent execution are non-polynomial for reachability and liveness problems [EN94]. If the P/T-Net class is restricted to bounded [4] nets several polynomial results exist. In the case of bounded nets the occurrence graph can be represented as a Finite State Automaton which can get very large but finite. The occurrence graph does not exceed the expressiveness of Finite State Automata. A major advantage of Finite State Automata compared to P/T-Nets is the decidability of equivalence and the corresponding minimization theory. Similar to P/T-Nets, the representation of parameter

[4] A net is bounded if it is has a finite set of possible markings.

constraints requires an extension based on guard functions using description logic with concrete domains. In addition, Finite State Automata do not distinguish between mandatory and optional transitions as required for deciding multi-lateral consistency. As a consequence, the Finite State Automaton model is extended by annotations of states explicating which transitions are mandatory and which are optional, being evaluated by the emptiness test.

The introduction of the formalism starts with an overview of the definitions introduced, followed by the introduction of classical Finite State Automata and their extension by annotations. Afterwards parameter constraints are introduced as guard functions, and the local consistency of multi-lateral collaborations is defined. Based on this foundation, the definition of cycle resolution and constraint propagation follows.

4.3.1 Overview of Definitions

In the following an overview of the different definitions and their interdependencies is given and summarized in Figure 4.8 containing a graphical representation including definition numbers. Local consistency based on a synchronous communication model is based on Finite State Automata (FSA) (Definition 4.22) as already illustrated above. Thus, first the formal definition of a FSA is introduced, followed by the intersection operation (Definition 4.23) and the emptiness test. As illustrated in Section 2.1, the expressiveness of FSA does not suffice to consistency of bilateral collaborations, thus, an extension is introduced fulfilling the requirements. In particular, states of a FSA are annotated by propositional formulas, where the variables used correspond to transition labels. The resulting approach is called annotated FSA (aFSA) (Definition 4.24), and the effects of the extension on the intersection operation (Definition 4.26) and the emptiness test are specified.

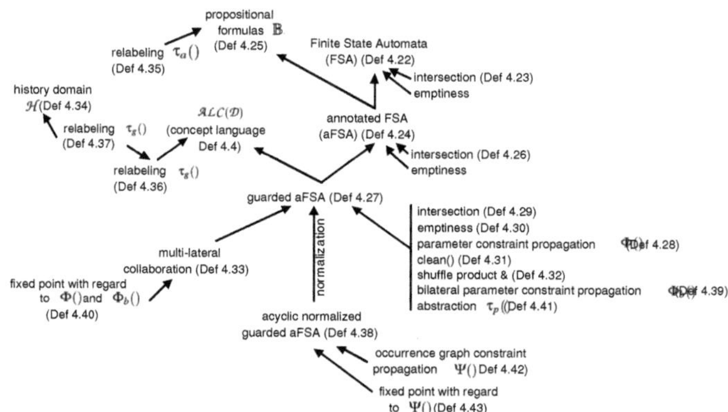

Figure 4.8: Map of Definitions for the Synchronous Model

Similar to the approach used in the asynchronous model, aFSA are extended by parameter constraints resulting in guarded aFSA (Definition 4.27). The parameter constraints are expressed in the concept language with concrete domains $\mathcal{ALC}(\mathcal{D})$ (Definition 4.4) as introduced in Section 4.1. Since the additional constraints affect the usage of transitions due to the constraints, the definitions of intersection (Definition 4.29) and emptiness test (Definition 4.30) have to be adapted. Further, a *clean*() operation (Definition 4.31) to reduce the number of transitions contained in a guarded aFSA is introduced. This operation takes into account the parameter constraints used and removes those, which can never be validated to true. This operation is later on used to realize emptiness testing based on structural aspects without an evaluation of parameter constraints called normalization (Definition 4.38) in accordance to the approach described for the asynchronous model.

To be able to express multi-lateral collaborations, the shuffle operation & (Definition 4.32) is required in accordance to the standard shuffle product definition in FSA extended by specifics of guarded aFSA. In particular, the shuffle product allows us to vary different execution sequences represented by FSA involved in a multi-lateral collaboration. The shuffle product is used to construct the execution sequences of a multi-lateral collaboration (Definition 4.33). In particular, the multi-lateral collaboration is locally consistent, if the constructed multi-lateral collaboration is not empty. Since this initial representation of a multi-lateral collaboration requires a lot of information on all FSA, the basis for an equivalent definition is provided by introducing abstractions of guarded aFSA $\tau_p()$ (Definition 4.41), of propositional formulas $\tau_a()$ (Definition 4.35), and constraints $\tau_g()$ (Definitions 4.36 and 4.37) based on the concept language $\mathcal{ALC}(\mathcal{D})$.

Finally, based on the formally introduced model of guarded aFSA, the steps outlined in Section 2.4 describing the overall approach are introduced. The first step is the resolution of cycles resulting in a acyclic normalized guarded aFSA. The second step is the propagation of parameter constraints, which is formalized in operations $\Phi()$ (Definition 4.28) and $\Phi_b()$ (Definition 4.39) realizing parameter constraint propagation within a single guarded aFSA and between two guarded aFSA respectively. The third step is the propagation of occurrence graph constraints, formalized in operation $\Psi()$ (Definition 4.42). Further, the fixed points are defined on these constraint propagation operations (Definitions 4.40 and 4.43).

4.3.2 Finite State Automaton

Finite State Automata (FSA) are well studied. Formally, Finite State Automata can be represented as follows [HMU01]:

Definition 4.22
A Finite State Automaton A is represented as a tuple $A = (Q, \Sigma, \Delta, q_0, F)$ where :

- Q is a finite set of states,
- Σ is a finite set of messages denoted *s#r#msg* with sender $s \in \mathcal{P}$ sending message *msg* to recipient $r \in \mathcal{P}$, with $\mathcal{P}$ being the set of all parties,
- $\Delta : Q \times \Sigma \times Q$ represents labeled transitions,
- q_0 a start state with $q_0 \in Q$, and
- $F \subseteq Q$ a set of final states.

The only difference to the standard definition of FSAs [HMU01] is that the alphabet Σ consists of messages constructed by a sender, a recipient, and a message name. However, for the purpose of consistency checking of business processes, these triples can be treated like atomic tokens: Two message triples are equal, if their sender, their recipient, and the message (with its parameters) are equal.

A FSA A generates a language $L(A)$ which enumerates the (possibly infinite) set of all message sequences supported by a business process. Two FSAs are consistent, if their languages have a non-empty intersection. The intersection of two FSAs is again a FSA, which can be determined with the usual cross product construction [HMU01] :

Definition 4.23
The intersection $A_1 \cap A_2$ of two automata $A_1 = (Q_1, \Sigma_1, \Delta_1, q_{10}, F_1)$, and $A_2 = (Q_2, \Sigma_2, \Delta_2, q_{20}, F_2)$ is $A = (Q, \Sigma, \Delta, q_0, F)$, with

- $Q = Q_1 \times Q_2$,
- $\Sigma = \Sigma_1 \cap \Sigma_2$,
- $\Delta((q_{11}, q_{21}), \alpha, (q_{12}, q_{22}))$ with $\Delta_1(q_{11}, \alpha, q_{12}) \wedge \Delta_2(q_{21}, \alpha, q_{22})$,
- $q_0 = (q_{10}, q_{20})$, and
- $F = F_1 \times F_2$.

If the resulting automaton does not contain at least one path (possibly of zero length) between the start state and an end state, its language is the empty language $\emptyset$. In this case, the business processes modeled by the FSAs are inconsistent, because they do not share a common message sequence.

An emptiness test algorithm like in [HMU01] is based on the reachability of states within an automaton starting from the start state q_0. The automaton accepts an empty language, if and only if no final state is within the set of reachable states.

A functional definition of an emptiness test is based on a recursive reachability function, where *curP* represents the current path of the recursion and q_i represents the current state. The function terminates, if a final state has been reached (first line of definition) or no further non-cyclic transition is available (third line). The function traverses the automaton in a depth-first manner (second line) searching for at least one path to a final state. An automaton is empty, that is, $Empt(A) := \neg Reach(\emptyset, q_0)$, if no final state is reachable. A formal definition is given below:

$$Reach(curP, q_i) := \begin{cases} true & if q_i \in F \\ \bigvee_{\{q_l | \Delta(q_i, l, q_l)\}} Reach(curP.q_i, q_l) & if q_i \notin F \wedge q_l \notin curP \\ false & otherwise \end{cases}$$

As discussed in Section 2.1,a standard automaton can not distinguish between mandatory and optional messages. Usually, a message in a standard FSA is regarded as an optional one. However, modeling business processes requires both mandatory and optional messages. It is not possible to represent this semantics in message sequences or FSA directly. Thus, an annotation containing this additional meta information is required relevant only for consistency checking.

4.3.3 Annotated Finite State Automaton

Based on the above observation, annotated FSA (aFSA) are introduced as a standard FSA (see Definition 4.22), where each state might be assigned a propositional logical term.

Definition 4.24
An annotated FSA A is represented as a tuple $A = (Q, \Sigma, \Delta, q_0, F, QA)$ where

- Q is a finite set of states,
- Σ is a finite set of messages denoted *s#r#msg* with sender $s \in \mathcal{P}$ sending message *msg* to recipient $r \in \mathcal{P}$, with $\mathcal{P}$ being the set of all parties,
- $\Delta : Q \times \Sigma \times Q$ represents transitions,
- q_0 a start state with $q_0 \in Q$,
- $F \subseteq Q$ a set of final states, and
- $QA : Q \times E$ is a finite relation of states and logical terms within the set E of propositional logic terms.

The terms in E are standard Boolean formulas, adapting the definition in [CS98] [5]:

Definition 4.25

The syntax of the supported logical formulas is given as follows:

- the constants *true* and *false* are formulas,
- the variables $v \in \Sigma$ are formulas,
- if ϕ is a formula, so is $\neg\phi$,
- if ϕ and ψ are formulas, so is $\phi \wedge \psi$ and $\phi \vee \psi$.

The set of all propositional formulas is denoted as $\mathbb{B}$.

The standard semantics of automata is an optional execution of transitions. This is observable also in the functional emptiness test definition given above: a single path to a final state returns a *true* causing the whole disjunction to return *true* in the reachability function. Thus, the logical mapping of automata to annotated automata is an annotation containing a disjunctive expression including all transition labels as depicted in Figure 4.9. For reasons of simplicity, the OR annotations are neglected in the following.

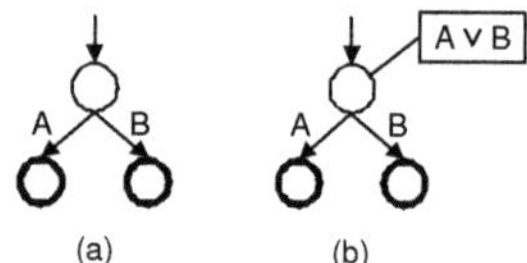

Figure 4.9: (a) Automaton (b) Annotated Automaton Equivalent to (a).

The definition of terms does not force a term to contain all labels of outgoing transitions of the associated state. Thus, annotations may be incomplete, that is, not containing all outgoing transition labels. Such incomplete annotations can be completed by extending them with a disjunction of all labels not contained yet. This method is explained on behalf of an example being an extension of the example introduced in Section 2.1.1 and being depicted in Figure 4.10(a). The process starts with a purchase order (*C#V#PO* message) sent by a customer, which is answered by the vendor via *V#C#delivery* message or an out of stock notification (*V#C#noStock* message) or can directly be canceled again by the customer sending a *C#V#cancel* message. Finally, the payment can be provided by credit card (*C#V#ccPay* message). The annotation provided represents that the vendor insists on having *V#C#delivery* and *V#C#noStock* messages supported. Message *C#V#cancel* is unrelated to messages *V#C#delivery* and *V#C#noStock*, thus, represents an independent alternative,which is combined with the existing term by a disjunction as depicted in Figure 4.10(b).

[5]The description logic $\mathcal{ALC}(\mathcal{D})$ is not used due to the later extension of the approach on a three valued logic (see also Section 4.3.5).

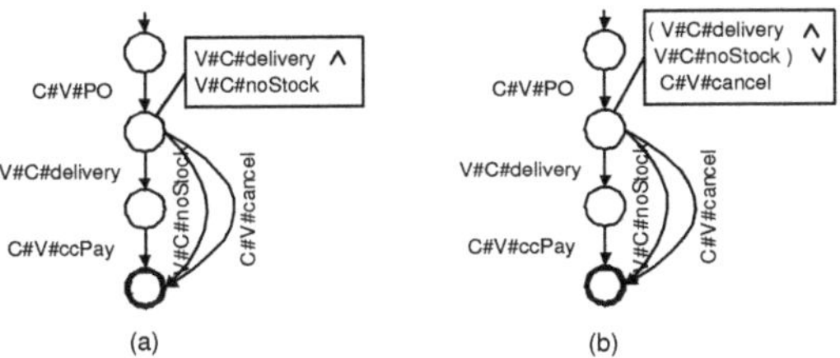

Figure 4.10: (a) Incomplete aFSA (b) Completely Annotated aFSA Equivalent to (a).

Extending terms of annotated automata is quite important for defining the emptiness test later on. The set of variables X^{q_i} corresponding to state q_i is defined as the set of outgoing transition labels of state q_i. Formally expressed as:

$$X^{q_i} := \{x^{q_i} \mid \exists q' \in Q.\Delta(q_i, x^{q_i}, q')\}$$

Similar to standard Boolean logic definitions *Var* is the set of all variables bound in a term t^{q_i} associated with a state q_i with $(q_i, t^{q_i}) \in QA$. Be aware, that the formula

$$Var(t^{q_i}) \subseteq X^{q_i}$$

is not necessarily true. There might exist variables in a term associated to a state q_i without a counterpart in outgoing transition labels. An example is depicted in Figure 4.11(a) and explained in Section 4.3.4 later on. As stated above, a term t^{q_i} might be incomplete, that is

$$X^{q_i} \backslash Var(t^{q_i}) \neq \emptyset$$

and must be extended. The completed term $\tilde{t}^{q_i}$ is defined as a disjunction of the annotated term t^{q_i} associated to state q_i and all outgoing transition labels not used in the term t^{q_i} so far. A formal definition is given below:

$$\tilde{t}^{q_i} := t^{q_i} \vee (\bigvee_{x \in X^{q_i} \backslash Var(t^{q_i})} x)$$

4.3.4 Intersection of Annotated Finite State Automaton

Matchmaking business processes has been defined as a non-empty intersection. The intersection automaton of two automata contains the language accepted by both automata. Therefore, the annotation of the result automaton must support the annotation of the first and the annotation of the second automaton. The intersection definition is given below:

Definition 4.26
The intersection $A_1 \cap A_2$ of two annotated automata $A_1 = (Q_1, \Sigma_1, \Delta_1, q_{10}, F_1, QA_1)$, and $A_2 = (Q_2, \Sigma_2, \Delta_2, q_{20}, F_2, QA_2)$ is $A = (Q, \Sigma, \Delta, q_0, F, QA)$, with

- $Q = Q_1 \times Q_2$,
- $\Sigma = \Sigma_1 \cap \Sigma_2$,
- $\Delta((q_{11}, q_{21}), \alpha, (q_{12}, q_{22}))$ with $\quad \Delta_1(q_{11}, \alpha, q_{12}) \wedge \Delta_2(q_{21}, \alpha, q_{22})$,
- $q_0 = (q_{10}, q_{20})$,
- $F = F_1 \times F_2$, and
- $$QA = \bigcup_{\substack{q_1 \in Q_1, \\ q_2 \in Q_2}} \begin{cases} ((q_1, q_2), e_1 \wedge e_2) & if (q_1, e_1) \in QA_1, (q_2, e_2) \in QA_2 \\ ((q_1, q_2), e_1) & if (q_1, e_1) \in QA_1, \ \nexists e'.(q_2, e') \in QA_2 \\ ((q_1, q_2), e_2) & if (q_2, e_2) \in QA_2, \ \nexists e'.(q_1, e') \in QA_1 \\ \emptyset \quad otherwise & \end{cases}$$

The intersection definition above is a slight extension of standard automaton intersection definition (see Definition 4.23). In particular, the annotations are maintained independently of the automaton structure itself. The evaluation of the resulting annotated automaton with regard to matchmaking is done in the emptiness test.

To illustrate this definition the example in Section 2.1.1 is reconsidered. The minimized intersection automaton of the vendor and customer process in Figure 2.2(a) and (b) is depicted in Figure 4.11(a). The resulting automaton is the standard automaton intersection plus the corresponding annotation. The annotation of the intersection automaton requires a *V#C#noStock* message, although the intersection automaton structure does not provide this transition. Figure 4.11(b) depicts the intersection automaton of the vendor and the customer process given in Figure 2.2(a) and (c). The resulting intersection automaton contains both required messages: *V#C#delivery* and *V#C#noStock*.

4.3.5 Emptiness Test of Annotated Finite State Automaton

So far, state annotations have been maintained, but not yet been evaluated. Within the emptiness test the annotated terms are now evaluated. The evaluation of annotated terms is done in accordance with standard logical interpretation as, e.g., defined in [CS98] where an interpretation is based on a valuation ν of variables. A variable is evaluated as *true* if and only if the target state of the transition labeled with the variable name can reach a final state. Thus, the word associated with the current state concatenated with the variable name is a prefix of at least one word accepted by the language of the automaton.

Based on this definition of truth of variables within annotated terms it is required to first determine whether the target state of outgoing transitions of a state can reach a final state before

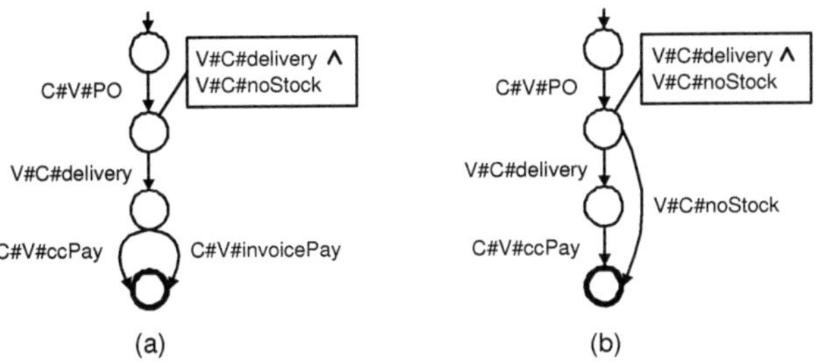

Figure 4.11: (a) Intersection of Vendor and Customer Process with Missing *V#C#noStock* Message. (b) Intersection of Vendor and Customer Process with *V#C#noStock* Message.

	$\neg_3$
f	t
t	f
i	i

$\vee_3$	f	t	i
f	f	t	f
t	t	t	t
i	f	t	i

$\wedge_3$	f	t	i
f	f	f	f
t	f	t	t
i	f	t	i

Table 4.1: Truth Tables of Three-valued Logic

evaluating the annotated term. This may result in cyclic dependencies, like for example observable in a self-loop, where the truth value of a state can not be determined, because the result depends on its own (not yet defined) truth value. This issue can be resolved by using a three-valued logic providing the standard truth values *true t* and *false f*, and in addition a value *intermediate i* used in case of recursion. This issue is well known from primitive recursive function theory. The formal definition of the emptiness test is based on a three-valued logic similar to Kleene's system of "strong connectives" [Pan98][6]. The corresponding operations of the three valued logic are negation $\neg_3$, disjunction $\vee_3$, and conjunction $\wedge_3$. The corresponding truth tables is depicted in Table 4.1.

The standard interpretation $||.||$ of the logic is based on the operations defined above, but must consider the current path *curP* of the evaluation to enable cycle detection. The characters t, t_1, t_2, and c represent terms and a constant respectively, while x represents a variable symbol.

$$\begin{aligned}
||\neg t||^{v}_{curP} &:= \neg_3 ||t||^{v}_{curP} \\
||t_1 \vee t_2||^{v}_{curP} &:= ||t_1||^{v}_{curP} \vee_3 ||t_2||^{v}_{curP} \\
||t_1 \wedge t_2||^{v}_{curP} &:= ||t_1||^{v}_{curP} \wedge_3 ||t_2||^{v}_{curP} \\
||true||^{v}_{curP} &:= t; ||false||^{v}_{curP} := f \\
||x||^{v}_{curP} &:= v_I \quad with \quad v_I \in \{t, f, i\}; x \in \Sigma
\end{aligned}$$

As stated above, the truth value of variables are derived by checking whether there exists a path to a final state starting from the current path *curP* extended by the current state q_i and following

[6]The special definition of implications of this system is not required in the presented approach.

the transition labeled with the name of the variable $x_j^{q_i}$. The value *intermediate i* is returned if the transition labeled $x_j^{q_i}$ has a target state contained in the current path *curP* concatenated with the current state q_i. This is, because the evaluation of the variable $x_j^{q_i}$ depends on its own evaluation. In case the target state of the transition labeled $x_j^{q_i}$ is not in the current path nor the current state q_i, the evaluation of $x_j^{q_i}$ is done by a function called $R()$ checking the reachability of a final state. The function is quite similar to the *Reach*() function specified in Section 4.3.2 and is defined in more detail later on. In case no transition labeled with $x_j^{q_i}$ exists the evaluation is *false f*. The formal definition of the valuation of variables is given below:

$$||x_j^{q_i}||_{curP}^{\vee} := \begin{cases} f & if \ \nexists q' \in Q.\Delta(q_i, x_j^{q_i}, q') \\ \bigvee_{\Delta(q_i, x_j^{q_i}, q')} & \begin{cases} i & if \ q' \in curP.q_i \\ R(curP.q_i, q') & otherwise \end{cases} \end{cases}$$

Based on this valuation definition emptiness in annotated automata denoted as $Empt'()$ is *false* if and only if the modified reachability function $R'()$ returns truth value t. Emptiness is defined by a comparison to ensure a Boolean result rather than a three-value logical result.

$$\begin{aligned} Empt'(A) \quad &:= R'(curP, q_i) \neq t \\ R'(curP, q_i) \quad &:= \begin{cases} t & if q_i \in F \\ ||\tilde{f}^{q_i}||_{curP}^{\vee} & otherwise \end{cases} \end{aligned}$$

The reachability function $R'()$ terminates with *true t* if the current state q_i is a final state. If the current state q_i is not a final state the completed annotation must be valuated.

4.3.6 Guarded Annotated Finite State Automaton

The current definition of annotated Finite State Automata lacks the possibility to represent parameter constraints. Similar to the introduction of guard functions in WF-Nets (see Definition 4.16) the aFSA definition can be extended by guard functions to represent parameter constraints within an aFSA. The guard function is used to introduce additional constraints on the enabling of transitions, thus, guard functions are annotated to transitions rather than to states as done by the annotations contained in aFSA already. A guarded aFSA is defined as follows:

Definition 4.27

A guarded aFSA $A_g := (Q, \Sigma, \Delta, q_0, F, QA, G, P)$, where $(Q, \Sigma, \Delta, q_0, F, QA)$ represents an annotated Finite State Automaton, $P \in \mathcal{P}$ a set of parties [7] whose local workflows are represented in A_g, and $G : \Delta \rightarrow \mathcal{ALC}(\mathcal{D})$ a guard function assigning each transition a guard expression denoted in description logic with concrete domain $\mathcal{D}$. The default guard expression assigned to a transition by a guard function is the tautology $\top$, which is not explicitly represented.

[7] Party names corresponds to the names of senders and recipients of messages (see Definition 4.22 and 4.24).

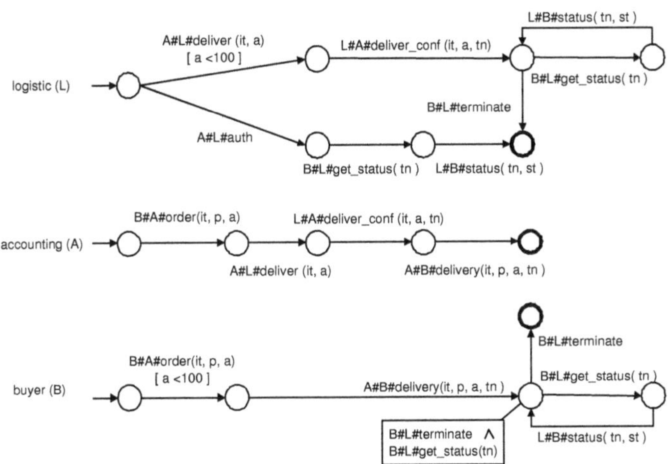

Figure 4.12: Guarded aFSA Representation of the Local Workflows

With regard to the example described in Section 2.3.1, the local workflows denoted as guarded aFSA are depicted in Figure 4.12, where WF-Net places are represented as automaton states and WF-Net transitions become automaton transitions[8]. The annotation for the buyer workflow represents the notion that the buyer has a choice of sending a message, where both options are mandatory and thus must be supported by a trading partner.

Similar to WF-Nets, the guard function is used to check satisfiability of guard expressions aggregated along a path, where unsatisfiable transitions can be omitted. The guard expressions are evaluated by every automaton operation. In particular, within the intersection calculation the guard expression of a transition, which does not fulfill the subsumption relation of a guard expression associated with an equally labeled transition within an intersection calculation is set to false $\perp$ and can be omitted afterwards. Further, guard expressions are evaluated during the recursive traversal within an emptiness test of a guarded aFSA. In either case, the basis for the operations are propagated guard expressions, that is, guard expressions along a message sequence of the guarded automaton are combined by conjunction, while different message sequences are represented as disjunctions. The formal definition of parameter constraint propagation is:

Definition 4.28

The parameter constraints contained in a guarded aFSA $A = (Q, \Sigma, \Delta, q_0, F, QA, G, P)$ can be propagated resulting in a guarded aFSA $A' := \Phi(A)$ with $A' = (Q, \Sigma, \Delta, q_0, F, QA, G', P)$. In particular, the guard expression of a transition $(q, \tilde{\alpha}, \tilde{q})$ is the disjunction of the conjunctions of guard expressions,

[8]This direct mapping is possible due to equivalence of the WF-Net model with the corresponding occurrence graph.

which correspond to transitions being part of a path, where the last transition is $(q,\tilde{\alpha},\tilde{q})$.

$$\forall(q,\tilde{\alpha},\tilde{q}) \in \Delta.G'((q,\tilde{\alpha},\tilde{q})) := \bigsqcup_{\sigma:=\langle(q_0,\alpha',q'),(q',\alpha'',q''),\ldots,(q,\tilde{\alpha},\tilde{q})\rangle} \sqcap_{t\in\sigma}G(t)$$

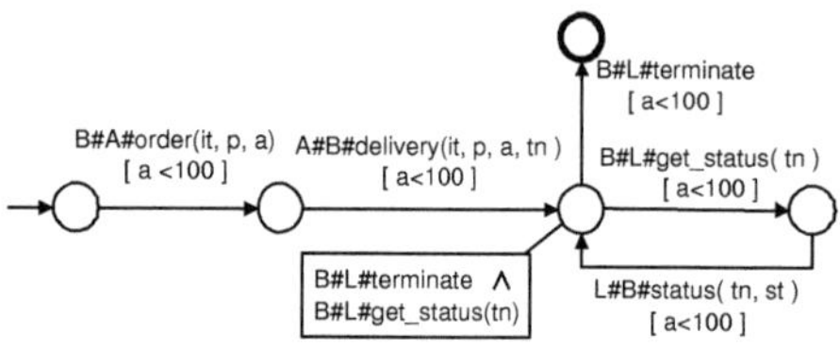

Figure 4.13: Parameter Constraint Propagated Buyer Workflow

Applying the parameter constraint propagation on the buyer workflow depicted in Figure 4.12 results in the guarded aFSA depicted in Figure 4.13.

Further, the intersection definition of aFSA (see Definition 4.26) can be extended to guarded aFSA. Intersection is based on the cross product of transitions and states, which means that two transitions are combined resulting in a single transition, thus, two guard expressions must be aggregated to a single one. However, there exists a subsumption relation between the guard expression of the sender of a message and the corresponding guard expression of the recipient, that is, the recipient must at least support those parameter combinations, which might be provided by the sender of the message. If this subsumption is not provided, the guard expression is set to false $\perp$, thus, the transition can be omitted.

Definition 4.29

The intersection $A_1 \cap A_2$ of two guarded aFSA with $A_1 = (Q_1,\Sigma_1,\Delta_1,q_{10},F_1,QA_1,G_1,P_1)$ and $A_2 = (Q_2,\Sigma_2,\Delta_2,q_{20},F_2,QA_2,G_2,P_2)$ is a guarded automaton $A = (Q,\Sigma,\Delta,q_0,F,QA,G,P)$, where the intersection of the annotated automata is defined as in Definition 4.26 and the intersection of the set of parties is $P := P_1 \cup P_2$, while the intersection of the guard functions is defined for a transition $t \in \Delta$ with $t := ((q_{1,1},q_{2,1}),s\#r\#msg,(q_{1,2},q_{2,2}))$ as

$$G(t) := \begin{cases} (t,G_1(t)) & if\ s \in P_1 \wedge r \in P_2 \wedge G_1((q_{1,1},s\#r\#msg,q_{1,2})) \sqsubseteq G_2((q_{2,1},s\#r\#msg,q_{2,2})) \\ (t,G_1(t)) & if\ (s \in P_1 \wedge r \notin P_2) \vee (s \notin P_2 \wedge r \in P_1) \\ (t,G_2(t)) & if\ s \in P_2 \wedge r \in P_1 \wedge G_2((q_{2,1},s\#r\#msg,q_{2,2})) \sqsubseteq G_1((q_{1,1},s\#r\#msg,q_{1,2})) \\ (t,G_2(t)) & if\ (s \in P_2 \wedge r \notin P_1) \vee (s \notin P_1 \wedge r \in P_2) \\ (t,\top) & if\ s \notin P_1 \cup P_2 \wedge r \notin P_1 \cup P_2 \\ (t,\perp) & otherwise \end{cases}$$

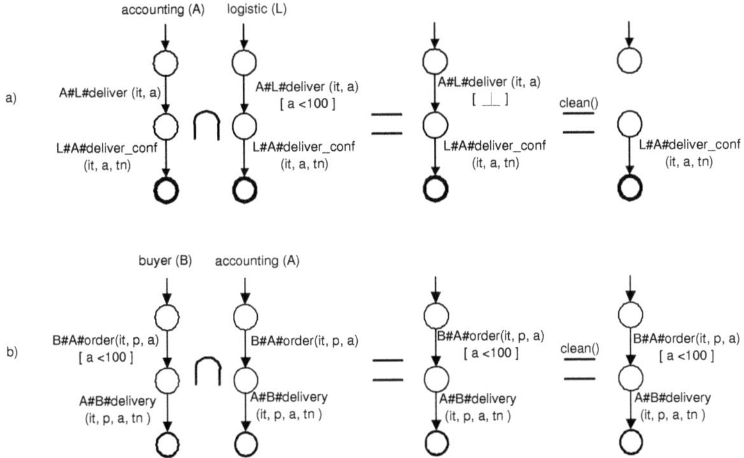

Figure 4.14: Guarded aFSA Intersection Examples: (a) Direct Accounting and Logistic Intersection (b) Direct Buyer and Accounting Intersection

To illustrate the intersection definition, the exemplary guarded aFSA depicted in Figure 4.12 are simplified by only containing two messages each directly corresponding to the trading partner. Figure 4.14(a) contains the *A#L#deliver()* and *L#A#deliver_conf()* messages, where receiving the *A#L#deliver()* message is constraint to an amount below 100 by the logistics department. In accordance to the intersection definition, the guard expression of the received message is not subsumed by the guard expression of the sending message, thus, the guard expression is changed to false. However, in Figure 4.14(b) the parameter constraint is specified by the sending party, which keeps the constraint in the intersection automaton.

Further, the emptiness test definition is adapted. In particular, the definition given in Section 4.3.5 has to be extended by following a transition only, if the corresponding guard expression is satisfiable.

Definition 4.30
Emptiness of a guarded aFSA A denoted as $Empt''(A)$ is $false$ if and only if the modified reachability function $R''()$ returns truth value t, where $Empt''(A) := R''(\emptyset, q_0) \neq t$ and

$$R''(curP, q_i) := \begin{cases} t & if q_i \in F \\ \|\vec{t}^{q_i}\|^{\vee}_{curP} & otherwise \end{cases}$$

with

$$\|x_j^{q_i}\|^{\vee}_{curP} := \begin{cases} f & if \ \nexists q' \in Q.\Delta(q_i, x_j^{q_i}, q') \\ \bigvee_{\Delta(q_i, x_j^{q_i}, q')} & \begin{cases} i & if \ q' \in curP.q_i \wedge G((q_i, x_j^{q_i}, q')) \text{ is satsifiable} \\ R(curP.q_i, q') & if \ q' \notin curP.q_i \wedge G((q_i, x_j^{q_i}, q')) \text{ is satsifiable} \\ f & otherwise \end{cases} \end{cases}$$

As a consequence, transitions assigned with unsatisfiable guard expressions can be omitted, thus, after calculating the intersection, a scan on the satisfiability of guard expressions assigned to a transition can remove irrelevant transitions.

Definition 4.31
A guarded aFSA $A = (Q, \Sigma, \Delta, q_0, F, QA, G, P)$ can be transformed into an equivalent guarded aFSA $A' = (Q, \Sigma, \Delta', q_0, F, QA, G', P)$ with $A' = clean(A)$ by the operation $clean()$, where all unsatisfiable transitions are removed and the guard function is adapted to the changed set of transitions. Thus, $\Delta' := \{t \in \Delta \mid G(t) \text{ is satisfiable}\}$ and $G' := G \cap (\Delta' \times \mathcal{ALC}(\mathcal{D}))$.

Based on the $clean()$ operation, the emptiness test of guarded aFSA can be represented as an emptiness test of aFSA introduced in Section 4.3.5 by $Empt''(\Phi(A)) = Empt'(clean(\Phi(A)))$. With regard to the intersection example depicted in Figure 4.14(a), the intersection is empty, although the structural emptiness test ($Empt'()$) applied to the intersection result derives a non-empty automaton, while $Empt''()$ derives the correct result of an empty automaton. However, applying the $clean()$ operation on the intersection result results in the last automaton in the row depicted in Figure 4.14(a), where also the structural emptiness test $Empt'()$ derives the correct result. In the case of non-empty automata the $clean()$ operation does not modify the automaton as depicted in Figure 4.14(b).

4.3.7 Consistency of a Multi-lateral Collaboration

Consistency of a multi-lateral collaboration can be specified as the non-empty intersection of the local workflows forming the collaboration. A message sequence accepted by an intersection automaton must be contained in each local workflow. However, a local workflow contains only messages, where the party providing the local workflow is either sender or recipient. As a consequence, the local workflows have to be extended by messages for which the local party is neither sender nor recipient to get an intersection result at all, where the additional messages might occur in arbitrary order.

The regular expression representing an arbitrary order of messages Σ_M contained in a multi-lateral collaboration A_M without the set of messages Σ_k contained in the local workflow A_k is specified by $(\Sigma_M \setminus \Sigma_k)^*$, which corresponds to an automaton with a single start state being also a final state having one transition per message $\alpha \in \Sigma_M \setminus \Sigma_k$ from the start state to the start state. In the following, the regular expression notation $(\Sigma_M \setminus \Sigma_k)^*$ is used to specify the equivalent automaton.

To combine the additional messages with the local workflow, the automaton theoretic shuffle product operation is used. In particular, the shuffle product of two message sequences results in a set of message sequences, where the order of messages contained in two message sequences remains unchanged in all constructed message sequences, while the interleaving of the message sequences is in arbitrary order. The formal definition of the shuffle product based on a standard definition [MMP+95] is:

Definition 4.32
The shuffle product $A := A_1 \& A_2$ of $A_1 = (Q_1, \Sigma_1, \Delta_1, q_{10}, F_1, QA_1, G_1, P_1)$, and $A_2 = (Q_2, \Sigma_2, \Delta_2, q_{20}, F_2, QA_2, G_2, P_2)$ is $A = (Q, \Sigma, \Delta, q_0, F, QA, G, P)$ with $Q := Q_1 \times Q_2$, $\Sigma := \Sigma_1 \cup \Sigma_2$, $q_0 := q_{10} \times q_{20}$, $F := F_1 \times F_2$, $P := P_1 \cup P_2$,

$$\begin{aligned}\Delta := \quad & \{((p,q_1),\alpha,(p,q_2)) \in (Q_1 \times Q_2) \times \Sigma_2 \times (Q_1 \times Q_2) \mid (q_1,\alpha,q_2) \in \Delta_2\} \\ \cup \quad & \{((p_1,q),\alpha,(p_2,q)) \in (Q_1 \times Q_2) \times \Sigma_1 \times (Q_1 \times Q_2) \mid (p_1,\alpha,p_2) \in \Delta_1\}\end{aligned}$$

$$QA = \bigcup_{\substack{q_1 \in Q_1, \\ q_2 \in Q_2}} \begin{cases} ((q_1,q_2),e_1 \wedge e_2) & if (q_1,e_1) \in QA_1 \ \wedge \ (q_2,e_2) \in QA_2 \\ ((q_1,q_2),e_1) & if (q_1,e_1) \in QA_1 \ \wedge \ \nexists e'.(q_2,e') \in QA_2 \\ ((q_1,q_2),e_2) & if (q_2,e_2) \in QA_2 \ \wedge \ \nexists e'.(q_1,e') \in QA_1 \\ \emptyset & otherwise \end{cases}$$

$G = (\Delta \times \mathcal{ALC}(\mathcal{D})) \cap G'$ where t is the transition constructed from t_1 and t_2 and

$$G' = \bigcup_{\substack{t_1 \in \Delta_1, \\ t_2 \in \Delta_2}} \begin{cases} (t,e_1 \sqcap e_2) & if (t_1,e_1) \in G_1 \ \wedge \ (t_2,e_2) \in G_2 \\ (t,e_1) & if (t_1,e_1) \in G_1 \ \wedge \ \nexists e'.(t_2,e') \in G_2 \\ (t,e_2) & if (t_2,e_2) \in G_2 \ \wedge \ \nexists e'.(t_1,e') \in G_1 \\ \emptyset & otherwise \end{cases}$$

Based on the shuffle product definition, the workflow of the multi-lateral collaboration can be defined as the intersection of the local workflows extended by all messages, where the local party is neither sender nor recipient.

Definition 4.33
Let $A_0, \ldots, A_{n-1}$ be a set of guarded aFSA representing local workflows respectively, then the workflow A_M of the multi-lateral collaboration M is defined as

$$A_M := \bigcap_{0 \leq j < n} \Phi(A_j) \& (\Sigma_M \setminus \Sigma_j)^*$$

where & is the shuffle product (see Definition 4.32), $*$ is the Kleene Operator known from regular expressions, and $\Sigma_M := \bigcup_{0 \leq j < n} \Sigma_j$ with Σ_j being the alphabet of automaton A_j and Σ_j is complete, that is, it contains all messages occurring in the multi-lateral collaboration. In particular, all messages of the collaboration are contained, which are sent or received by a party being involved in messages used by automaton A_j, that is, $\Sigma_j = \{s\#r\#msg \in \Sigma_M \mid s \in P_j \vee r \in P_j\}$. The multi-lateral collaboration is consistent if the multi-lateral workflow is non-empty, that is, $L(A_M) \neq \emptyset$.

With regard to the example described in Section 2.3.1, the local workflows denoted as guarded aFSA are depicted in Figure 4.12, while the corresponding non-empty minimized multi-lateral workflow is depicted in Figure 4.15, which is consistent.

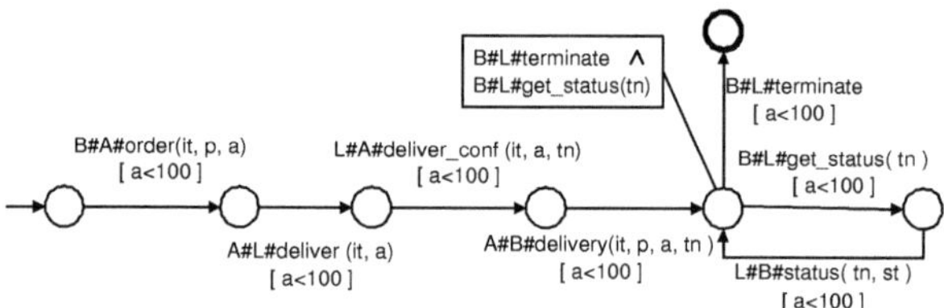

Figure 4.15: Minimized Guarded aFSA Representation of the Multi-lateral Collaboration

According to the consistency definition of multi-lateral workflows, bilateral consistency can be defined quite similarly. In particular, bilateral consistency checking can be realized by extending the local party's workflow and that of the trading partner, calculating the intersection, and checking the result for emptiness. The local workflow is consistent, if the intersection automaton is non-empty. This bilateral consistency definition fulfills the requirements stated in Section 2.1.2 by representing message sequences in terms of Finite State Automata and explicating optional and mandatory messages within annotations of states.

However, the current consistency definition is not yet complete as illustrated by the following example. Let's consider a three party scenario as depicted in Figure 4.16, where the multi-lateral workflow is equivalent to the local workflow of party B. Although, the multi-lateral workflow is non-empty, it expects message *B#C#msg*2 to be sent by party B before message *A#B#msg*3 is received by party B. Due to party A being independent of party B for sending message *A#B#msg*3, party A might send the message before party B has sent message *B#C#msg*2, thus, in this case the execution

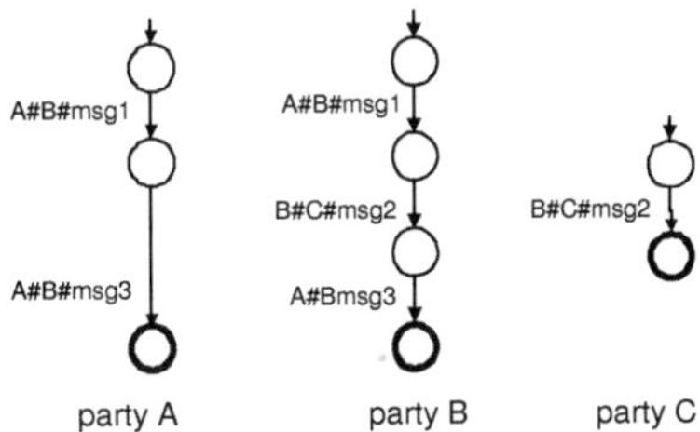

Figure 4.16: Guarded aFSA Representation of Local Workflows

of the multi-lateral collaboration fails. In particular, such unsynchronized dependencies of message exchanges make a multi-lateral collaboration inconsistent, thus, must result in an empty multi-lateral workflow.

To take this observation into account for locally checking consistency, a notion of history is introduced in terms of a history domain integrated in the description logic framework via a functional role history h, where the history domain represents the alphabet of the multi-lateral collaboration. The history functional roles are added to the guard expressions of each transition, where initially the guard expression of each transition is conjuncted with the functional role history $\exists h.\alpha$, where α is the transition label. Via propagation of guard expressions using $\Phi()$, the guard expression is extended by a conjunction of history predicates representing the list of transition labels (messages) that have been passed to reach the current transition. Formally, the concrete history domain $\mathcal{H}$ is defined to be used via the history functional role h within description logic based guard expressions.

Definition 4.34

The history domain $\mathcal{H}$ consists of a set of constants, where each constant represents a single message, thus, the set of constants is the union of all alphabets.

Applying this extension to the above example results in the automaton depicted in Figure 4.17. The intersection of the aFSA of party A and B results in a falsified $\perp$ guard expression of the transition labeled $A\#B\#msg3$, because

$$\exists h.A\#B\#msg1 \sqcap \exists h.A\#B\#msg3 \not\sqsubseteq \exists h.A\#B\#msg1 \sqcap \exists h.B\#C\#msg2 \sqcup \exists h.A\#B\#msg3$$

Thus, the multi-lateral workflow is empty, that is, is now classified correctly.

Based on the definition of consistency of multi-lateral collaborations, the operations needed to decentrally decide on consistency of the multi-lateral collaboration in accordance with the approach described in Section 2.4 are introduced next, that is, resolution of cycles, propagation of parameter and occurrence graph constraints.

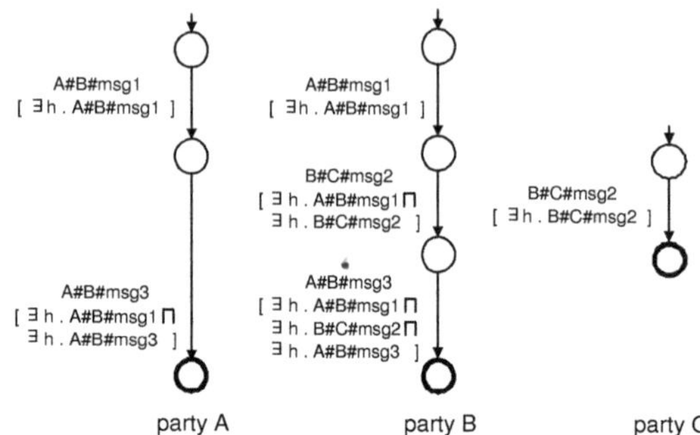

Figure 4.17: Guarded aFSA Representation of Local Workflows Extended by History Annotation and Propagated Guard Expressions

4.3.8 Resolution of Cycles

Cycles have to be removed since parameter constraints within different steps of a cycle may vary. An illustrative example is discussed in Appendix A.1. Thus, the goal of the resolution of cycles is to make the language accepted by the automata finite and to ensure that a message occurring several times within a message sequence are distinguishable, that is, to make messages unique on a path, while all paths are finite. To achieve this there exist two possibilities: the first one keeps the parameter names and changes the message name, while the second approach changes parameters and leaves message names unchanged. In either case guard functions as well as annotations have to be changed. While the first approach assumes that parameters named equally on a global level are considered to be equivalent, the second case considers each variable to be unique, while relations between the different parameters have to be made explicit by equivalence relations. In either case messages are unique, although the first case is easier to handle, which will be followed in the further discussion.

As stated above, changing the message name also implies changing the annotations. Thus, a definition of replacing a variable, that is, a message name by a new message name has to be provided. Since it might be necessary to change several messages during the traversal of an annotation or guard expression respectively, the required replacements are represented by a substitution defined as $\theta := \{\alpha_0 \to \beta_0, \dots, \alpha_{m-1} \to \beta_{m-1}\}$

Definition 4.35

The recursive operation τ_a based on the substitution $\theta := \{\alpha_0 \to \beta_0, \dots, \alpha_{m-1} \to \beta_{m-1}\}$ substitutes the variable α_i by another variable β_i within a three-valued logical expression $e \in \mathbb{B}$ in accordance with Definition 4.25 to an expression $e' := \tau_a(e, \theta)$ as follows:

- $\tau_a(e \wedge e', \theta) := \tau_a(e, \theta) \wedge \tau_a(e', \theta)$,

- $\tau_a(e \vee e', \theta) := \tau_a(e, \theta) \vee \tau_a(e', \theta)$,
- $\tau_a(\neg e, \theta) := \neg \tau_a(e, \theta)$,
- $\tau_a(true, \theta) := true$, $\tau_a(false, \theta) := false$, $\tau_a(intermediate, \theta) := intermediate$,
- $\tau_a(\gamma, \theta) := \gamma$ if $\forall \alpha \rightarrow \beta \in \theta. \gamma \neq \alpha$
- $\tau_a(\alpha, \theta) := \beta$ where $\alpha \rightarrow \beta \in \theta$

A similar definition is provided for renaming the constants of the history domain within the functional roles of a guard expression denoted in description logic with concrete domains as follows:

Definition 4.36
The recursive operation τ_g based on the substitution $\theta := \{\alpha_0 \rightarrow \beta_0, \ldots, \alpha_{m-1} \rightarrow \beta_{m-1}\}$ substitutes occurrences of α_i within a guard expression $e \in \mathcal{ALC}(\mathcal{D})$ by β_i in accordance with Definition 4.4 to a guard expression $e' := \tau_g(e, \theta)$ as follows:

- $\tau_g(e \sqcup e', \theta) := \tau_g(e, \theta) \sqcup \tau_g(e', \theta)$,
- $\tau_g(e \sqcap e', \theta) := \tau_g(e, \theta) \sqcap \tau_g(e', \theta)$,
- $\tau_g(\neg e, \theta) := \neg \tau_g(e, \theta)$,
- $\tau_g(\top, \theta) := \top$, $\tau_g(\bot, \theta) := \bot$
- $\tau_g(\forall r.e, \theta) := \forall \tau_g(r, \theta).\tau_g(e, \theta)$,
- $\tau_g(\exists r.e, \theta) := \exists \tau_g(r, \theta).\tau_g(e, \theta)$,
- $\tau_g(\exists(u_1, \ldots, u_n).e, \theta) := \exists(\tau_g(u_1, \theta), \ldots, \tau_g(u_n, \theta)).\tau_g(e, \theta)$,

The substitution of messages within the history domain is specified as follows:

Definition 4.37
The recursive operation τ_g based on the substitution $\theta := \{\alpha_0 \rightarrow \beta_0, \ldots, \alpha_{m-1} \rightarrow \beta_{m-1}\}$ substitutes the element $\alpha_i \in \mathcal{H}$ of the history domain $\mathcal{H}$ by another element $\beta_i \in \mathcal{H}$ as follows:

$$\tau_g(\gamma, \theta) := \begin{cases} \gamma & if\ \forall \alpha \rightarrow \beta \in \theta. \gamma \neq \alpha \\ \beta & if\ \gamma \rightarrow \beta \in \theta \end{cases}$$

Based on these definitions the construction of a acyclic automaton derived from a cyclic one can be defined by limiting the maximum number of iterations of a cycle to a constant N and explicitly enumerating all remaining execution sequences of the cycle. The construction process of the acyclic automaton subscribes each message name by the occurrence of that message name in the path that has been traversed to reach the transition. Further, the construction process ensures that the guard expressions of each transition of the constructed automaton consists of conjunctions only, that is, one transition is introduced per disjunction taken from the disjunctive normal form of the original guard expression of the transition. This construction results in a normalized acyclic tree-structured automaton accepting a reasonable subset of the language accepted by the original automaton [9]. A definition of the normalization operation Θ is given in Appendix A.2. In the following, the properties of an acyclic normalized guarded aFSA are defined.

Definition 4.38
A normalized guarded aFSA $A = (Q,\Sigma,\Delta,q_0,F,QA,G,P)$ provides the following properties:

- it is acyclic, that, is, cycles are resolved by at most N iteration steps, and
- all guard expressions are conjunctions only.

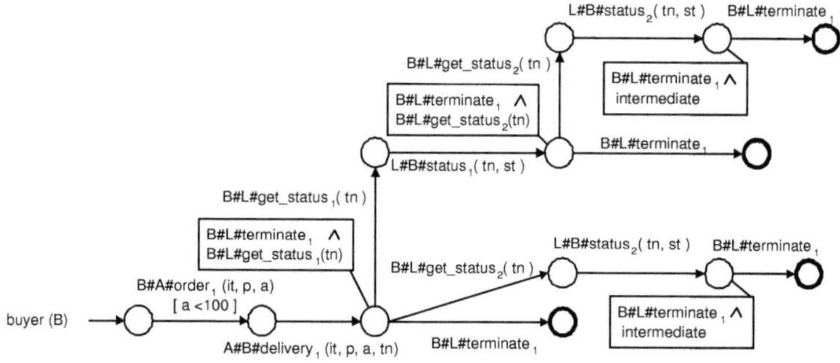

Figure 4.18: Buyer Acyclic Workflow with a Maximum Iteration of 2.

With regard to the example described in Section 2.3.1, the local workflows depicted in Figure 4.12 of the buyer and the logistics department have been used as the the basis for constructing normalized guarded aFSAs depicted in Figure 4.18 and 4.19 respectively. To make the figures less complex, the history functional roles as introduced in the previous section are not shown. In particular, within this example, the history functional roles are not required to derive a correct consistency decision.

[9] A similar approach of representing parameter constraints as automaton structure has been used by [FBS04] called "determinization". However, the approach seems to be too restrictive, since for a single state either sending transitions or receiving ones are allowed, but not a combination of both.

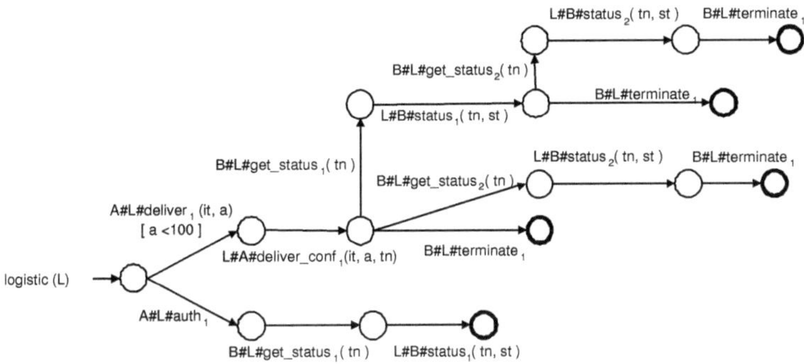

Figure 4.19: Logistics Department Acyclic Workflow with a Maximum Iteration of 2.

4.3.9 Propagation of Parameter Constraints

Based on the acyclic aFSA the parameter constraint propagation can be performed resulting in a fixed point as outlined in Section 2.4.2. Parameter constraint propagation consists of the propagation of constraints within the local workflow, which has already been defined in Section 4.3.6 (see Definition 4.28), and the propagation of parameter constraints from one local workflow to another local workflow. This bilateral parameter constraint propagation collects all parameter constraints, which are introduced by the trading partner sending a message being received by the local party. Because only constraints of sending messages are propagated while constraints of receiving messages are ignored, the propagation operation is asymmetric. In particular, the asymmetry is the consequence of the asymmetry of a message exchange, that is, one party sends the message, while it is received by another party. The formal definition is given below.

Definition 4.39
Let A_1 and A_2 be two guarded aFSA with $A_i = (Q_i, \Sigma_i, \Delta_i, q_{0i}, F_i, QA_i, G_i, P_i)$ with $i = 1,2$. Then, the bilateral parameter constraint propagation Φ_b transforming A_1 into A'_1 with $A'_1 := \Phi_b(A_1, A_2)$ where the guarded aFSA $A'_1 = (Q_1, \Sigma_1, \Delta_1, q_{01}, F_1, QA_1, G'_1, P_1)$ redefines the guard expressions of the guarded aFSA A_1 as follows:

$$G'_1 := \bigcup_{((q_1,\alpha,q'_1),e_1)\in G_1} \left\{ \left((q_1, \alpha, q'_1), e_1 \sqcap \Big(\bigsqcup_{\substack{((q_2,\alpha,q'_2),e_2) \in G_2 \\ \alpha = s\#r\#msg \wedge r \in P_1}} e_2 \Big) \right) \right\}$$

where G_2 is the guard function of A_2.

The combination of local and bilateral parameter constraint propagation results in a fixed point formally specified as follows:

Definition 4.40
Let A_M be a multi-lateral collaboration A_M consisting of $A_0, \dots, A_{n-1}$ local workflows, then A_M is a fixed point, if and only if

$$\forall 0 \leq k < n. \forall 0 \leq j < n, j \neq k. A_k = \Phi(\Phi_b(A_k, A_j))$$

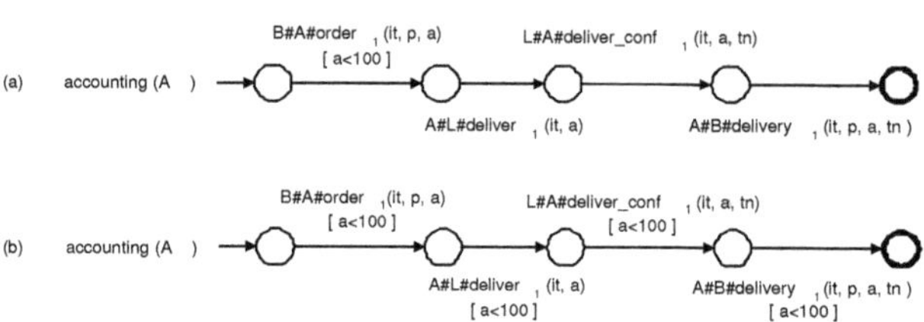

Figure 4.20: Accounting Department Workflow with Propagation - (a)$A := \Phi_b(A, B)$ With A and B From Figure 4.12 and (b)$A := \Phi(A)$ With A From (a)

With regard to the example described in Section 2.3.1 and in accordance to the local workflows depicted in Figure 4.12, constraint propagation is performed on acyclic normalized guarded aFSA. The acyclic normalized guarded aFSA of buyer and logistics department are depicted in Figure 4.18 and 4.19 respectively. Since the accounting department workflow is already acyclic, the normalized guarded aFSA equals the guarded aFSA depicted in Figure 2.3.1 except that every message is subscribed by a one since every message occurs exactly once.

The bilateral propagation of accounting and logistics departments applied in either direction keeps the local workflows unchanged. Also the buyer workflow remains unchanged in the bilateral propagation with the accounting department. However, the bilateral propagation of accounting department and buyer assigns the transition labeled $B\#A\#order_1(it, p, a)$ a parameter constraint on restricting the amount to at most 99, that is, $a < 100$. The resulting accounting department workflow is depicted in Figure 4.20(a). Applying local propagation on this accounting department workflow results in a workflow depicted in Figure 4.20(b). The application of local propagation on the buyer and logistics department workflow spreads the constraint on the amount a, that is, $a < 100$, to all transitions following $B\#A\#order_1(it, p, a)$ and $A\#L\#deliver_1(it, a)$ respectively.

After this parameter constraint propagation, the fixed point has already been reached, because further propagation of parameter constraints does not change any workflow further. Thus, the next step can be applied, that is, occurrence graph constraint propagation.

4.3.10 Propagation of Occurrence Graph Constraints

Propagation of occurrence graph constraints as outlined in Section 2.4.3 means that only those message sequences are considered by the trading parties which are supported by both trading partners.

This is exactly the definition of intersection. Thus, the definition introduced for consistency checking are reused for propagation of occurrence graph constraints.

In particular, propagation of occurrence graph constraints is based on the intersection of the extended local workflows of trading partners of a local party p and a final removal of all messages, which are unrelated to the party p's local workflow, which has been informally introduced in Section 2.4.3 as abstraction τ_p. The abstraction can formally be defined as a replacement of transition labels (messages) not related to party p by an silent transition ε [10]. In particular, the extension of the silent transition ε by the transition label is required to enable ε-removal operation on an aFSA effecting annotation.

Definition 4.41
A guarded aFSA $A' = (Q, \Sigma', \Delta', q_0, F, QA', P)$ with $A' = \tau_p(A)$ is an abstraction of a guarded aFSA $A = (Q, \Sigma, \Delta, q_0, F, QA, P)$ with regard to a party p, where

$$\tau_p(s\#r\#msg) := \begin{cases} s\#r\#msg & if\ (s = p) \vee (r = p) \\ \varepsilon_{s\#r\#msg} & otherwise \end{cases}$$

and $\Sigma' := \{\tau_p(\alpha) \mid \alpha \in \Sigma\}$, $\Delta' := \{(q, \tau_p(\alpha), q') \mid (q, \alpha, q') \in \Delta\}$, $QA' := \{(q, \tau_p(e)) \mid (q, e) \in QA\}$ with
$\tau_p(e \wedge e') := \tau_p(e) \wedge \tau_p(e')$,
$\tau_p(e \vee e') := \tau_p(e) \vee \tau_p(e')$,
$\tau_p(\neg e) := \neg \tau_p(e)$,
$\tau_p(true) := true$, $\tau_p(false) := false$, $\tau_p(intermediate) := intermediate$

Due to the introduction of silent transitions ε the definition of intersection (see Definition 4.29) has to be slightly extended by copying the ε transitions of each guarded aFSA to the intersection automaton, such that, the resulting transition Δ is defined as

$$\begin{aligned} \Delta := \quad & \{((q_{11}, q_{21}), \alpha, (q_{12}, q_{22})) \mid (q_{11}, \alpha, q_{12}) \in \Delta_1 \wedge (q_{21}, \alpha, q_{22}) \in \Delta_2\} \\ \cup \quad & \{((q_{11}, q), \alpha, (q_{12}, q)) \mid (q_{11}, \alpha, q_{12}) \in \Delta_1 \wedge q \in Q_2\} \\ \cup \quad & \{((q, q_{21}), \alpha, (q, q_{22})) \mid q \in Q_1 \wedge (q_{21}, \alpha, q_{22}) \in \Delta_2\} \end{aligned}$$

Based on the definition of abstraction the propagation of occurrence graph constraints can be defined as follows:

Definition 4.42
Let A_M be a multi-lateral collaboration consisting of $A_0, \ldots, A_{n-1}$, where each A_i is a normalized acyclic guarded aFSA with A_i being fixed point with regard to parameter constraint propagation. Further, let party p having the local workflow A_k and $\{A_{i_p(0)}, \ldots, A_{i_p(m_p)}\} := \{A_j \mid 0 \leq j <$

[10] In WF-Net theory the silent transition is τ, while automata theory uses ε to represent silent transitions [HMU01].

$n \wedge \Sigma_j \cap \Sigma_p \neq \emptyset\}$ be the set of party p's trading partner workflows. The propagated occurrence graph constraints of A_k result in an acyclic guarded aFSA $A'_k = \Psi(A_k)$ with

$$A'_k := \tau_p\Big(\bigcap_{0 \leq j < m_p} A_{i_p(j)} \& (\Sigma_{M_p} \setminus \Sigma_{i_p(j)})^* \Big)$$

where & is the shuffle product (see Definition 4.32), $*$ is the Kleene Operator known from regular expressions, and $\Sigma_{M_p} := \bigcup_{0 \leq j < m_p} \Sigma_{i_p(j)}$ with $\Sigma_{i_p(j)}$ being the alphabet of automaton $A_{i_p(j)}$.

The propagation definition requires normalization to ensure that the handling of the guard expressions within the intersection operation is in accordance with the intended semantics as discussed in Section 4.2.6. The iterative application of occurrence graph constraint propagation results finally in a fixed point defined as:

Definition 4.43
Let A_M be a multi-lateral collaboration A_M consisting of $A_0, \dots, A_{n-1}$ local workflows, where each A_i is a normalized acyclic guarded aFSA with A_i being fixed point with regard to parameter constraint propagation. Then A_M is fixed point, if and only if

$$\forall 0 \leq k < n. A_k = \Psi(A_k)$$

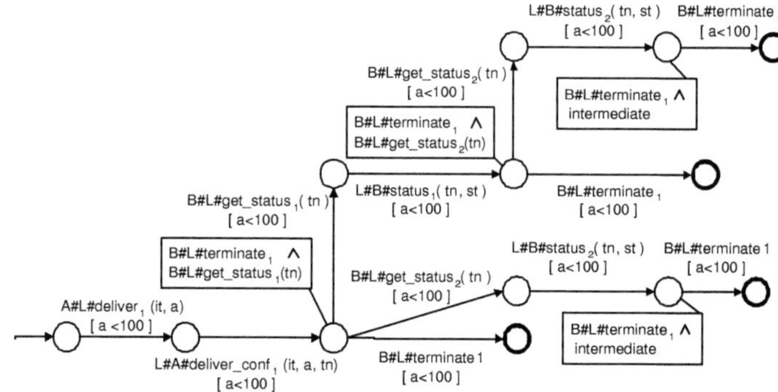

Figure 4.21: Minimized Logistics Department Propagated Occurrence Graph Constraints

Returning to the example from the previous section, the buyer and accounting department workflow are already fixed point, however, the logistics workflow as depicted in Figure 4.19 but with propagated parameter constraints of $a < 100$ is not fixed point for occurrence graph constraint propagation. The intersection automaton of the extended buyer, logistics and accounting department workflow does not contain the transition labeled $A\#L\#auth_1$ since the accounting department workflow does not provide an equally labeled transition. Thus, the message sequence starting with this transition is not contained in the intersection automaton. Applying the abstraction to the intersection automaton results in the propagated logistics department workflow depicted in Figure 4.21, where the branch providing the parcel tracking option after authentication by the accounting department has been removed. After this occurrence graph constraint propagation, the fixed point has already been reached. The fixed point workflows of the three parties are localy consistent, thus, the multi-lateral collaboration is also consistent.

4.4 Summary

Local consistency checking as introduced in this chapter can be investigated based on an asynchronous or synchronous communication model. While there exist sufficient proposals for the asynchronous communication model like, for example, Workflow Nets (WF-Nets), none are available for the synchronous case (see also Chapter 3). In either case, a representation of message parameters and constraints on these parameters is required, which must be extendable to support domain specific predicates. The selected logical model is description logic with concrete domains, because subsumption in description logic is decidable and the extensibility by domain specific predicates via concrete domains is provided.

Local consistency checking on an asynchronous communication model is based on guarded WF-Nets, that is, a WF-Net extended by parameter constraints denoted in description logic with concrete domains. To apply standard WF-Net consistency definition on guarded WF-Nets, parameter constraints have to be structurally represented as normalized guarded occurrence graphs, thus, consistency checking does not require evaluation of parameter constraints anymore.

Local consistency checking on a synchronous communication model is based on a Finite State Automaton (FSA) workflow model. Since no sufficient bilateral consistency definition exists for FSA, the model is extended to annotated FSA by an explicit notion of mandatory and optional messages. In particular, states are annotated by logical expressions containing outgoing message names as predicates, where mandatory messages are combined by conjunctions and optional message names are combined by disjunction. In accordance with the extension of WF-Nets, annotated FSA are also extended to guarded annotated FSA, that is, annotated FSA where transitions are assigned with parameter constraints denoted in description logic with concrete domains. Based on this formal model the required operations are formally defined:

- propagation of parameter constraints within a single local workflow as well as between two local workflows,
- bilateral and multi-lateral consistency as non-empty intersection of local workflows extended by messages the local party is neither sender nor receiver,

- resolution of cycles by at most N iteration steps of a cycle,
- propagation of occurrence graph constraints as intersection of local workflows extended by messages the local party is neither sender nor receiver

Based on these definitions the approach presented in Section 2.4 can be implemented.

So far, guarded WF-Nets and guarded annotated FSA have been defined for asynchronous and synchronous communication models respectively, while the necessary proofs for convergence and correctness of the proposed approach are addressed in the next chapter.

Chapter 5

Decentralized Consistency Checking

In the previous chapter workflow models for asynchronous and synchronous communications were introduced, that is, Workflow Nets (WF-Nets) and annotated Finite State Automata (aFSA) respectively. Based on these workflow models multi-lateral collaborations have been introduced and local consistency has been defined. Further, operations for the resolution of cycles, the propagation of parameter and occurrence graph constraints have been specified for the aFSA in accordance with the basic steps outlined in the description of the overall approach in Section 2.4. However, these steps have not been defined on WF-Nets. Further, it has not been shown so far that local consistency checking derives the same results as decentralized consistency checking. The further discussion remains quite informal to improve readability in contrast to the formal definitions in the previous chapter, where the aim was to provide a clear semantics of the introduced models.

In the following, a guarded WF-Net model representing asynchronous communication is mapped to guarded annotated Finite State Automata as introduced in Section 4.3.6 due to non-constructive operations in WF-Nets. Based on this mapping, the aFSA definitions specified for the synchronous communication model providing the cycle resolution and constraint propagation operations also apply to the asynchronous case.

Another issue is the formal proof based on the aFSA operations of the equivalence of local multi-lateral collaboration consistency. The consistency of the multi-lateral collaboration is derived from the fixed point of the parameter and occurrence graph constraint propagation.

5.1 Mapping Asynchronous Model

The formal specification of the asynchronous communication introduced in Section 4.2 is based on guarded Workflow Nets (WF-Nets). However, checking of WF-Net properties is performed on an occurrence graph (see Definition 4.21), that is, a graph representing all message sequences supported by the WF-Net. Due to the notion of message sequences, the mapping of an occurrence graph to an aFSA is straightforward. The formal definition is given as

Definition 5.1
Let N be a normalized acyclic guarded WF-Net with $N = (P,T,F,\ell,C,G,E)$ (see Definition 4.16) representing party p's local workflow and $OG = (V,A,Node,Guard)$ (see Definition 4.21) the corresponding guarded occurrence graph. The mapping of the guarded occurrence graph OG to a guarded aFSA $\tilde{A} = (Q,\Sigma,q_0,F,\Delta,QA,G,P)$ is as follows:

- the set of states Q equals the set of vertices V, that is, $Q = V$,
- the alphabet Σ comprises the transition labels $\ell(t)$ of all transitions T, that is, $\Sigma = \{\ell(t) \mid t \in T\}$,
- the start state q_0 is the initial marking of the guarded WF-Net $([i],\top)$ where $[i]$ represents a single token in the initial place of the WF-Net and $\top$ means that there are no constraints, that is, $q_0 = ([i],\top)$,
- the set of final states F consists of all leaf vertices of the occurrence graph, that is, $F = \{s \in V \mid \nexists s' \in V, t \in T.(s,t,s') \in A\}$,
- the set of transitions Δ equals the arcs of the occurrence graph, that is, $\Delta = \{(s,\ell(t),s') \mid (s,t,s') \in A'\}$,
- the set of annotations QA is the conjunction of all outgoing transitions of a vertex, that is, $QA = \bigcup_{s \in V}\{(s, \bigwedge_{(s,t,s') \in A} \ell(t)\}$,
- the guard expressions G are taken from the WF-Net guard expressions, that is, $G = \bigcup_{t \in T}\{((s,\ell(t),s'),G(t)) \mid (s,t,s') \in A\}$, and
- the set of parties P is the local part p, that is, $P = \{p\}$.

Based on this mapping it has to be shown that the definition of soundness as defined on WF-Nets corresponds to the consistency of aFSA, that is, the non-emptiness of aFSA.

Lemma 5.1 A normalized acyclic guarded WF-Net is sound if and only if the corresponding guarded aFSA is non-empty.

Proof: In accordance with WF-Net soundness (see Definition 4.12) a WF-Net is sound if it is safe and each path has a proper completion. Safeness is guaranteed by the structure of an acyclic WF-Net since no recursion can occur and the fact that a transition and a place are at most connected by a single arc. As a consequence the corresponding occurrence graph (see Definition 4.21) of an acyclic guarded WF-Net is sound if each path of the occurrence graph ends in a final marking containing a single token in the output place o and a satisfiable expression, which corresponds to a final place.

As a result of the construction of the aFSA, each path of the occurrence graph OG corresponds to a path in the aFSA A. Due to the annotations of the guarded aFSA the automaton is non-empty if all transitions of a source state support a path to a final state. Because each state is annotated by a conjunction of all outgoing transitions, the automaton is non-empty if and only if all paths result in a final state. □

In addition to consistency of a WF-Net as stated in the lemma above, consistency of a multi-lateral collaboration is based on IO-soundness of an Interorganizational Workflow Net in the notion of WF-Nets and non-empty intersection in the notion of aFSAs. Thus, in the case of a multi-lateral collaboration different requirements exist on the occurrence graph mapping to the aFSA. In particular, it is common to both representations that transitions sent by the local party are considered to be mandatory, while receiving transitions are considered optional.

Definition 5.2

Let N be a normalized acyclic guarded WF-Net with $N = (P,T,F,\ell,C,G,E)$ representing party p's local workflow and $OG = (V,A,Node,Guard)$ the corresponding guarded occurrence graph. The mapping of the guarded occurrence graph OG to a guarded aFSA $\tilde{A} = Occ(OG)$ with $\tilde{A} = (Q,\Sigma,q_0,F,\Delta,QA,G,P)$ is as follows:

- the set of states Q equals the set of vertices V, that is, $Q = V$,
- the alphabet Σ equals the transition labels $\ell(t)$ of all transitions T, that is, $\Sigma = \{\ell(t) \mid t \in T\}$,
- the start state q_0 is the initial marking of the guarded WF-Net $([i],\top)$ where $[i]$ represents a single token in the initial place of the WF-Net and $\top$ means that there are no constraints, that is, $q_0 = ([i],\top)$,
- the set of final states F consists of all leaf vertices of the occurrence graph, that is, $F = \{s \in V \mid \nexists s' \in V, t \in T.(s,t,s') \in A\}$,
- the set of transitions Δ equals the arcs of the occurrence graph, that is, $\Delta = \{(s,\ell(t),s') \mid (s,t,s') \in A'\}$,
- the set of annotations QA is the conjunction of all outgoing transitions of a vertex send by the local party, that is, $QA = \bigcup_{s \in V}\{(s, \bigwedge_{t \in QA_s} t)\}$ with $QA_s := \{t \in T \mid (s,t,s') \in A \wedge t = p\#r\#msg\}$ and p is the local party name,
- the guard expressions G are taken from the WF-Net guard expressions, that is, $G = \bigcup_{t \in T}\{((s,\ell(t),s'),G(t)) \mid (s,t,s') \in A\}$, and
- the set of parties P is the local part p, that is, $P = \{p\}$.

Though, the mapping seems to be appropriate, the consistency of aFSA is not yet equivalent to soundess of an interorganizational workflow as illustrated by the following example.

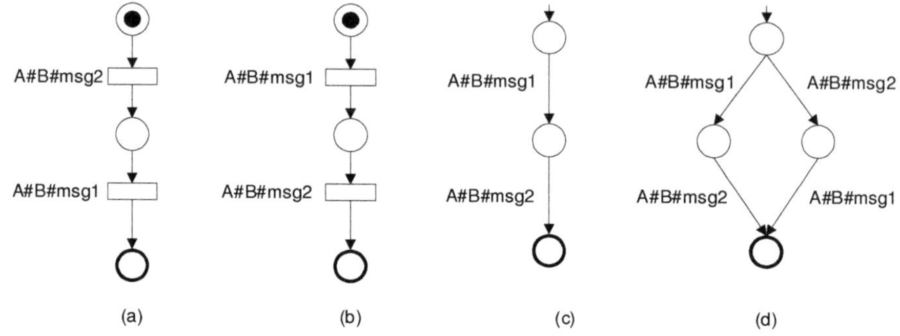

Figure 5.1: (a) WF-Net of Party A, (b) WF-Net of Party B, (c) aFSA Representation of the Occurrence Graph of (b), (d) aFSA Representation of the Complete Occurrence Graph of (b)

The example is based on a party B's local workflow depicted in Figure 5.1(b) used within the asynchronous WF-Net example depicted in Figure 4.1. In particular, party B receives message *A#B#msg*1 before message *A#B#msg*2, however, due to the asynchronous communication model the bilateral WF-Net is consistent if party A sends these messages either in same or in reverse order.

A mapping of the WF-Net to aFSA in accordance to Definition 5.2 results in the aFSA depicted in Figure 5.1(c). The intersection automaton of party B's local workflow with party A's (equal to the one depicted in Figure 5.1(b)) having the same order of messages is non-empty, that is, the bilateral collaboration is consistent. If the party A sends the messages in reverse order (depicted in Figure 5.1(a)) the intersection result is empty, making the bilateral collaboration inconsistent, while it should be consistent. As a consequence, the aFSA representing occurrence graphs must be extended by additional paths, where the order of two messages subsequently received by the local party is inverted. The complete aFSA representing an occurrence graph of a WF-Net is depicted in 5.1(d). Since only receiving messages are used for the restructuring of the aFSA and the fact that receiving messages are considered to be optional, the annotations remain unchanged. A formal definition of a complete aFSA is given as follows:

Definition 5.3

An aFSA is complete, if and only if for any two preceding transitions $(q, \alpha, q'), (q', \alpha', q'') \in \Delta$ with $\alpha = s\#r\#msg$ and $\alpha' = s'\#r'\#msg'$, where $r \in P$ and $r' \in P$, the inverse order of messages is also contained in Δ, that is, there exist also transitions $(q, \alpha', \tilde{q}), (\tilde{q}, \alpha, q'') \in \Delta$.

Every aFSA representing an occurrence graph can be transformed into a complete aFSA by shuffling the relevant transitions. This is comparable to parallel processing of receiving transitions in the corresponding WF-Net, that is, not considering the order in which the different messages are received.

Based on these definitions, the consistency of a multi-lateral collaboration consisting of $N_0,\ldots,N_{n-1}$ WF-Nets can be represented as global soundness of an Interorganizational Workflow Net (IOWF-Net) $IOWF = (C, F_C, n, N_0, \ldots, N_{n-1})$ in accordance with Definition 4.13. In particular, the set of channels C corresponds to the set of messages exchanged between the WF-Nets $N_0,\ldots,N_{n-1}$. Each channel represents a single message exchange, thus the channels are named $c_{s\#r\#msg}$ where the character c is subscripted by the corresponding message name. Finally, each channel is represented by a place with the same label as the channel itself and arcs connecting the place with the sending and receiving transitions of the local workflows. Hence, the directed arcs specified by F_C connect the place representing the channel with two WF-Nets N_k and N_l related to party p_k and p_l exchanging the message. This can be formalized as $C := \{c_{\ell(t)} \mid t \in T\}$ and

$$F_C := \bigcup_{0 \le k < l < n} \begin{aligned} \{(t, c_{\ell(t)}), (c_{\ell(t)}, t') \mid \; & c_{\ell(t)} \in C \wedge N_k = (P, T, F, \ell) \wedge N_l = (P', T', F', \ell') \wedge \\ & t \in T \wedge t' \in T' \wedge \ell(t) = \ell'(t') = s\#r\#msg \wedge s = p_k \wedge r = p_l\} \end{aligned}$$

Based on this representation of a multi-lateral collaboration as an IOWF-Net consistency of the collaboration can be specified as soundness of the flattened IOWF-Net constructed via the $flat()$ operation (see Definition 4.14).

Lemma 5.2 Let $IOWF = (C, F_C, n, N_0, \ldots, N_{n-1})$ be an acyclic interorganizational workflow with OG_k being the occurrence graph of WF-Net N_k $(0 \le k < N)$, and A_k be a complete aFSA representation of OG_k with Σ_k being the alphabet of A_k $\Sigma_M := \bigcup_{0 \le k < n} \Sigma_k$, then

$$\emptyset \neq \bigcap_{0 \le k < n} \Phi(A_k) \& (\Sigma_M \setminus \Sigma_i)^* \longleftrightarrow flat(IOWF) \text{is sound}$$

where & is the shuffle product (see Definition 4.32) and $*$ the Kleene operator known from regular expressions.

Proof: By the definition of $flat()$, a sending transition labeled with message α inserts a token in place c_α, which can only be removed by a receiving transition labeled with message α again. Should the receiving transition be missing, the place c_α contains a token until the end of the firing sequence, making the WF-Net non-sound. Thus, in a sound WF-Net constructed by $flat(IOWF)$ every sending transition has to be followed by a receiving transition.

Let's assume that the WF-Net $flat(IOWF)$ is not sound, that is, there exists a path where no receiving message α follows the corresponding sending message α. Thus, the local workflow does not support receiving of α in this particular firing sequence.

If and only if this is the case, then the recipient's completed local workflow does not contain message α in the corresponding firing sequences and, thus, the intersection calculation removes α

within this path at the intersection automaton. Due to the annotations introduced by $Occ()$ of a sending message being mandatory, there exists a state in the intersection automaton annotated with α being mandatory, although the corresponding transition has been removed. As a consequence the emptiness test evaluates to true indicating a non-consistent workflow.

If the WF-Net $flat(IOWF)$ is sound, no such firing sequence exists where a receiving message is missing, thus the intersection will not remove the corresponding message in the automaton of the receiving party and the emptiness test will be false.

The correct order of sending and receiving messages is guaranteed, since the definition of F_C is such that in a firing sequence of a bilateral communication, all messages sent from a party A to another party B have to be received before party B can respond to party A. Thus, the order in which messages can be received may vary in a firing sequence, however, before sending another message all messages in the firing sequence waiting to be received must be received first. This observation corresponds to the definition of completed aFSAs representing occurrence graphs introduced in Definition 5.3 and covers the variation of message order provided by the $flat()$ operation. □

The above lemma also explains the relation of the two mapping Definitions 5.1 and 5.2. Definition 5.2 specifies a mapping of each WF-Net to an aFSA, where the intersection of these extended aFSAs is equivalent to the aFSA generated by Definition 5.1 applied on the WF-Net resulting from $flat(IOWF)$. Thus, the second mapping is relevant for the decentralized collaboration establishment addressed in this thesis.

An additional consequence of the previous lemma is that consistency of both communication models can be represented as the non-empty intersection of extended aFSA. Thus, further discussion is based on the notion of aFSA.

5.2 Correctness of the Approach

The overall goal is to decide consistency of multi-lateral collaborations in a decentralized way. In the previous chapter several definitions were provided and illustrated with the help of examples, however, a formal proof is missing. In particular, the following statements have to be proven:

- The propagation of constraints guarantees convergence, thus, the fixed point can always be reached.
- The local workflow A_k can be constructed by those parties having direct interaction with A_k as specified in Definition 4.42. Thus, the constructed workflow is equivalent to corresponding workflow projected from the global workflow.
- The definition of multi-lateral consistency as defined in Definition 4.33 has to be mapped to the consensus of all parties on consistency of the fixed point local workflows.

These issues are addressed in the following sections.

5.2.1 Convergence of Constraint Propagation

In the following, it is shown that the definition of parameter constraint propagation as defined in Definition 4.28 and 4.39 guarantees convergence, such that the fixed point definition (see Definition 4.40) can always be reached.

Lemma 5.3 For all A_M being a multi-lateral collaboration consisting of $A_0,\ldots,A_{n-1}$ local workflows A_M always reaches the fixed point

$$\forall 0 \leq k < n. \forall 0 \leq j < n, j \neq k. A_k = \Phi(\Phi_b(A_k, A_j))$$

Proof: Local propagation of parameter constraints changes the resulting automaton if there exists a transition in the former version of the automaton, which does not contain a guard expression provided by a transition passed on the message sequence already. In case of bilateral parameter constraint propagation, the resulting automaton changes, if there exists a transition in the previous version of the automaton, which does not contain a guard expression provided by the corresponding transition of a trading partners local workflow.

In either case, guard expressions are not created, but existing ones are used to extend the ones assigned to a transition already. In particular, the resulting guard expression subsumes the former guard expression due to the construction of the propagation via conjunctions (see Definition 4.28 and 4.39). As a consequence the change of the local workflow A_k is monotonic, because within a multi-lateral collaboration the set of potential guard expressions is finite and the guard expressions from one propagation step to another are subsumed, thus, the propagation converges. □

In addition to the convergence of parameter constraint propagation, it can be shown that the propagation of occurrence graph constraints as defined in Definition 4.42 based on the fixed point of parameter constraint propagation guarantees convergence, such that fixed point definition (see Definition 4.43) can always be reached.

Lemma 5.4 For all A_M being a multi-lateral collaboration consisting of $A_0,\ldots,A_{n-1}$ local workflows, where each A_i is a normalized acyclic guarded aFSA with A_i being a fixed point with regard to parameter constraint propagation, A_M always reaches the fixed point

$$\forall 0 \leq k < n. \forall 0 \leq j < n, j \neq k. A_k = \Psi(A_k)$$

Proof: Propagation of occurrence graph constraints is based on the intersection of extended automata of a local workflow and the trading partners corresponding local workflows. Since intersection of an automaton with other automata guarantees that the original one subsumes the intersection automaton, the propagation operation Ψ is monotonic, thus, the occurrence graph constraint propagation converges. □

5.2.2 Alternative Consistency Definition

The propagation results in a fixed point as stated above. However, it has to be shown that the fixed point local workflows of a multi-lateral collaboration are equivalent to the corresponding party's projection of the multi-lateral collaboration. This proof requires an intermediate step of showing that a party p's projection of the intersection of the multi-lateral collaborations extended local workflows is equivalent to the intersection of party p's local workflow with the shuffle product of party p's projection of the remaining local workflows of the collaboration. To show this equivalence, the two implications forming the equivalence are separated by the following two lemmas.

Lemma 5.5 Let A_M be a multi-lateral collaboration consisting of $A_0,\ldots,A_{n-1}$ with A_j being the local workflow of party j and A_j being parameter and occurrence graph constraint fixed point, then for every $0 \leq k < n$ and for every message sequence ω accepted by A_k, the message sequence can be represented as the shuffle product of the projections $\tau_j(\omega)$ with $0 \leq j < n$ and $j \neq k$, that is,

$$\forall 0 \leq k < n. \forall \omega \in L(A_k). \omega \in L(\&_{0 \leq j < n, j \neq k} \tau_j(\omega))$$

Proof: Since ω contains messages, which are exchanged between A_k and another party A_j, the messages used by different j in $\tau_j(\omega)$ are disjoint. As a consequence, ω is in the language created by the combination of these messages, where a potential order per trading partner is already considered, that is, $\omega \in L(\&_{0 \leq j < n, j \neq k} \tau_j(\omega))$. □

While the above lemma is quite straightforward, the following has to show that each word which can be created by the shuffle product providing non-contradicting guard expressions implies that the word is contained in the local workflow.

Lemma 5.6 Let A_M be a multi-lateral collaboration consisting of $A_0,\ldots,A_{n-1}$ with A_j being the local workflow of party j and A_j being parameter and occurrence graph constraint fixed point, then for every $0 \leq k < n$ and for every message sequence ω accepted by $A'_k := \tau_k\Big(\bigcap_{0 \leq j < n} \Phi(A_j) \& (\Sigma_M \setminus \Sigma_j)^*\Big)$, all message sequences ω', which can be constructed by the shuffle product of the projections $\tau_j(\omega)$ with $0 \leq j < n$ and $j \neq k$ fulfilling the local parameter constraint propagation, that is, $\omega' = clean(\omega')$, are contained in $L(A'_k)$. That is,

$$\forall 0 \leq k < n. \forall \omega \in L(A'_k). \forall \omega' \in L\Big(\Phi(\&_{0 \leq j < n, j \neq k} \tau_j(\omega))\Big). \omega' = clean(\omega') \rightarrow \omega' \in L(A'_k)$$

Proof: Due to the definition of A'_k being the projection τ_k of the multi-lateral workflow (see Definition 4.33), that is,

$$A'_k := \tau_k\Big(\bigcap_{0\leq j<n} \Phi(A_j)\&(\Sigma_M \setminus \Sigma_j)^*\Big) \tag{5.1}$$

and the requirement of $\omega \in L(A'_k)$ every local workflow A_j with $0 \leq j < n$ accepts a message sequence ω_j, which shares the same order of messages exchanged between A_k and A_j, that is,

$$\forall 0 \leq j < n. \exists \omega_j \in L(\Phi(A_j)). \tau_k(\omega_j) = \tau_j(\omega) \tag{5.2}$$

If this condition is not fulfilled, then the intersection in equation 5.1 would be empty and, thus, ω would not be contained in $L(A'_k)$ as stated in the requirement. As a consequence, such a message sequence ω_j exists for every local workflow A_j in the multi-lateral collaboration.

Each message used in ω has a sender and a recipient, where party k is either but not both of them. As a consequence, the set of messages used in message sequences $\tau_k(\omega_j)$ and $\tau_k(\omega_i)$ are disjoint, where $0 \leq j < i < n, i \neq k, j \neq k$. Based on the construction of ω' (see equation 5.3) by the shuffle product of the disjoint message sequences $\tau_j(\omega)$

$$\omega' \in L\Big(\Phi(\&_{0\leq j<n, j\neq k} \tau_j(\omega)\,)\Big) \tag{5.3}$$

the requirement of $\omega' = clean(\omega')$, that is, having satisfiable guard expressions within ω', and the fact that $\tau_j(\omega)$ equals $\tau_k(\omega_j)$ by equation 5.2 it follows that

$$\omega' \in L\Big(\Phi(\&_{0\leq j<n, j\neq k} \tau_k(\omega_j)\,)\Big) \tag{5.4}$$

Since $\tau_k(\omega_j)$ are pairwise disjoint, the following equation can be stated:

$$\forall 0 \leq j < n, j \neq k. \tau_k(\omega_j) = \tau_j(\omega') \tag{5.5}$$

Due to the construction of ω' (see equation 5.3) the parameter constraint propagation has already been applied, thus, with the assumption of the lemma that all automata are fixed points with parameter constraints $\omega' = \Phi(\omega')$ it follows that this equation also holds for the projection of ω' such that $\tau_j(\omega') = \Phi(\tau_j(\omega'))$, which can be rephrased by using equation 5.5 as

$$\forall 0 \leq j < n. \tau_k(\omega_j) = \Phi(\tau_k(\omega_j)) \tag{5.6}$$

Let's assume equation 5.6 is not valid, then ω_j can not be accepted by A_j, which contradicts equation 5.2. Thus, the above equation is valid. As a consequence of this argumentation, the following equation is valid, too:

$$\forall 0 \leq j < n, j \neq k. \omega_j = \Phi(\omega_j) \tag{5.7}$$

ω_j is contained in $L(A_j)$, which is constructed in the same way as A_k, that is, recursively via the intersection calculation. Since $\omega_j \in L(A_j)$ the intersection of A_j with the remaining parties as specified in equation 5.1 accept the message sequence ω_j due to the fixed point assumption, otherwise ω_j would not be contained in $L(A_j)$. As a consequence, the intersection of the extended ω_j cannot be empty, thus,

$$\omega' := \bigcap_{0\leq j<n, j\neq k} \Phi(\omega_j \& (\Sigma_M \setminus \Sigma_j)^*) \tag{5.8}$$

which by requirement $\omega' = clean(\omega')$ and equation 5.1 means that $\omega' \in L(A'_k)$, while ω' has been constructed by the shuffle product (see equation 5.3). □

Based on the previous lemmas, the initial aim of this section can be formally stated as a theorem:

Theorem 5.1
Let A_M be a multi-lateral collaboration consisting of $A_0,\ldots,A_{n-1}$ with A_j being the local workflow of party j and A_j being parameter and occurrence graph constraint fixed point, then the local workflow resulting from the projection of the multi-lateral workflow is equivalent to the one constructed by the intersection of the local workflow with the shuffle product of the local party's projection of the remaining local workflows, that is,

$$\tau_k\Big(\bigcap_{0\leq j<n} \Phi(A_j \& (\Sigma_M \setminus \Sigma_j)^*)\Big) \equiv clean\Big(\Phi(A_k) \cap \Phi\Big(\&_{0\leq j<n, j\neq k} \tau_k(A_j)\Big)\Big)$$

Proof: Two automata are equivalent if the corresponding languages are equivalent. Thus, every message sequence is accepted by the right hand side if and only if the message sequence is also accepted by the left hand side.

The implication from left to right can easily be shown, since $\omega \in L(A_k)$ with $\omega = clean(\omega)$ and by Lemma 5.5 $\omega \in L\Big(\Phi(\&_{0\leq j<n, j\neq k} \tau_k(A_j))\Big)$. As a consequence of $\omega \in L(A_k)$, ω is also contained in the language resulting from $clean\Big(\Phi(A_k) \cap \Phi\Big(\&_{0\leq j<n, j\neq k} \tau_k(A_j)\Big)\Big)$.

The implication from right to left can be shown using Lemma 5.6. Since ω is contained in the intersection language of $\Phi(A_k)$ and $\Phi(\&_{0\leq j<n, j\neq k} \tau_k(A_j))$ with $\omega = clean(\omega)$, ω is contained in either language. Further, since ω is contained in $\Phi(A_k)$ the equation $\omega = \Phi(\omega)$ is also valid.

As a consequence, it has been shown that $\omega \in \Phi(A_k)$ and $\omega = \Phi(\omega)$ which are the prerequisites for Lemma 5.6, implying that $\omega \in \tau_k(L(\bigcap_{0\leq j<n} \Phi(A_j \& (\Sigma_M \setminus \Sigma_j)^*)))$ □

The current definition of the fixed point calculation requires a local workflow A_p to recognize all messages of the trading partners to be able to extend its local workflow before doing the intersection calculation (see also Definition 4.42). This seems inappropriate since the decentralization requirement forces us to stick to local knowledge. As a consequence, an equivalent representation of this propagation rule is introduced.

Lemma 5.7 Let A_M be a multi-lateral collaboration consisting of $A_0,\ldots,A_{n-1}$ with A_j being the local workflow of party j and A_j being parameter and occurrence graph constraint fixed point. The trading partner's workflows of a party k are the subset of all local workflows, where the corresponding alphabets have at least a single message in common, that is, $\{A_{i_k(0)},\ldots,A_{i_k(m_k)}\} := \{A_j \mid 0 \leq j < n \wedge j \neq k \wedge \Sigma_j \cap \Sigma_k \neq \emptyset\}$. The following equivalence holds:

$$\&_{0 \leq j < n, j \neq k} \tau_k(A_j) \equiv \&_{0 \leq l < m_k, l \neq k} \tau_k(A_{i_k(l)})$$

Proof: Based on $\&_{0 \leq j<n, j \neq k} \tau_k(A_j)$ two cases have to be distinguished: In the first case, A_j represents a local workflow of a trading partner, that is, $\Sigma_j \cap \Sigma_k \neq \emptyset$ which maps to a workflow contained in the subset $\{A_{i_k(0)},\ldots,A_{i_k(m_k)}\}$ with $j = i_k(l)$. Thus, the automaton is represented at either side of the equivalence.

In the second case, A_j represents a local workflow of a party being not a trading partner, that is, $\Sigma_j \cap \Sigma_k = \emptyset$. Thus, there exists no mapping of A_j to a workflow contained in the subset $\{A_{i_k(0)},\ldots,A_{i_k(m_k)}\}$ with $j = i_k(l)$. Therefore, the workflow A_j appears only on the left hand side of the equivalence. However, due to $\Sigma_j \cap \Sigma_k = \emptyset$ the abstraction $\tau_k(A_j)$ of the local workflow A_j results in an empty message sequence. Thus, the projection does not contribute any messages to the construction of the workflow by the shuffle product and therefore can be neglected.

In case the language of the local workflow A_j is empty, the multi-lateral collaboration A_M must also be empty since $A_j = \tau_j(A_M)$. Thus, all automata A_j are empty making the right hand side also empty. □

Based on this lemma and the above Theorem 5.1 it follows that the fixed point local workflows A_j are equivalent to $\tau_j(A_M)$.

5.2.3 Decentralized Consistency

The overall goal of this thesis is to decide consistency of multi-lateral collaborations in a decentralized way. The definition of consistency of a multi-lateral collaboration has been stated in Definition 4.33 [1]. In addition, the relation between multi-lateral workflow and fixed point local workflows was discussed in the previous section. As a consequence, the decentralization aspect of deciding consistency has to be addressed next.

In Definition 4.33 consistency of a multi-lateral collaboration has been defined as the non-empty intersection of the local workflows extended by all messages that the party is not directly involved in. Due to this definition, it can be shown that in case of a single automaton being empty, that is, inconsistent, the multi-lateral collaboration is also empty, that is, inconsistent. The first lemma shows that a single local workflow being empty implies that also the multi-lateral workflow is empty.

[1] While this definition specifies consistency for the synchronous communication model based on aFSA, the asynchronous case has also been mapped to aFSA as discussed in Section 5.1.

Lemma 5.8 Let A_M be a multi-lateral collaboration based on the local workflows $A_0,\dots,A_{n-1}$ with A_j being the local workflow of party j and A_j being parameter and occurrence graph constraint fixed point. The multi-lateral collaboration A_M is empty, if at least one local workflow A_j is empty, that is

$$\exists 0 \leq j < n.L(A_j) = \emptyset \longrightarrow L(A_M) = \emptyset$$

Proof: Since the multi-lateral workflow is defined as the intersection of the extended local workflows, an empty local workflow can not be extended, thus, the intersection of languages where one is empty results in an empty intersection language. □

The second lemma shows the opposite direction by proving that in case all automata are non-empty, also the multi-lateral workflow is non-empty.

Lemma 5.9 Let A_M be a multi-lateral collaboration based on the local workflows $A_0,\dots,A_{n-1}$ with A_j being the local workflow of party j and A_j being parameter and occurrence graph constraint fixed point. The multi-lateral collaboration A_M is non-empty, if all local workflows A_j are non-empty, that is

$$\forall 0 \leq j < n.L(A_j) \neq \emptyset \longrightarrow L(A_M) \neq \emptyset$$

Proof: Based on Theorem 5.1 and the fixed point of A_j each A_j is equivalent to the projection $\tau_j(A_M)$ of the multi-lateral workflow. Since all workflows are non-empty, the multi-lateral collaboration A_M is also non-empty. □

As a consequence of these two lemma, the following theorem can be shown:

Theorem 5.2

Let A_M be a multi-lateral collaboration based on the local workflows $A_0,\dots,A_{n-1}$ with A_j being the local workflow of party j and A_j being parameter and occurrence graph constraint fixed point. The multi-lateral collaboration A_M is consistent, if and only if all local workflows A_j with $0 \leq j < n$ are consistent.

Proof: Since consistency is non-emptiness of the corresponding automaton and based on Lemma 5.8 and 5.9 the theorem is valid. □

Since non-emptiness is not a structural property of FSA, it does not propagate like the guard expressions do. Thus, finally the consensus making step is needed to decide consistency of a multi-lateral collaboration in a decentralized way.

5.3 Consensus Making

Consensus making describes the problem of eliciting all parties involved in the process whether all of them agree on a certain fact. With regard to decentralized collaboration establishment, the consensus has to be achieved between the parties involved in the multi-lateral collaboration, while the fact they have to agree on is local consistency. However, local consistency is based on an emptiness test of fixed point local workflows. In particular,the emptiness test evaluates annotations of a guarded aFSA, which can only be locally checked and do not influence the structure of an automaton.

To avoid explicitly introducing a protocol implementing consensus making, the evaluation of annotations must also affect the structure of an automaton, thus being propagated during the fixed point calculation. In particular, an annotation normalized form of an automaton is introduced, where a state annotation is represented in disjunctive normal form and in the normalized automaton one state per conjunction is introduced. Thus, annotations in an annotation normalized guarded aFSA contain only conjunctions. Based on this annotation for normalized aFSA a clean operation can be defined, removing those states which are annotated with an unsatisfiable expression, thus affecting the structure of the aFSA. By applying the propagation it can be shown that either all local workflows are empty or none of them are.

Definition 5.4
A normalized acyclic guarded aFSA $A = (Q, \Sigma, \Delta, q_0, F, QA, G, P)$ can be transformed into an equivalent annotation normalized acyclic guarded aFSA $A' = (\underline{Q} \cup \{\bar{q}\}, \underline{\Sigma}, \underline{\Delta}, \bar{q}, \underline{F}, \underline{QA}, \underline{G}, P)$ with $\underline{A} := \Upsilon(A, q_0, \varepsilon, \bar{q}, \varepsilon)$ with $\bar{q}$ being a new unique state and using the recursive definition of Υ defined as follows:

$$\Upsilon(A, q_{cur}, \alpha_{last}, q_{last}, \tilde{e}) := \bigcup_{e'_i} \begin{pmatrix} \{q'\} \cup \bigcup_{\{(q_{cur},\alpha,q)\in\Delta|\alpha\in Var(e'_i)\}} Q'' \\ \Sigma \\ \{(q_{last}, \alpha_{last}, q')\} \cup \bigcup_{\{(q_{cur},\alpha,q)\in\Delta|\alpha\in Var(e'_i)\}} \Delta'' \\ \bar{q} \\ \left(\bigcup_{\{(q_{cur},\alpha,q)\in\Delta|\alpha\in Var(e'_i)\}} F''\right) \cup \begin{cases} \{q'\} & if\ q_{cur} \in F \\ \emptyset & otherwise \end{cases} \\ \{(q', e'_i)\} \cup \bigcup_{\{(q_{cur},\alpha,q)\in\Delta|\alpha\in Var(e'_i)\}} QA'' \\ \{((q_{last}, \alpha_{last}, q'), \tilde{e})\} \cup \bigcup_{\{(q_{cur},\alpha,q)\in\Delta|\alpha\in Var(e'_i)\}} G \\ P \end{pmatrix}^T$$

where q_{cur} is the current state of the original automaton A being represented in the result automaton as a new unique state q'. Further, the state q_{last} represents the state within the result automaton calling this recursion via a transition labeled α_{last} with guard expression $\tilde{e}$. The current state q_{cur}'s annotation e can be normalized in disjunctive normal form resulting in a disjunction of conjunctions $e' = e'_1 \vee \ldots \vee e'_n$, while each e'_i is treated explicitly. The automaton $A'' = (Q'', \Sigma, \Delta'', \bar{q}, F'', QA'', G'', P)$ is derived by the recursion $A'' = \Upsilon(A, q, \alpha, q', \tilde{e}')$ with $\tilde{e}' = G((q_{cur}, \alpha, q))$.

This definition ensures that annotations used within an automaton consists of conjunctions only. It is achieved by transforming annotations in disjunctive normal form and introducing a new state for each conjunction. As a consequence, due to the newly introduced states a deterministic automaton may result in an annotation normalized non-deterministic automaton.

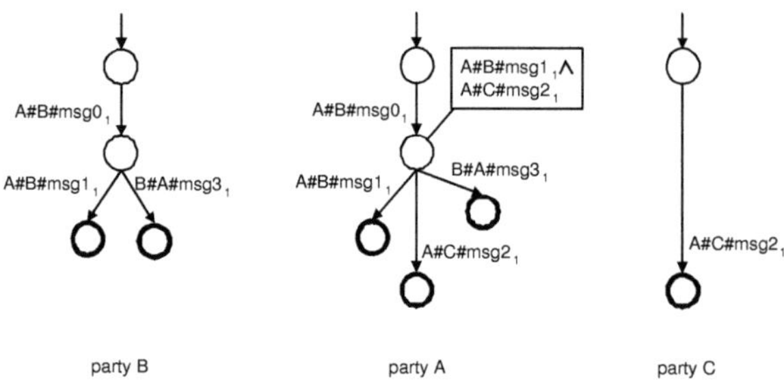

Figure 5.2: Normalized Acyclic Guarded aFSA Example

To illustrate the definition an example depicted in Figure 5.2 is introduced. The example consists of a multi-lateral collaboration of party A, B, and C, where the process starts with party A sending message *A#B#msg*0 to party B, followed by party A sending either message *A#B#msg*1 or *A#C#msg*2 resulting in the annotation at party A. However, party A alternatively may receive message *B#A#msg*3. It can easily be shown that the multi-lateral collaboration is inconsistent.

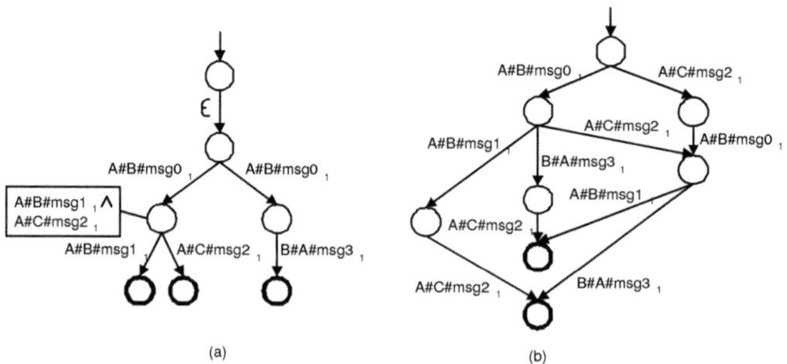

Figure 5.3: Normalized Acyclic Guarded aFSA: (a) Annotation Normalization of Party A (b) Shuffle Product of A's Projection on Party B's and C's Workflow

Applying the annotation normalization definition to party A's workflow results in the guarded aFSA depicted in Figure 5.3(a). The ε transition has been introduced to allow normalization of annotations at the start state. The annotation $A\#B\#msg1 \wedge A\#C\#msg2$ must been extended to $(A\#B\#msg1 \wedge A\#C\#msg2) \vee B\#A\#msg3$ because the transition $B\#A\#msg3$ is not already contained in the annotation and therefore must be added by a disjunction (see also Section 4.3.3). Since the extended annotation $(A\#B\#msg1 \wedge A\#C\#msg2) \vee B\#A\#msg3$ is already in disjunctive normal form it can be split into two "conjunctive parts", that is, $A\#B\#msg1 \wedge A\#C\#msg2$ and $B\#A\#msg3$ each associated to a state on its own.

The occurrence graph constraint propagation requires part A's workflow to intersect with the shuffle product of party A's trading partners workflows projected for party A (see also Theorem 5.1). Figure 5.3(b) depicts the shuffle product of A's projection on the workflows of party B and C. Intersecting the aFSA depicted in Figure 5.3(a) and (b) results in the aFSA depicted in Figure 5.4(a). Due to the occurrence graph constraint propagation, the target state of the transition labeled $A\#C\#msg2$ is not final any more. As a consequence, the evaluation of the annotation $A\#B\#msg1 \wedge A\#C\#msg2$ is false, thus, the transitions following the annotated state can be omitted as depicted in Figure 5.4(b). The operation for cleaning the automaton is $clean_a()$ formally defined as:

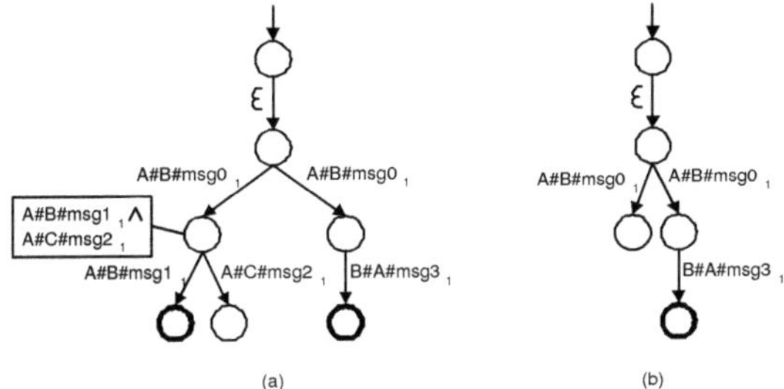

Figure 5.4: Normalized Acyclic Guarded aFSA: (a) Occurrence Graph Constraint Propagation on Party A's Workflow (b) $clean_a() of (a)$

Definition 5.5

An annotation normalized acyclic guarded aFSA $A = (Q, \Sigma, \Delta, q_0, F, QA, G, P)$ can be transformed into an equivalent annotation normalized acyclic guarded aFSA $A' = (Q, \Sigma, \Delta', q_0, F, QA, G', P)$ with $A' := clean_a(A)$ by the operation $clean_a()$, where all transitions are omitted which leave a state with a falsified annotation, that is, an annotation which can never be evaluated to true. The guard function is adapted to the changed set of transitions. Thus, $\Delta' := clean_a(q_0)$ with

$$clean_a(q) := \begin{cases} \bigcup_{(q,\alpha,q') \in \Delta} \{(q,\alpha,q')\} \cup clean_a(q') & if \ \|\tilde{r}^q\|_{\emptyset}^{\mathsf{v}} = t \\ \emptyset & otherwise \end{cases}$$

and $G' := G \cap (\Delta' \times \mathcal{ALC}(\mathcal{D}))$.

Continuing the fixed point calculation based on party A's workflow depicted in Figure 5.4(b) makes the remaining final state of party A non final. This is due to the intersection with the shuffle product of the projections on party B's and C's workflow. Finally, applying occurrence graph constraint propagation to party B and C again results in local workflows not containing any final state, too, as depicted in Figure 5.5.

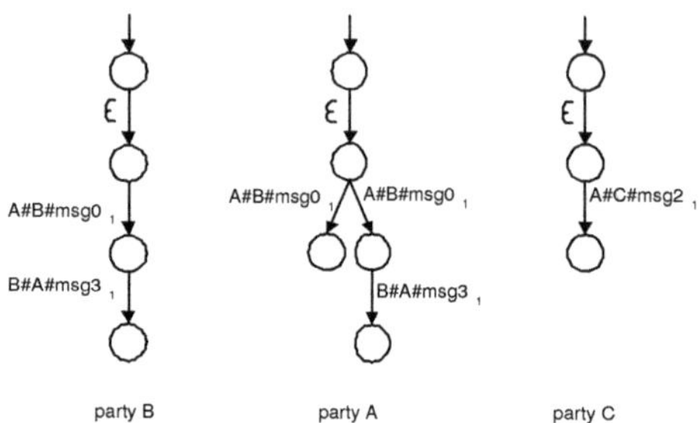

Figure 5.5: Fixed Point Local Workflows of Multi-lateral Collaboration

Applying $clean_a()$ again, each local workflow consists of a single state, which is not a final state. This is because all states are removed which have an annotation which cannot be evaluated to true. In the example none of the automata has a final state anyway, thus there is no path at all resulting in a final state, which results in removing all states except the start state (by definition). As a consequence, an automaton containing only a single state which is not a final one, indicates that the workflow is inconsistent. Changing the original workflow of Party C by making the start state also a final state results in a consistent collaboration, where the local workflows are not drilled down to a single state.

In the following, it is proven that the observed behavior always works, thus, being an alternative to introducing a consensus making protocol.

Lemma 5.10 Let A_k be an annotation normalized acyclic guarded aFSA, then

$$L(A_k) = \emptyset \longleftrightarrow L(clean_a(clean(A_k))) = \emptyset$$

where the emptiness test on the left hand side is based on Definition 4.30 considering annotations, and where the emptiness test on the right hand side is a standard automaton emptiness test as introduced in Section 4.3.2 without consideration of annotations.

Proof: Applying the $clean()$ operation on A_k removes all transitions with unsatisfiable guard expressions, thus, all transitions contained in the resulting automaton have to be considered for emptiness testing. This fits the emptiness test used on the left hand side, since by this definition unsatisfiable transitions are also ruled out.

Since A_k is annotation normalized, every annotation associated with a state is a conjunction of transition labels. Thus, based on the emptiness definition on the left hand side, the annotation evaluates to true if and only if all transitions are on a path to a final state and no additional transition labels are contained in the annotation. Because an annotation associated to a state not evaluating to true results in omitting all outgoing transitions of the state, thus, the state does not provide any transition afterwards ensuring that the state is only on a path to a final state if the annotation is valid. As a consequence, the left and the right hand side are equivalent. □

Using this lemma it can be shown that multi-lateral consistency is equivalent to consistency of fixed point local workflows. As a consequence no consensus making protocol is required.

Theorem 5.3
Let A_M be a multi-lateral collaboration based on the local workflows $A_0,\ldots,A_{n-1}$ with A_j being the local workflow of party j and each A_j being a fixed point annotation normalized acyclic guarded aFSA. The multi-lateral collaboration is inconsistent if and only if all local workflows are inconsistent.

Proof: It has to be shown that the multi-lateral workflow is empty if and only if all local workflows are empty. Based on Theorem 5.2 the multi-lateral collaboration is consistent if and only if all local workflows are consistent. Thus, the multi-lateral collaboration is inconsistent, if and only if at least a single workflow is inconsistent. Based on Lemma 5.10 the evaluation of annotations within the emptiness test has been represented on structural properties of the aFSA. Thus, let's assume a local workflow A_k is empty in accordance with the standard automaton emptiness test, that is, $L(A_k) = \emptyset$. Then, for every local workflow A_j within the multi-lateral collaboration $L(A_j) = \emptyset$ due to $A_j = \bigcap_{0 \leq l < n} \Sigma_l$ which also includes A_k. □

5.4 Summary

Multi-lateral collaborations may be based on asynchronous or synchronous communication models. In the synchronous case guarded annotated Finite State Automata (guarded aFSA) were introduced in the previous chapter, while guarded Workflow Nets (WF-Nets) are used in the asynchronous case. Since checking guarded WF-Nets properties is based on analyzing the corresponding occurrence graph, which has the same expressiveness as guarded FSA, a mapping from guarded WF-Nets to guarded FSA is provided, thus, the further analysis and required definitions have to be provided only on the guarded FSA workflow model. In particular, a proof for the equivalence of guarded WF-Net consistency with guarded FSA consistency is provided.

To validate the correctness of the proposed approach the convergence of the constraint propagation to a fixed point and the equivalence of multi-lateral consistency and the consensus of all parties on local consistency is shown. Since multi-lateral consistency checking is based on local workflows extended with messages not used by a trading partner himself, each party has to know all messages used within the multi-lateral collaboration. An alternative approach has been presented, where multi-lateral consistency is defined as the non-empty intersection of a party P's local workflow and the combination of the trading partners abstracted local workflows, where those messages are represented as silent transitions which are neither sent nor received by party P. This definition increases the applicability of the approach presented because information not related to trading partners is kept private. It has been shown that these two definitions of multi-lateral consistency are equivalent.

Finally, it is shown that the evaluation of state annotations of a guarded aFSA performed during an emptiness test can also be represented within FSA structure by omitting those transitions leaving a state and being related to an annotation not evaluating to true. Based on this structural representation of state annotations, emptiness of a single local workflow results in emptiness of all local workflows of a multi-lateral collaboration within a fixed point. Thus, a multi-lateral collaboration is inconsistent, if and only if a fixed point has been reached and a party's own local workflow is consistent.

Chapter 6

Implementation and Evaluation

The aim of this chapter is twofold: (i) to describe the implementation of the approach presented for the synchronous communication model based on annotated Finite State Automata (aFSA) as introduced in Section 5.1, and (ii) to evaluate the implementation and the formal model based on a set of realistic workflow models derived from the Internet Open Trading Protocol (IOTP) workflows. The entire evaluation is performed in the domain of Web Services.

The description of the implementation starts with the introduction of a mapping from a workflow modeling language called Business Process Execution Language for Web Services (BPEL) to the annotated Finite State Automata (aFSA) model. This section includes an evaluation of the expressiveness of aFSA by showing that all workflows derivable from the IOTP specification can be represented. Next, the implementation of the bilateral consistency checking is implemented, which uses the previously introduced mapping component. Finally, the complete process of establishing consistent multi-lateral collaborations in a decentralized way is described.

6.1 Workflow Modeling Language Transformation

As stated above, the following discussion is based on Web Service technology. The main standards in this domain at present are

- XML as a common alphabet,
- SOAP as a common interface to communication protocols (like e.g. HTTP),
- WSDL as an interface definition language,
- UDDI as a service repository interface, and
- BPEL as a workflow model specification language.

To illustrate the applicability of the approach presented in the thesis, a mapping of the workflow modeling language BPEL to annotated Finite State Automata is presented and explained following an example.[1]

6.1.1 Example

With regard to the example in Section 2.3.1 the interface definition provided by WSDL is simplified by neglecting the concrete message structure and simplifying the message names. Concrete message structures could, for example, be taken from the RosettaNet Partner Interface Processes (PIPs) 3A4 (Request Purchase Order), 3A7 (Notify of Purchase Order Update), 3B2 (Notify of Advanced Shipment) [Ros04] or from the Internet Open Trading Protocol (IOTP) [Bur00].

```
<portType name="logBuyer">
    <operation name="getStatusOp">
        <input message="tns:getStatus"/>
    </operation>
    <operation name="terminateOp">
        <input message="tns:terminate"/>
    </operation>
</portType>
<portType name="buyer">
    <operation name="statusOp">
        <output message="tns:status"/>
    </operation>
</portType>
<portType name="logAccounting">
    <operation name="authOp">
        <input message="tns:auth"/>
    </operation>
    <operation name="deliverOp">
        <input message="tns:deliver"/>
    </operation>
</portType>
<portType name="accounting">
    <operation name="deliverConfOp">
        <output message="tns:deliver_conf"/>
    </operation>
</portType>
```

```
<plnk:partnerLinkType name="BuyLog">
  <plnk:role name="buyer">
    <plnk:portType name="tns:buyer"/>
  </plnk:role>
  <plnk:role name="logistics">
    <plnk:portType name="tns:logBuyer"/>
  </plnk:role>
</plnk:partnerLinkType>
<plnk:partnerLinkType name="AccLog">
    <plnk:role name="accounting">
        <plnk:portType name="tns:accounting"/>
  </plnk:role>
  <plnk:role name="logistics">
    <plnk:portType name="tns:logAccounting"/>
  </plnk:role>
</plnk:partnerLinkType>
```

Figure 6.1: WSDL Porttype Definition

Within Web Service specifications one or more messages specify an operation representing a potential message exchange. If an operation contains only a single input message, then the operation is asynchronous, otherwise the operation is synchronous[2]. A portType contains a set of operations supported by a service provider which is specified in the corresponding WSDL file. Figure 6.1 depicts the operations and the related messages used in the example logistics department BPEL description, where the messages are labeled in accordance with messages in the global workflow depicted in Figure 2.4. The *buyer* and the *accounting* portTypes represent the operations provided by the corresponding department service, that is, contain messages that are received by the buyer and accounting department respectively. Consequently, the *logBuyer* and *logAccounting* portTypes contain operations received by the logistics department and sent by the buyer and the accounting

[1]Major parts of this section have been published in [WFN04].

[2]Synchronous and asynchronous messages specify the behavior of the process execution rather than the underlying communication protocol. In particular, synchronous messages mean that the execution of the process is pending until the response message has been received.

department respectively. The partnerLinkType is a WSDL extension introduced by BPEL relating partTypes to roles. In particular, the partnerLinkType *BuyLog* represents communication between buyer and logistics department, where the messages received by the buyer are specified in portType *buyer* associated with role *buyer*, while the portType *logBuyer* is associated with role *logistics*. The partnerLinkType accordingly specifies the communication between accounting and logistics department.

As stated above, the description of local workflows is based on these portType definitions by directly referencing them. Local workflows are denoted in BPEL [ACD+03], where a workflow is specified in terms of tasks (named *activities* in BPEL terminology) representing basic pieces of work to be performed by potentially nested services. The control flow of a BPEL process constrains the performance of tasks by selective (*switch* and *pick* activities), sequence (*sequence* activity), and parallel (*flow* activity) execution. In addition, a BPEL process also defines the data flow (variable handling and *assign* activity) of the business process regardless of concrete implementation of tasks. Based on this understanding, a workflow model includes activities realizing the interaction with partners represented by exchanging messages (*receive*, *reply*, *invoke*, and *pick* activities).

```
<process>
.....
 <pick createInstance="yes" name="start process">
   <onMessage partnerLink="AccLog" portType="tns:logAccounting" operation="deliverOp">
     <switch name="amount smaller than 100">
       <case condition="a &lt; 100">
         <sequence>
           <invoke name="deliver_conf" partnerLink="AccLog" portType="tns:accounting"
                   operation="deliverConfOp"/>
           <while name="parcel tracking" condition="1=1">
             <pick>
               <onMessage name="getStatus" partnerLink="BuyLog" portType="tns:logBuyer"
                             operation="getStatusOp" variable="getStatus">
                 <reply name="status" partnerLink="BuyLog" portType="tns:buyer"
                        operation="statusOp" variable="status"/>
               </onMessage>
               <onMessage partnerLink="BuyLog" portType="tns:logBuyer"
                          operation="terminateOp" variable="terminate">
                   <terminate/>
               </onMessage>
             </pick>
           </while>
         </sequence>
       </case>
     </switch>
   </onMessage>
   <onMessage name="auth" partnerLink="AccLog" portType="tns:logAccounting"
              operation="authOp" variable="auth">
     <sequence>
       <receive name="get_status" partnerLink="BuyLog" portType="tns:logBuyer"
                operation="getStatusOp" variable="getStatus"/>
       <reply name="status" partnerLink="BuyLog" portType="tns:buyer"
              operation="statusOp" variable="status"/>
     </sequence>
   </onMessage>
 </pick>
</process>
```

Figure 6.2: BPEL Notation of the Logistics Department Workflow

The BPEL specification of the logistics department workflow described in Section 2.3.1 is depicted in Figure 6.2. The partnerLink definition associates a partner name with a bilateral interaction between two roles. In particular, a partnerLink references a corresponding partnerLinkType within the related WSDL document. The roles can be derived from the WSDL document by checking the partnerLinkType using the portType information.

BPEL is a specification evolving from a standardization process. However, the specification is informal and there is no formal model underlying the BPEL specification [Aal03]. Thus, to provide a matchmaking definition for service discovery, or to enable decentralized collaboration establishment a subset of a BPEL specification is mapped to a guarded aFSA representation. Since BPEL specifies an executable business process, the workflow specification that is published by a service provider is limited. In particular, business critical information such as conditions under which a customer is willing to perform a payment, or the number of negotiation steps a party is willing to accept have to remain private. As a consequence, the following transformation approach omits this kind of information, that is, does not transform conditions in BPEL representation to guard expressions in aFSA representation.

The transformation from BPEL to aFSA notation is quite similar to transformations, for example, from regular expressions to finite state automata (see for example the Berry-Sethi Algorithm [BS86]). The approach performs the structural traversal of the BPEL XML document and recursively transforms an activity by interrelating the already transformed child activities. Thus, an activity is transformed by representing it in a partial structure combined with the partial structures of the child activities. These partial structures must maintain an input state q_{in} representing the state to enter the partial structure and an output state q_{out} representing the state to leave the partial structure finally. This partial structure is called partial aFSA and is formally defined in the next section.

The recursion has to start with the first activity within the BPEL document being a child element of the *<process>* element. So, the transformation of the *<process>* is different from that of the activity elements, because here the recursion is initiated by creating a start and final state passed to the partial structure used in the recursion as input and output places. Finally, the mapping from the partial aFSA to an aFSA structure is performed.

6.1.2 Model Extension

The partial aFSA is defined based on the definition of aFSA (see Section 4.3.3). As stated above, this structure is used by the recursive transformation of the BPEL description to aFSA notation, where the input state and the output state represent the states for entering/leaving the partial structure used within the recursion step.

Definition 6.1
A partial aFSA *PA* is an aFSA extended by an output state $q_{out} \in Q$ and an input state q_{in} by not passing the start state q_0. The resulting signature is $PA = (Q, \Sigma, \Delta, q_{in}, q_{out}, F, QA)$.

When constructing a partial aFSA by combining lower level partial aFSAs, the corresponding input and output states must for example be interrelated to form a sequence. In case of the sequence, the output state of the preceding partial aFSA is equivalent to the input state of the succeeding partial aFSA, thus, one of them need to be renamed by another one. So, a renaming function $\tilde{\tau} : (Q \cup \{\varepsilon\}) \times (Q \times Q) \rightarrow (Q \cup \{\varepsilon\})$ of states on partial aFSAs is defined, where ε represents a non-existent state.

Definition 6.2
A state q is renamed q' by function $\tilde{\tau}$ defined for a state $\tilde{q}$ with

$$\tilde{\tau}(\tilde{q}, q \rightarrow q') := \begin{cases} q' & if\ \tilde{q} = q \\ \tilde{q} & otherwise \end{cases}$$

Extending the above definition to partial automata results in a renaming function $\tilde{\tau} : PA \times (Q \times Q) \rightarrow PA$ which renames a state of the input annotated automaton PA resulting in a new automaton PA' by renaming the set of states of PA', all source and target states in transitions of PA', and the corresponding variables within annotations of PA'.

Definition 6.3
Let $PA = (Q, \Sigma, \Delta, q_{in}, q_{out}, F, QA)$ and $PA' = (Q', \Sigma, \Delta', q'_{in}, q'_{out}, F', QA')$ be partial automata. Then, $PA' := \tilde{\tau}(PA, q \rightarrow q')$ where

- the set of states Q' where $Q' := \{\tilde{\tau}(\tilde{q}, q \rightarrow q') \mid \tilde{q} \in Q\}$,
- the set of transitions Δ' where $\Delta' := \{(\tilde{\tau}(q_1, q \rightarrow q'), l, \tilde{\tau}(q_2, q \rightarrow q')) \mid (q_1, l, q_2) \in \Delta\}$,
- the input state q'_{in} where $q'_{in} := \tilde{\tau}(q_{in}, q \rightarrow q')$,
- the output state q'_{out} where $q'_{out} := \tilde{\tau}(q_{out}, q \rightarrow q')$,
- the set of final states F' where $F' := \{\tilde{\tau}(\tilde{q}, q \rightarrow q') \mid \tilde{q} \in F\}$, and
- the annotations QA' where $QA' := \bigcup_{(\tilde{q},\tilde{e}) \in QA \setminus \{(q',e')\}} \begin{cases} \{(q', e' \wedge \tilde{e})\} & if\ \tilde{q} = q \\ \emptyset & if\ \tilde{q} = \varepsilon \\ \{(\tilde{q}, \tilde{e})\} & otherwise \end{cases}$

6.1.3 Transformation Overview

The transformation translates BPEL syntax to aFSA. In particular, the transformation represents messages that might be sent by a party at a particular state as messages that *must* be supported by the corresponding receiving party. This is because the sender has the choice to select a particular message to be sent, while the receiving party must be able to handle all possible choices of the sender. This is modeled by the sender workflow annotating each choice of sending messages as mandatory transitions, that is a conjunction of message labels. In contrast, a receiving party represents all supported options as genuine alternatives via a disjunction of message labels.

For example, the logistics department workflow as depicted in Figure 6.2 can be translated into an aFSA by the following mapping of BPEL activities:

- represent *send*, *receive*, *pick*, and *invoke* activities as transitions
- *switch* and *pick* activities represent choices, that is modeled as several transitions each connected with the current place by an input arc

- a *flow* activity represents a parallel execution, that is modeled by enumerating all possible execution sequences of the parallel execution
- a *sequence* activity connects is modeled by renaming the input state by the output state of a preceding activity
- a *while* activity represents a repeated execution, that is modeled by renaming the output state by the input state of the included partial activity forming a loop
- data management operations like *assign* are neglected

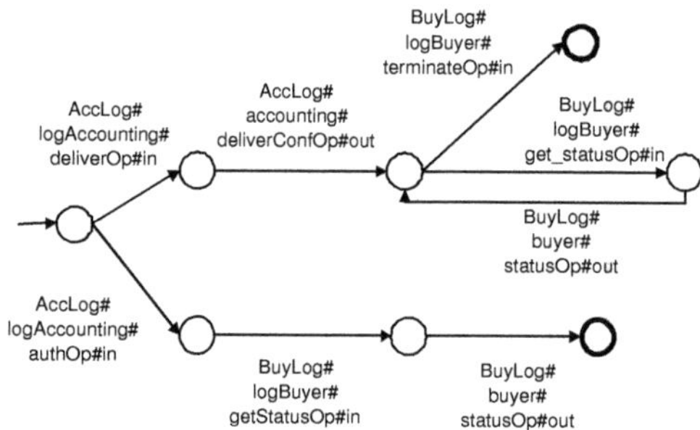

Figure 6.3: aFSA Notation of Logistics Department Workflow

The aFSA model derived by this transformation without resolution of message names is depicted in Figure 6.3 where transition labels *pl#pt#op#dir* represent partnerLink *pl*, portType *pt*, operation *op*, and direction *dir* of the message flow. The final aFSA model after message name resolution Γ is depicted in Figure 6.4, where the annotation of transitions *s#r#msg* contains sender, recipient and message name.

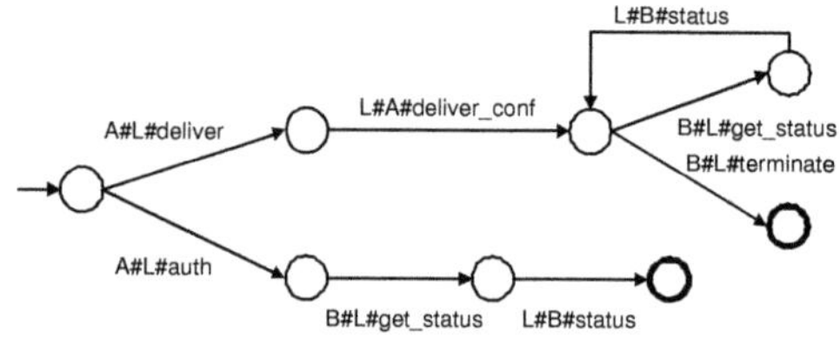

Figure 6.4: aFSA Notation with Message Name Resolution

A detailed formal description of the transformation is given below.

6.1.4 Message Transformation

The representation of interactions in BPEL and aFSA differ, because BPEL is based on communication activities while aFSA is based on messages exchanged between trading partners. Communication activities are either synchronous or asynchronous, and the specification is done in terms of partnerLink, portType and operation, which are specified in a corresponding WSDL file (as already discussed in section 6.1.1). While asynchronous communication can be characterized by portType and operation executed via a partnerLink, synchronous communication requires a differentiation between outgoing and incoming message. This is because a receiving trading partner models synchronous communication by two separate activities (*receive* and *reply*). Thus, an additional parameter '*in*' or '*out*' expressing the direction of the sender of the synchronous exchange is added to the corresponding message. Thus, an exchange within a bilateral interaction is characterized by: partnerLink, portType, operation, and direction. However, the message format *s#r#msg* with sender *s*, recipient *r* and message name *msg* as used in aFSA can be derived based on the above information. In particular, the resolution of message names *s#r#msg* $= \Gamma(pl, pt, op, dir)$ can be informally specified as:

- The sender and recipient can be derived by following the partnerLink to the corresponding partnerLinkType in the WSDL document, which has two *role* child elements representing sender *r* and recipient *r* of the message, while the recipient is the role having the *portType* with name *pt* as a child element.

- The message name is derived from the WSDL document again, where the portType specification is used. In particular, the *portType* element named *pt* is selected, where the child element *operation* is named *op*. The message name *msg* is the message attribute of the *input* element in the case of input direction *dir=in*, or is the message attribute of the *output* element otherwise.

The underlying assumption here is that the two processes to be compared reference the same WSDL document, thus guaranteeing that partnerLinkType, portType and operation are referencing to commonly agreed messages by the bilateral trading parties.

6.1.5 Process Element Transformation

The recursive transformation starts at the top level element *<process>* of BPEL resulting in a partial aFSA representing the child activity.

<process> activity </process>

The recursion starts by transforming the *activity* by the rules below resulting in a partial aFSA *PA*, which can be represented as an aFSA *A* by adding the output state q_{out} to the set of final states and assigning the input state q_{in} as the start state q_0 resulting in an aFSA $A = (Q, \Sigma, \Delta, q_{in}, F \cup \{q_{out}\}, QA)$ with $PA := (Q, \Sigma, \Delta, q_{in}, q_{out}, F, QA)$.

6.1.6 Internal and Simple Activity Transformation

Internal activities do not need to be represented in a description of the bilateral interaction. Such activities are: *scope*, *assign*, or *wait*. To provide a full composability of the transformation, internal activities are represented by an *empty* activity.

Simple activities are related to a single state without having a transition, thus, the corresponding annotation to the state is $true$. Simple activities are *empty* and *termination* activity.

empty activity denoted in BPEL as *<empty/>* is represented as a partial aFSA by a single state only:

$$PA = (\{s_0\}, \emptyset, \emptyset, s_0, s_0, \emptyset, \{(s_0, true)\})$$

terminate activity denoted in BPEL as *<terminate/>* is modeled by a single state, where no further activity can be appended, thus, the output state is an non-existent state ε. Further, the input state is marked final.

$$PA = (\{s_0\}, \emptyset, \emptyset, s_0, \varepsilon, \{s_0\}, \{(s_0, true)\})$$

6.1.7 Communication Activity Transformation

Communication activities exchange messages with trading parties. They are represented as partial aFSAs with a single transition per exchanged message, while the corresponding state is annotated with the transition label in the case of sending activities, or with true in the case of receiving activities. The output state is the state reached after the last message has been exchanged.

reply and asynchronous invocation activities denoted in BPEL as

<reply partnerLink="pl" portType="pt" operation="op" variable="var"/>
<invoke partnerLink="pl" portType="pt" operation="op" inputVariable="var"/>

are modeled as a single transition with an message label at the transition source state represented as

$$\begin{aligned} PA = (& \{s_0, s_1\}, \{\Gamma(pl, pt, op, out)\}, \{(s_0, \Gamma(pl, pt, op, out), s_1)\}, \\ & s_0, s_1, \emptyset, \{(s_0, \Gamma(pl, pt, op, out)), (s_1, true)\}) \end{aligned}$$

receive activity denoted in BPEL as

<receive partnerLink="pl" portType="pt" operation="op" variable="var"/>

is modeled as a single transition annotated with true represented as

$$PA = (\{s_0, s_1\}, \{\Gamma(pl, pt, op, in)\}, \{(s_0, \Gamma(pl, pt, op, in), s_1)\}, s_0, s_1, \emptyset, \{(s_0, true), (s_1, true)\})$$

synchronous invoke activity denoted in BPEL as

<invoke partnerLink="pl" portType="pt" operation="op" inputVariable="var" outputVariable="var2"/>

is modeled by two transitions, while the first one is a sending transition annotated with the message name, the second one is a receiving transition annotated with true. The resulting partial aFSA is represented as

$$\begin{aligned} PA = (& \{s_0, s_1, s_2\}, \{\Gamma(pl, pt, op, in), \Gamma(pl, pt, op, out)\}, \\ & \{(s_0, \Gamma(pl, pt, op, in), s_1), (s_1, \Gamma(pl, pt, op, out), s_2)\}, \\ & s_0, s_2, \emptyset, \{(s_0, \Gamma(pl, pt, op, in)), (s_1, true), (s_2, true)\}) \end{aligned}$$

The remaining communication activity *pick* will be discussed later, because it is a mix of structural and communication activities.

6.1.8 Structural Activity Transformation

Structural activities are *sequence*, *while*, *switch*, and *flow*. They take some partial automata $PA_0, \ldots, PA_n$ and combine them into a new partial automaton PA with $PA_i := (Q_i, \Sigma_i, \Delta_i, q_{in,i}, q_{out,i}, F_i, QA_i)$ for $i = 0, \ldots, n$ and $PA = (Q, \Sigma, \Delta, q_{in}, q_{out}, F, QA)$.

while activity denoted in BPEL by *<while condition="cond">* PA_1 </while> allows a single activity inside the *while* activity only. The loop is created in the partial aFSA by replacing the output state with the input state, formally denoted as

$$PA = \tilde{\tau}(PA_1, q_{out,1} \rightarrow q_{in,1})$$

The previous output state $q_{out,1}$ is disabled. As discussed in Section 6.1.1, the termination condition of the loop is not represented in the aFSA to ensure that business critical information is not published. As a consequence, the loops modeled in aFSA are infinite loops which have to be terminated by explicitly sending a message.

sequence activity denoted in BPEL by *<sequence>* PA_1 PA_2 ... PA_n *</sequence>* connects the independent partial aFSAs by renaming the input state of PA_{i+1} with the output state of PA_i of all partial aFSAs except the last one, that is, PA_n which remains unchanged. The formal specification is

$$PA = PA_n \cup (\bigcup_{i=1}^{n-1} \tilde{\tau}(PA_i, q_{out,i} \rightarrow q_{in,i+1}))$$

flow activity denoted in BPEL by *<flow>* PA_1 PA_2 ... PA_n *</flow>* specifies parallel execution of the partial automata $PA_1, \ldots, PA_n$. Automata do not provide means to model parallel execution, thus, the resulting execution sequences must be enumerated. A well known operation to generate these enumeration is the shuffle product as introduced in Section 4.3.7. In particular, the shuffle product keeps the message order within each message sequence, but combines two message sequences in all possible combinations. The adaptation of the provided definition to partial aFSA is:

Definition 6.4
The shuffle product $PA := PA_1 \& PA_2$ of two partial aFSA PA_1 and PA_2 is defined as

- the set of states Q where $Q := Q_1 \times Q_2$,
- the alphabet Σ where $\Sigma := \Sigma_1 \cup \Sigma_2$,
- the input state q_{in} where $q_{in} := q_{in,1} \times q_{in,2}$,
- the output state q_{out} where $q_{out} := q_{out,1} \times q_{out,2}$,
- the set of final states F where $F := F_1 \times F_2$,
- the set of transitions Δ where
$$\begin{aligned} \Delta := \quad & \{((p,q_1),\alpha,(p,q_2)) \in (Q_1 \times Q_2) \times \Sigma_2 \times (Q_1 \times Q_2) \mid (q_1,\alpha,q_2) \in \Delta_2\} \\ \cup \quad & \{((p_1,q),\alpha,(p_2,q)) \in (Q_1 \times Q_2) \times \Sigma_1 \times (Q_1 \times Q_2) \mid (p_1,\alpha,p_2) \in \Delta_1\} \end{aligned}$$
- the set of annotations QA where $QA = \bigcup_{(q_1,e_1) \in QA_1,(q_2,e_2) \in QA_2}((q_1,q_2), e_1 \wedge e_2)$

Based on the shuffle product definition the *flow* activity can easily be transformed into partial aFSA by shuffling all partial automata and finally renaming the combination of the input states of all automata with a new input state, and the combination of all output states with a new output state respectively. The formal definition is given below

$$PA = \tilde{\tau}\Big(\tilde{\tau}(\&_{i=1}^{n} PA_i, (q_{in,1}, \ldots, q_{in,n}) \rightarrow q_{in}), (q_{out,1}, \ldots, q_{out,n}) \rightarrow q_{out}\Big)$$

switch activity denoted in BPEL by

<switch>
<case condition="cond$_1$"> PA_1 </case>
<case condition="cond$_2$"> PA_2 </case>
⋮
<case condition="cond$_n$"> PA_n </case>
<otherwise> PA_0 </otherwise>
</switch>

specifies an internal choice performed by evaluating the condition statements which are XPath 1.0 Boolean expressions. This choice is represented in partial aFSAs by introducing a new input state

q_{in} and an output state q_{out}, and renaming input and output states of $PA_0, \ldots, PA_n$ by q_{in} and q_{out} respectively. Again, the conditions of the choice are not represented in aFSA to ensure that business critical information is not published. The formal definition is

$$PA = \bigcup_{i=0}^{n} \tilde{\tau}(\tilde{\tau}(PA_i, q_{in,i} \to q_{in}), q_{out,i} \to q_{out})$$

The approach presented is based on the assumption that all conditions are pairwise disjoint. If this condition is not fulfilled the disjoint partitioning of the conditions are represented as a conjunction in the state annotations, while the different partitions are combined by disjunctions. Due to the incomplete representation of relations between parameters within a BPEL document, pairwise disjointness becomes a requirement.

pick activity denoted in BPEL as

<pick>
  <onMessage partnerLink="pl_1" portType="pt_1"
    operation="op_1" variable="var_1"> PA_1 </onMessage>
    ⋮
  <onMessage partnerLink="pl_n" portType="pt_n"
    operation="op_n" variable="var_n"> PA_n </onMessage>
  <onAlarm> PA''_0 </onAlarm>
</pick>

is a combination of a *switch* activity applied to several sequences of a *receive* activity and a partial automaton PA_i. In the current modeling the time constraints which might be expressible in *onAlarm*, that is *for* and *until* , are not considered.

Each *onMessage* element is modeled as a single receive transition formally described as

$$\begin{aligned} PA'_j := \; & (\{s_0, s_1\}, \{\Gamma(pl_j, pt_j, op_j, in)\}, \{(s_{0,j}, \Gamma(pl_j, pt_j, op_j, in), s_{1,j})\}, s_{0,j}, s_{1,j}, \emptyset, \\ & \{(s_{0,j}, true), (s_{1,j}, true)\}) \end{aligned}$$

Each of these receive transitions is sequentially combined with the corresponding PA_j in accordance with the *sequence* activity formally described as

$$PA''_j := \tilde{\tau}(PA'_j \cup PA_j, q'_{out,j} \to q_{in,j})$$

Finally, the above constructed sequences are combined by a choice resulting in the final partial automaton formally denoted as

$$PA := \bigcup_{i=0}^{n} \tilde{\tau}(\tilde{\tau}(PA''_i, q''_{in,i} \to q_{in}), q''_{out,i} \to q_{out})$$

6.1.9 Limitations

The transformation defined above is partial, in particular, the attributes *joinCondition* and *suppressJoinFailure*, as well as the elements *link* and *throw* have not been considered. The first ones are relevant to process execution only and thus do not affect the matchmaking. The latter ones are introducing additional dependencies between the different activities, which cannot be resolved in a recursive traversal of the BPEL, but require post-processing to reflect these additional constraints.

The structural activity *while* supports the termination of a loop based on an internal global variable, that is, a counter or a flag. This kind of predetermined loop termination can be represented in guarded aFSA by combining the states derived by the defined mapping with the potential values of the global variable. Since a change of the global variable is effected by sending or receiving a message, the change of the global variable is reflected by a corresponding state change in the guarded aFSA. As a consequence the guarded aFSA model complexity increases dramatically. However, time dependent changes of a global variable cannot be encoded in guarded aFSA due to the lack of a representation of time. Further, the automatic mapping of such a loop construction to guarded aFSA requires a very good understanding of changes of the global variable. As a consequence of this discussion it is impractical to automatically transform loop conditions, therefore the mapping process from BPEL to aFSA can be realized semi-automatically if conditioned loops are used. From a pragmatic point of view, an explicit modeling of time as for example in timed Petri-Nets [Jen92] introduces very high computational complexity, which makes these approaches impractical. Further, the usage of loop termination conditions in workflows executed by a party is quite common, although these conditions are usually not provided to trading partners, because they contain business critical information. Therefore, the impact of this limitation in general to concrete applications of the proposed mapping is low.

6.1.10 Expressiveness of Guarded aFSA

The evaluation of the expressiveness of the aFSA model is based on a data set of local workflows in accordance with the Internet Open Trading Protocol (IOTP) [Bur00]. The IOTP specification is provided by the Network Working Group of the Internet Engineering Task Force (IETF) [IET], in which companies like IBM, Commerce One, HP, Oracle, MasterCard, Modex, Motorola, and Sun have been involved. It describes a framework for e-commerce supporting classical trading scenarios, like purchase, deposit, refund, withdrawal, monetary exchange, and inquiry. To describe these trading scenarios, IOTP provides three generic roles, that is, merchant, payment and delivery handler, which are used to construct concrete scenarios on behalf of a set of so called "basic message exchanges". Each "basic message exchange" consists of several messages exchanged between different parties, where

- the authentication exchange supports the authentication of one trading partner,

- the brand dependent/independent offer exchange represents signing an offer with/without a predefined payment method,
- the payment exchange and delivery exchange represent exchange of payment and delivery information respectively, and
- the payment and delivery exchange is a shortcut for the payment exchange followed by a delivery exchange.

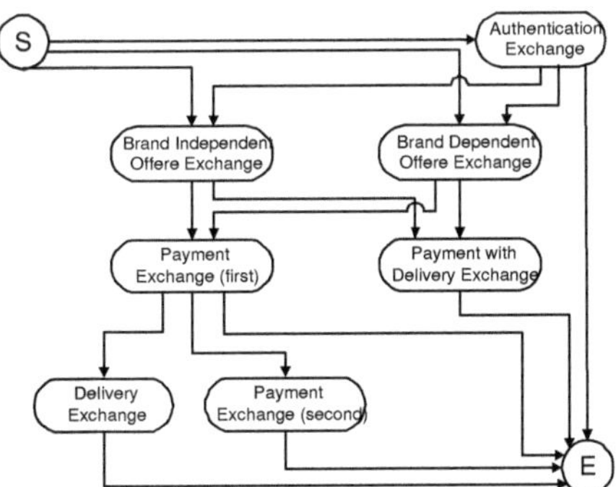

Figure 6.5: IOTP Message Exchange Structure

The way in which the different exchanges can be combined is depicted in Figure 6.5. The circle labeled with **S** represents the start state, while that labeled with **E** represents the end state. A valid workflow has at least one path starting from the start state and terminating in the end state. The total number of workflows that can be constructed by the combination of the different path is 726 workflows. However, to check the expressiveness of aFSA it suffices to check each individual path on its own and to check the combination of two example paths.

As described in detail in [Sch04], the IOTP workflows have been formally specified in terms of colored P/T-Nets and subsequently mapped to BPEL. Finally, the BPEL transformation described in the previous section has been used to represent workflows as guarded annotated finite state automata and the correctness of the mapping has been manually checked.

As an outcome of this analysis, no single workflow can be constructed based on the IOTP specification resulting in a local workflow that is not expressible as guarded annotated finite state automata. Thus, the model has shown its applicability to real world e-commerce scenarios. In particular, a total of 726 workflows has been generated, where in total 23 different messages have been used per workflow. The complexity of the constructed workflows with regard to number of transitions is depicted in Figure 6.6.

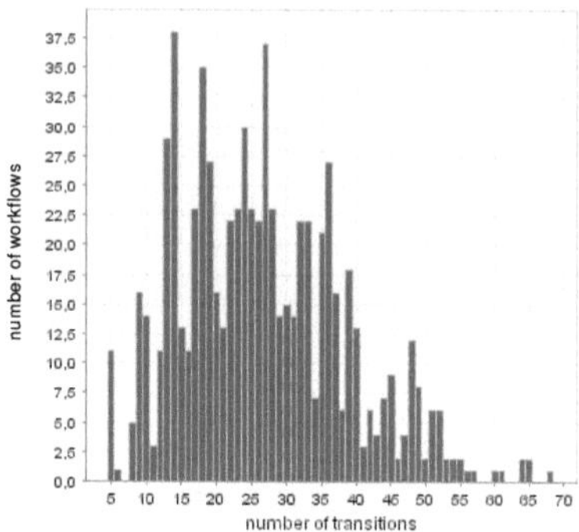

Figure 6.6: Plot of Number of Workflows versus Number of Transitions

The figure shows that most workflows have between 13 and 40 transitions, with the simplest workflow having five transitions and the most complex having nearly 70 transitions[3]. The highest number of workflows having the same number of transitions was 38, with 14 transitions.

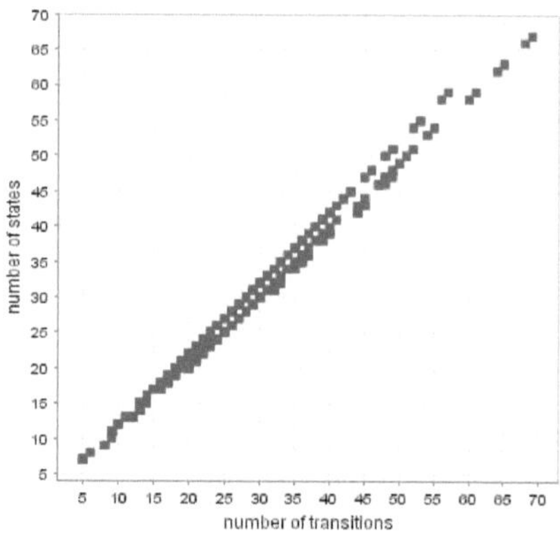

Figure 6.7: Plot of Number of States versus Number of Transitions

To get an impression of the structure of the automata constructed, Figure 6.7 shows a plot of the number of states against number of transitions. The plot shows an almost linear relationship between the number of states and number of transitions. Two lines with different slopes can be

[3]Be aware, that for example the IOTP delivery exchange represents several message exchanges in the sense of the automata model used in this thesis.

observed. The line with a steeper slope represents those workflows without cycles, due to the reuse of states by cyclic transitions. The line whose slope is less steep represents workflows with cycles. The length of the cycles in the IOTP workflows used is always one or two, accounting for the small difference in the slopes.

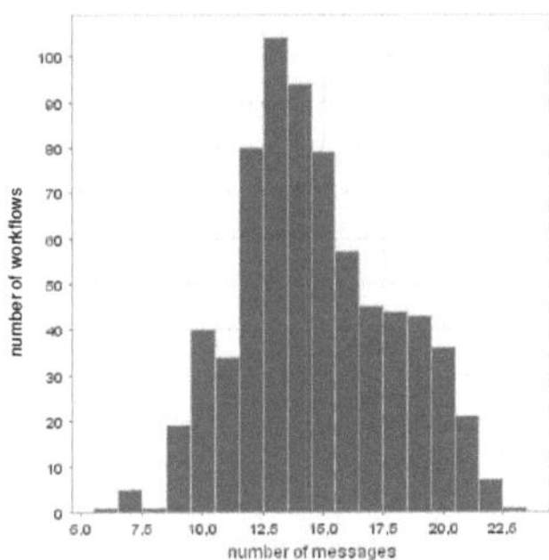

Figure 6.8: Plot of Number of Workflows versus Number of Messages

Figure 6.8 shows a plot of the number of workflows against the number of messages. Most workflows have between 9 and 20 messages. The workflow with the smallest number of messages has five messages, while that with the highest number of messages has 23. A total of 104 workflows comprised 13 messages. The much higher number of transitions compared to the number of messages used in a single workflow indicates a high reuse of messages within a single workflow.

6.2 Bilateral Consistency Checking

Based on the transformation from BPEL to annotated Finite State Automata and the creation of a concrete data set, bilateral consistency checking can be implemented and used to search for and find potential trading partners that might be involved in a multi-lateral collaboration later on.[4] In particular, bilateral consistency checking can be understood as a specific case of multi-lateral consistency checking as introduced in Section 4.3.7. In addition, bilateral consistency checking, that is checking for the non-empty intersection of automata has been the basis for decentralized consistency checking as discussed in Section 5.2.2.

Bilateral consistency is discussed in the application domain of Web Services, thus, the example in Section 6.1.1 is picked up again. In particular, the logistics department workflow was introduced, which interacts with a buyer and an accounting department. To establish a potential collaboration, the logistics department has to query potential trading partners at a service repository, which is performed on a bilateral basis. As discussed in Section 6.1.1, the local workflow of the logistics

[4]Major parts of this work have been published in [WMN04].

department is specified in BPEL with a corresponding WSDL file. An example query issued by the logistics department constrains the list of potential service providers to those which

1. support the role of an accounting department represented by the value *accounting* in the categorization *de.ipsi.oasys.ipsi-pf:IOTP:Role*,

2. are provided by a business entity located in Germany represented by the value *de* in the categorization *iso-ch:3166-1999*, and

3. are consistent with the logistics local workflow specified by a BPEL process and the corresponding WSDL document.

6.2.1 Approach

Analyzing the above query shows that the first two constraints can already be served by a UDDI repository being the proposed service repository within a standard Web Service infrastructure. The last constraint cannot be handled by a UDDI repository, because the required comparison operation is more complex than string comparison as provided by a UDDI repository. The IPSI Process Finder matchmaking engine (IPSI-PF) extends a UDDI repository by a feature for matching workflow descriptions. In particular, a query posed to IPSI-PF is split (decomposed) into a UDDI and a local workflow sub-query. The UDDI subquery is processed by a classical UDDI and the local workflow subquery by the IPSI-PF matchmaking engine. The final query result is derived by combining the partial results which is known in the database community as a natural join, where the business service key maintained by a UDDI and being unique for each service instance within a UDDI is used to relate the partial results to each other (primary key). The local workflow sub-query uses the business service key for referencing the service description (foreign key). In addition to querying IPSI-PF provides also a publish functionality, which is not discussed in detail within this thesis. In particular, the publish process is neglected, because it is performed only once per service instance, while querying a service is performed much more often and is much more performance critical.

UDDI Sub-query

The UDDI query is based on the standard UDDI API, that is a *find_service* SOAP call [IMH+02]. The call related to the above example is depicted in Figure 6.9. In this example, the categorization of the service providers geographical location is realized by the common taxonomy based on ISO 3166-1999 which is predefined in the UDDI repository. The taxonomy of roles is implemented as a 'private' taxonomy described in more detail in Section 6.2.2.

Local Workflow Sub-query

BPEL [ACD+03] and the corresponding WSDL document specify a workflow in terms of tasks (activities in BPEL terminology) representing basic pieces of work to be performed by potentially

```
<find_service generic="2.0" xmlns="urn:uddi-org:api_v2">
    <findQualifiers>
        <findQualifier>caseSensitiveMatch</findQualifier>
    </findQualifiers>
    <name>%</name>
    <categoryBag>
        <keyedReference keyName="de.fhg.ipsi.oasys.ipsi-pf:IOTP:Role" keyValue="accounting"
                        tModelKey="uuid:A035A07C-F362-44DD-8F95-E2B134BF43B4"/>
        <keyedReference keyName="uddi-org:iso-ch:3166-1999" keyValue="de"
                        tModelKey="uuid:4E49A8D6-D5A2-4FC2-93A0-0411D8D19E88"/>
    </categoryBag>
</find_service>
```

Figure 6.9: UDDI Query

nested services. A more detailed discussion on BPEL can be found in Section 6.1. When searching for potential service providers from the workflow point of view, it is necessary that the exchanged message sequences of the query process are consistent with a potential trading partner's message sequences derived from his local workflow. To be able to check consistency, the following aspects must be considered:

- Due to the fact that BPEL lacks a formal model [Aal03], a definition of a compatibility operation might be quite vague. It is preferable to have the match operation defined on a solid formal model based on sets of message sequences.
- Testing consistency is a binary operation, that is all elements contained in a message sequence not related to the opponent must be omitted. Thus, a partner specific view on his own supported message sequence must be calculated.
- The match operation compares the set of message sequences provided by a service provider and contained in the database with the relevant set of message sequences related to the query process.

6.2.2 Architecture

This section describes the architecture and implementation of the IPSI Process Finder (IPSI-PF), realizing a service discovery for state dependent Web Services supporting UDDI queries extended by workflow descriptions. As stated in the previous section, the input query has two parts: (i) the BPEL [ACD$^+$03] with corresponding WSDL part and (ii) the UDDI [IMH$^+$02] part. The BPEL part contains process-related descriptions of the query and the UDDI part provides information that is traditionally provided via the UDDI repository, e.g., business service categories.

Framework

Processing the query is initiated by submitting a form as depicted in the example in Figure 6.10. Triggered by this page, the data flow of the architecture depicted in Figure 6.11 is started, which is realized as an Apache Cocoon pipeline. Apache Cocoon was chosen since the data flow between the different processing steps is XML based and thus allows for good support by Cocoon. In particular, the pipeline realizes the query decomposition as well as the result list merge component depicted in Figure 6.11. A query decomposition component separates the three parts as follows:the BPEL part is sent to the matchmaking engine via a transformation component, BPEL→formal model, while the UDDI part is sent to the category matchmaking component being realized by a Cocoon LogicalSheet in the pipeline calling the Web Services based UDDI API. Finally, the merging of the results is also part of this pipeline and is realized by using XSLT.

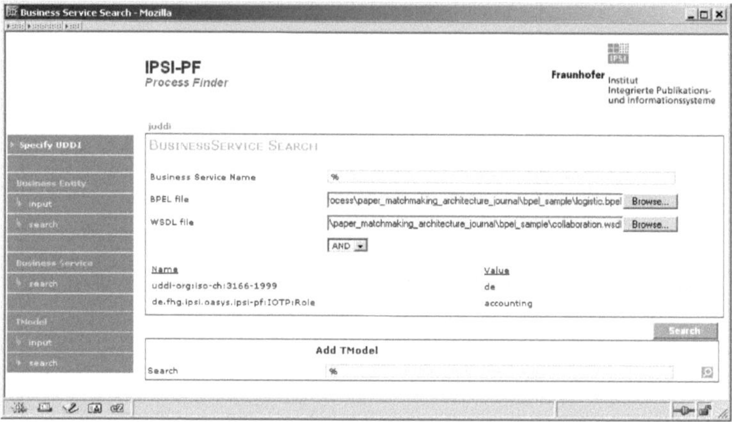

Figure 6.10: Example Query Form

A more expressive framework such as Struts or a workflow engine is not appropriate, because the remaining user interactions within the IPSI-PF are much simpler.

The implementation is based on Apache Cocoon 2.1.2. The above described pipeline uses *cinclude*, *XSLT* and *session* transformers. A *cinclude* transformer allows the loading of content from different web resources into a single document. An *XSLT* transformer applies a specified XSLT stylesheet to the intermediate version of the document passed through the pipeline and a *session* transformer grants access to data contained in an HTTP request and stores intermediate results in a session container.

BPEL→Formal Model Component

The role of the BPEL→formal model component is to transform the BPEL and the corresponding WSDL document into a formal model suitable for calculating process matches. The underlying formal model is annotated Finite State Automata (aFSA) (see also Section 4.3.3) and the mapping used is described in detail in Section 6.1. The resulting aFSA is used as input to the matchmaking engine for deciding the match of processes. This component has been implemented in Java and is part of the process matchmaking engine component described next.

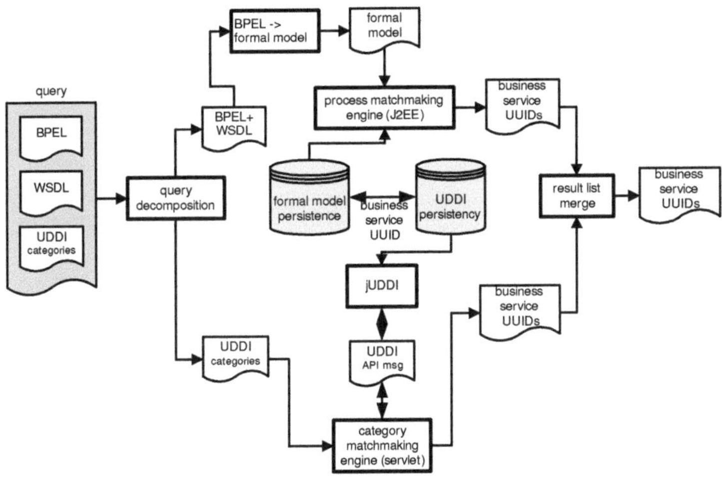

Figure 6.11: Architecture

Process Matchmaking Engine Component

The Process Matchmaking Engine Component is in charge of performing the comparison of the query workflow with the workflows stored in the IPSI-PF. Based on the constructed aFSA, the component performs a sequential scan on all stored aFSA and returns those being bilaterally consistent as defined in Section 4.3.7.

Each business process in the collection is associated with category data in the UDDI repository via a business service UUID used as a foreign key (see also Figure 6.11) to join the partial results as described above.

The matchmaking engine is implemented based on J2EE architecture. The application server used is JBoss. The main matchmaking component is an Enterprise Java Bean (EJB) and a web client (not included in Figure 6.11) is used for administering the server. Persistence is achieved by J2EE container managed persistence relying on a MySQL database system.

UDDI Category Matchmaking Engine Component

The Category Matchmaking component relies on a UDDI repository, which maintains most of the information queried by a UDDI subquery as categorization bags. A categorization is a *name-value* pair assigned to a service entity, where the *name* is the name of the taxonomy used and the *value* is a taxonomy value. The UDDI specification provides a number of predefined, common taxonomies, like for example ISO 3166-1999, a taxonomy for geographical locations. To establish such a taxonomy within a UDDI repository, a publication process has been specified [IMH$^+$02] to ensure that only those taxonomies are published which are relevant to the user group of the UDDI repository. In particular, the registrar has to approve the relevance of the taxonomy for the UDDI repository.

With regard to the example, a taxonomy representing the roles within the fictional procurement scenario will not get approval for a global taxonomy, because it is used only by a specific virtual enterprise. To allow users to introduce private categorization of services within a local UDDI repository the UDDI specification provides an alternative approach named "General Keywords taxonomy". Similar to the general taxonomy approach *name-value* pairs are maintained, where the *names* must be prefixed with the organization's own namespace and the supported *values* must be published in the virtual organization internally. In the prototype implementation the open source UDDI repository jUDDI [jud] has been used.

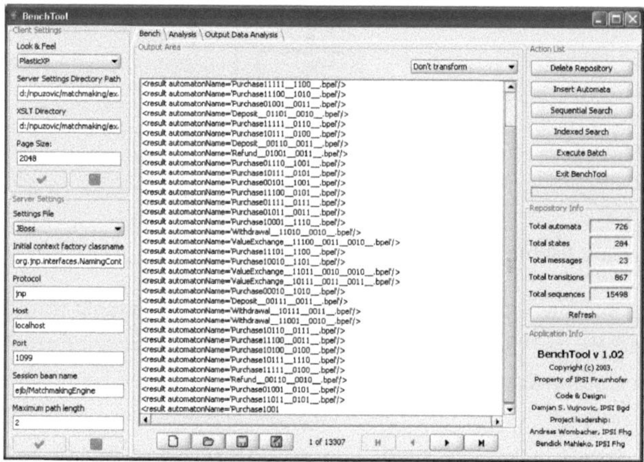

Figure 6.12: Benchmark Tool

Administration Tool

The administration tool (Figure 6.12) has been developed as part of the IPSI-PF project to support the testing and evaluation of the IPSI-PF. The functionality provided by this tools is

- the construction of example data sets, which is based on a general specification of potential message sequences and assigned probabilities on different branches,
- the analysis of the constructed data sets,
- the performance of a bunch of queries, measuring the individual results, and providing different analysis of the response times, and

- the maintenance of the database, that is, the bulk up-load of data into IPSI-PF, the clean-up of IPSI-PF, and providing status information on the number of stored objects in IPSI-PF.

The architecture described above has been implemented and tests have been performed. In the following, a discussion of the applicability of the concept and the implementation is presented as well as performance test results.

6.2.3 Discussion

The conceptual approach presented requires robust local workflows, that is, local workflows which are unconstrained in receiving messages. This limitation ensures that no explicit handling of conditions has to be established for checking consistency of bilateral interaction of services. Finally, the approach is based on a subsumption relation on message names. In particular, the subsumption relation used in the proposed approach is string equivalence, although other approaches are possible, such as those addressed by the Semantic Web community.

An advantage of the concept is that it relies on existing UDDI infrastructure extended by querying of workflow models. In particular, the provided match operation increases the precision of the query results and avoids false matches - that is finding service providers which claim to be consistent without being it - and without having false misses - that is not returning service providers, which are consistent but have not been found by the match operation.

As stated in Section 6.2.2 the persistence implementation of the process matchmaking engine is based on container managed persistence. This design decision has been made for ease of use and in the knowledge that the persistence model will have to be re-implemented in the next release after gaining initial experience with the process matchmaking component.

6.2.4 Performance Measurements

The main goal of the evaluation was to find out the major factors influencing performance. Measurements were conducted on a Dell machine, with a 2.00GHz clock speed Pentium 4 processor and 512 MB RAM. The total disk space was 74 GB. The machine was running under the Windows XP operating system. MySQL server version 4.0 was the used database engine. The machine was also running the JBOSS 3.2.3 application server which provided the J2EE environment for the IPSI-PF process matchmaking engine. The matchmaking engine is implemented on the same data model and level of abstraction using container managed persistence. All tests are performed without buffering/caching of results, thus, all tests were run under cold start conditions.

The performance measurement is based on the data set generated based on the IOTP specification as described in Section 6.1.10 consisting of 726 workflow models. During the evaluation of the proposed system, the highest measured response time for the UDDI part was about 2.7 seconds, while the matchmaking engine component required 40 seconds. As a consequence, the UDDI part is considered to be less critical and thus the further description of performance results focuses on the evaluation on the matchmaking engine component. The minimum response time for the data set was about three seconds, the maximum 40 seconds, and the mean response time was almost 18 seconds.

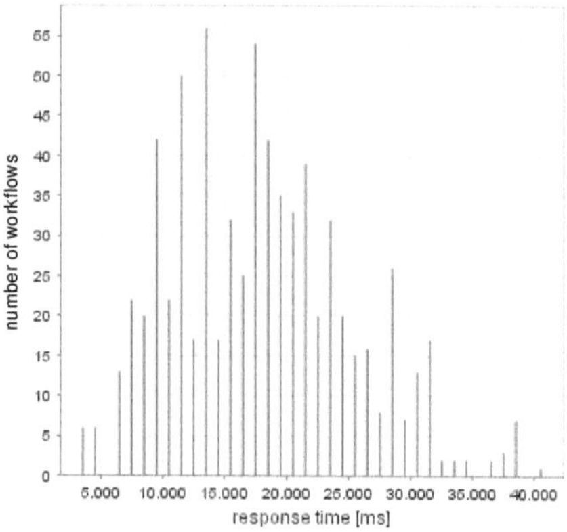

Figure 6.13: Query Response Time

Figure 6.13 shows the distribution of response times on workflows. The figure shows that most workflows had a response time between 6 and 32 seconds. The pattern of this distribution is very similar to the distribution of number of transitions on workflows (Figure 6.6), suggesting a possible influence of the number of transitions in a workflow on the response time. As discussed in more detail in [WMN04], the performance of the matchmaking engine component linearly depends on the number of transitions of the query automaton in case of a fixed data set.

However, this performance evaluation shows that the performance of the matchmaking engine is not sufficient for online service discovery, thus, future work requires an indexing mechanism to speed up the consistency checking.

6.3 Decentralized Multi-lateral Collaboration Establishment

Multi-lateral collaboration establishment as described in Section 2.4 is based on a set of local workflows forming a multi-lateral collaboration. Based on this collaboration, cycles can be resolved (see Section 4.3.8) and constraint propagation can be applied resulting in a fixed point determining whether the multi-lateral collaboration is consistent or not (see Sections 4.3.9, 4.3.10, 5.2.2 and 5.2.3). However, since a single local workflow might be involved in several multi-lateral collaborations, a unique collaboration identification can be used to resolve concurrency of a local workflow. Because none of the parties involved in a collaboration know all trading parties due to the decentralization requirement, an additional processing step is required to construct potential collaborations and assign unique identifications to them, which are known by all parties involved in the collaboration. Based on a single collaboration, the resolution of cycles and the propagation of constraints can be performed resulting in a fixed point. The determination of a fixed point, that is checking and informing the involved parties is another step. In the following, a concrete example in the application domain of Web Services is introduced before the different steps of decentralized establishment of multi-lateral collaborations are described.

6.3.1 Example

The scenario illustrating the concurrency effect of collaborations is based on the one introduced in Section 2.3.1 and its application to the Web Service domain in Section 6.1.1 extended by having several service providers for accounting and logistics department as well as buyers. In particular, the scenario consists of two accounting departments $A1$ and $A2$, two buyers $B1$ and $B2$, and three logistics departments $L1$, $L2$, and $L3$, where the local workflows of $A2$, $L2$, $L3$, and $B2$ require parcel tracking, and the local workflows of $L1$ and $B1$ do not support parcel tracking at all, while the local workflow $A1$ support both options. Further, let the service providers of $A1$, $L1$, $L2$, and $B1$ be located in Germany, while the service providers of $A2$, $L3$, and $B2$ are located in the US. In addition, buyer $B1$ wants to interact only with local service providers, that is, service providers located in Germany, while $B2$ does not have this restriction. The collaborations which can be constructed based on these requirements are depicted in Figure 6.14.

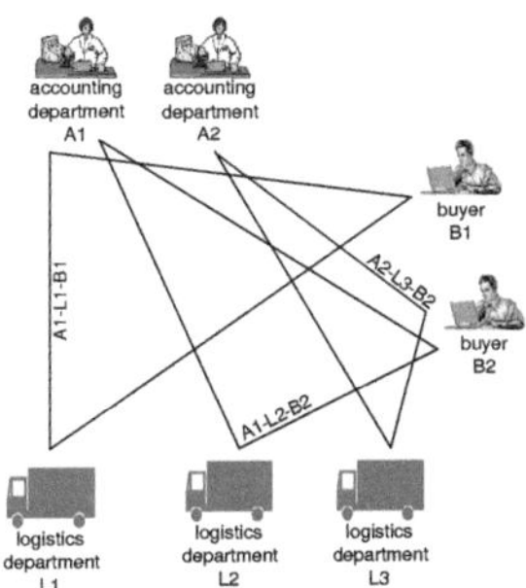

Figure 6.14: Concurrent Example with Three Collaborations

The collaboration $A1 - L1 - B1$ does not support parcel tracking and consists of service providers all located in Germany. In contrast, the remaining two collaborations $A1 - L2 - B2$ and $A2 - L3 - B2$ support parcel tracking, while the location of the service provider is irrelevant. In the following, the approach to deriving these three collaborations is discussed informally.

party	role: matching service providers	role: matching service providers
B1	accounting: A1	logistics: L1
B2	accounting: A1,A2	logistics: L2,L3
A1	buyer: B1,B2	logistics: L1,L2
A2	buyer: B2	logistics: L3
L1	accounting: A1	buyer: B1
L2	accounting: A1	buyer: B2
L3	accounting: A2	buyer: B2

Table 6.1: Bilateral Service Discovery Results

6.3.2 Finding Relevant Trading Partners

Establishing multi-lateral collaborations is based on bilateral collaborations, which are constructed between two trading partners. Thus, the first step is to find potential trading partners, which is known as bilateral service discovery introduced in Section 6.2 and based on Sections 4.3.7 and 5.2.2. With regard to the above example, the buyer $B1$ needs to interact only with service providers located in Germany. As a consequence, $A1$ can be used as an accounting department, and $L1$ and $L2$ can be used as logistics departments. In addition, $B1$'s workflow does not support parcel tracking, which limits the potential trading partners to $A1$ for the accounting department, and $L1$ for the logistics department. With regard to buyer $B2$, no regional constraint is specified, but the local workflow requires parcel tracking, which is supported by $A1$ and $A2$ as accounting department, $L2$ and $L3$ as logistics department.

In particular, buyer $B1$ and $B2$ have to perform bilateral service discovery for each role involved in the local workflow, that is, the accounting and logistics department respectively. In Section 6.2 IPSI-PF has been introduced as an implementation of bilateral service discovery based on annotated Finite State Automata. Applying this tool to the different parties' results in Table 6.1 containing the list of matching service providers for each local party and role.

6.3.3 Establishment of Potential Multi-lateral Collaborations

Based on the determined bilaterally matching services, a collaboration has to be established in a decentralized way. In particular, all parties involved in the collaboration need to know the identification of the collaboration and it has to be ensured that each party guarantees that each role is assigned exactly one service. Further, it is assumed that the underlying communication is asynchronous but reliable, while services are always available. These assumptions ease the approach, while it remains applicable for example in virtual enterprise scenarios. More general requirements result quite rapidly in impossible consensus problems (see also [Lyn96]).

The generic problem description is to calculate a spanning tree of services forming a potential multi-lateral collaboration. For each of these constructed trees representing a collaboration a consensus has to be achieved on whether each service involved has exactly one assignment of a trading partner role to an external service. While a spanning tree is constructed step by step via the services derived in the bilateral service discovery, the consensus is realized by forwarding local decisions similar to a simple flooding approach.

During the construction of the spanning trees several concurrent instances have to be handled by the different parties. To differentiate the collaborations each is assigned with a unique set of globally unique IDs, each representing a bilateral collaboration. Thus, the construction of a spanning tree is based on bilaterally matching services representing a bilateral collaboration (see Sections 6.2, 4.3.7 and 5.2.2), which is identified by a set containing a single globally unique ID. A spanning tree can be extended by a party, if the party contains a role, which has not been assigned to a bilateral collaboration contained in spanning tree right now.

With regard to the example, the bilateral collaboration of accounting department $A1$ and logistics department $L1$ is represented as $\{(A1,L1)\}$ being a tuple of the two service providers being equivalent to $\{(L1,A1)\}$. Based on bilateral collaborations accounting department $A1$ can combine the two bilateral collaborations $\{(A1,L1)\}$ and $\{(A1,B1)\}$ to the collaboration $\{(A1,L1),(A1,B1)\}$, which can be extended by buyer $B1$ via the bilateral collaboration $\{(B1,L1)\}$ to the multi-lateral collaboration $A1-L1-B1$ represented as $\{(A1,L1),(A1,B1),(B1,L1)\}$. This collaboration has exactly one service assigned to each party's roles. In contrast, the collaboration $\{(B1,L1),(L1,A1),(A1,B2),(B2,L3),(L3,A2)\}$ can be constructed which is still invalid because the logistics role for buyer $B1$ and the buyer role for accounting department $A2$ are still unspecified. However, extending the spanning tree by an additional bilateral collaboration results in an over-specification of a party's role. For example, adding the bilateral collaboration $\{A2,B2\}$ results in the buyer $B2$'s accounting role being assigned with accounting department $A1$ and $A2$ making the collaboration invalid.

Based on this specification all multi-lateral collaborations can be constructed and the construction process terminates due to the finite set of combinations that can be created from the bilateral service discovery. Due to the lack of a coordinator of the collaboration establishment, the number of potential collaborations to be checked is exponential with the number of available services. However, the number of relevant combinations is much lower. As a consequence, strategies must be developed which help to prune away irrelevant combinations as soon as possible, which are out of the scope of this thesis. A framework for testing and comparing different strategies has been proposed in [Wom05a] based on the implementation of the Web Services based specification described in more detail in [Wom05b].

6.3.4 Deciding Consistency of a Multi-lateral Collaboration

After multi-lateral collaborations have been established, the decentralized consistency checking can be applied by first resolving cycles, continued by propagating parameter constraints, and finally propagating occurrence graph constraints as introduced in Section 2.4.

Since the current scenario has been defined in the domain of Web Services specifying workflows in terms of BPEL documents, a formal representation in terms of guarded annotated Finite State

Automaton (aFSA) A has to be derived in accordance with the mapping introduced in Section 6.1. As a consequence, the following steps can be performed locally by each party on guarded aFSA. Due to the concurrency of collaborations handled by each party the ambiguities of communication with trading parties is resolved by using the globally unique collaboration ID.

The processing starts with a normalized acyclic guarded aFSA A' in accordance with Definition 4.38 (see Section 4.3.8). Based on this acyclic guarded aFSA parameter constraint propagation as given below

$$\forall 0 \leq k < n. \forall 0 \leq j < n, j \neq k. A'_k = \Phi(\Phi_b(A_k, A_j))$$

in accordance with Definitions 4.39 and 4.28 (see Sections 4.3.9 and 4.3.6)is applied repeatedly until a fixed point has been reached.

The parameter constraint fixed point acyclic guarded aFSA is normalized again to ensure that the parameter constraints are simple conjunctions enabling occurrence graph constraint propagation defined as

$$\forall 0 \leq k < n. A_k = \Psi(A_k)$$

in accordance with Definition 4.42. Based on Theorem 5.1 (see Section 5.2.2) occurrence graph constraint propagation can be restated as

$$A'_k = clean\Big(\Phi(A_k) \cap \Phi\Big(\&_{0 \leq j < n, j \neq k} \tau_k(A_j)\Big)\Big)$$

which keeps more information of trading partner's workflows private and reduces the complexity of the automata. Combining the above statement with the structural representation of emptiness in accordance with Lemma 5.10 (see Section 5.3) adds the $clean_a$ operation (see Definition 4.31 in Section 4.3.6) to the propagation operation resulting in

$$A'_k = clean_a\Big(clean\Big(\Phi(A_k) \cap \Phi\Big(\&_{0 \leq j < n, j \neq k} \tau_k(A_j)\Big)\Big)\Big)$$

This propagation operation is performed until a fixed point has been reached. If the resulting guarded aFSA representing the fixed point local workflow is empty, the multi-lateral collaboration is inconsistent.

If the multi-lateral collaboration is consistent, the process can be started and a successful business interaction is guaranteed.

6.3.5 Determination of a Fixed Point

The current description of the approach lacks a confident decentralized decision making as to whether a fixed point has already been reached or additional steps are necessary. In particular, this issue can be understood as a kind of a distributed transaction of changing all local states of the fixed point calculation from *running* to *terminated*. A common approach to solving this problem is the linear 2-Phase-Commit (2PC) protocol [ÖV99], which assumes a linear ordering of parties involved in the collaboration [5]. However, the collaboration does not explicitly provide such a structure of parties, although, the collaboration ID can be used to define a linear ordering of parties. Since the collaboration ID consists of bilateral collaboration IDs, these IDs can be sorted resulting in a linear order due to the global uniqueness of each ID. In addition, a bilateral collaboration is initiated by one of the parties being involved, while it is accepted by the corresponding trading partner. As a consequence, the initiator of a collaboration ID is listed before the accepting party resulting in a linear ordering of parties. Since initiator and the accepting party of two preceding collaboration IDs may not be trading partners, a routing protocol based on subsets of collaboration IDs, as for example known from prefix based routing in static peer-to-peer networks such as in [PRR97], has to be realized. Based on this communication extension, the linear 2PC protocol can be implemented determining whether all parties consider the fixed point to have been reached already.

6.4 Summary

Decentralized establishment of consistent, multi-lateral collaborations as proposed in this thesis requires a mapping from a workflow model used in the application domain to the formal model used of annotated Finite State Automata (aFSA). Based on this transformation, a component has been implemented providing bilateral consistency checking which has been integrated into an application domain specific search environment. Finally, this search and bilateral consistency checking component is used to describe the realization of the overall approach of decentralized consistency checking for multi-lateral collaborations including the determination of potential multi-lateral collaborations, the constraint propagation, and the final decision making. The proof of concept of the ideas contained in this thesis is implemented on the basis of Web Services, a realization of a service oriented architecture. Finally, the evaluation of the approach uses the Internet Open Trading Protocol since it specified a set of workflows which are derived from classical business processes. It has been illustrated that the expressiveness of aFSA suffices to represent all potential workflows, thus, aFSA are a usable workflow model as a basis for decentralized establishment of consistent multi-lateral consistency.

[5] The linear 2PC protocol is quite similar to hierarchical 2PC [CDK01] or nested 2PC [Gra78].

Chapter 7

Conclusion

The conclusions of this thesis start with a short summary of the presented achievements, a discussion of additional application scenarios, and finally gives an outlook on open issues and future directions for research.

7.1 Achievements of the Thesis

The contribution of this thesis is a uniform representation of workflows based on synchronous or asynchronous communication model in terms of guarded annotated Finite State Automata (aFSA) being an extension of standard Finite State Automata. In particular, aFSA support a differentiation of transitions as mandatory or optional, which has been identified as an essential workflow modeling property to realize bilateral consistency checking. Further, aFSA have been extended by a notion of parameters called guarded aFSA, which constrains the execution of transitions by parameter values. While guarded aFSA have been directly used to represent workflows based on a synchronous communication model, an approach based on v.d.Aalst's Workflow Nets (WF-Nets) has been used as a basis for the asynchronous communication model. Consistency checking for WF-Nets is performed on the occurrence graph derived from the WF-Net. Such an occurrence graph has equivalent expressiveness to guarded aFSA. Using this equivalence a mapping between WF-Nets and aFSA has been defined, and the equivalence of the corresponding consistency definitions has been presented. Hence, a uniform modeling of workflows independent of the underlying communication model has been achieved.

Based on this uniform model, decentralized consistency checking has been addressed. In particular, a definition of bilateral and multi-lateral consistency has been defined. Bilateral consistency specifies whether two trading partners can interact successfully given the assumption of a successful interaction with the remaining trading partners. Initially, bilateral consistency has been defined as the non-empty intersection of two local workflows extended by messages where the corresponding local workflow is neither sender nor receiver of the message. Because this definition entails informing a trading partner about all messages used in the local workflow, information not directly related to the trading partner is provided to him, which might give him a competitive advantage. An equivalent definition of bilateral consistency has therefore been proposed which is based on the non-empty intersection of the local workflow and the workflow constructed from the local parties' view on the trading partner's workflow. Thus, only the relevant information is provided by a party to its trading partners hiding more business critical information. In particular, it has been shown that these definitions are equivalent.

Multi-lateral consistency specifies whether several local workflows forming a multi-lateral collaboration guarantee successful interaction. Initially, multi-lateral consistency has been defined in a centralized way, since it is used for as a reference to proof equivalence with the decentralized multi-lateral consistency approach. In particular, centralized multi-lateral consistency has been defined similar to the initial bilateral consistency definition as the non-empty intersection of the local workflows extended by messages where the corresponding local workflow is neither sender nor receiver of the message. The decentralized multi-lateral consistency checking can not be decided by a single party, but requires a repetitive process of consolidating the local workflows by performing constraint propagation resulting in a fixed point. In particular, the required constraints to be propagated are parameter and occurrence graph constraints. While the first is needed to ensure a correct subsumption decision on parameter constraints related to a sent and received message, the second guarantees the omission of transitions within a local workflow that are unreachable within the multi-lateral collaboration. Within this thesis it has been shown that constraint propagation always converges and hence decentralized and centralized multi-lateral consistency are equivalent.

Finally, the theoretical approach presented has been applied to the concrete domain of Web Services, where a mapping from a workflow modeling language to aFSA has been introduced, the applicability of the expressiveness of the aFSA workflow model has been illustrated, and the different parts needed to realize decentralized establishment of multi-lateral collaborations have been described. In particular, an implementation of a service discovery involving the previously mentioned mapping has been presented, a protocol to derive multi-lateral collaborations based on bilateral ones in a decentralized way has been outlined, constraint propagation definitions have been summarized, and determining whether a fixed point has already been reached has been discussed.

7.2 Additional Application Areas

The main contribution of this thesis is demonstrating that decentralized consistency checking is an essential part of establishing multi-lateral collaborations in a decentralized way. In keeping with the application of this approach to the domain of Web Services, it can also be applied to similar technologies such as ebXML, Grid, or Peer-to-Peer (P2P) environments, which all have a necessity of forming multi-lateral collaborations in common. However, the approach can also be applied on other conceptual levels to, for example software engineering or e-contracting.

Technology

The electronic business XML initiative (ebXML) [ebX04] is one potential additional technology where decentralized collaboration establishment is applied. The ebXML specification provides a framework supporting XML based exchange of business data [Bus03]. In particular, Collaboration Partner Profiles (CPP) and Collaboration Partner Agreements (CPA) are part of this framework which reflect the description of a party and the subset of this description to be used within a concrete collaboration. Although Patil and Newcomer [PN03] consider ebXML as a top-down collaboration establishment approach, this is not enforced by the framework since no centralized coordinator of a collaboration has to be specified and the assignment of potential trading partners supports late binding similar to the service discovery phase in Web Service.

Another technology is a Grid infrastructure. Foster defines in [FKT01] the Grid as "coordinated resource sharing and problem solving in dynamic, multi-institutional virtual organizations". In particular, different organizations provide resources and request capacities for solving problems. However, the different parties are independent of each other although they agreed to participate in the Grid, which is currently a quite static relationship with centralized coordination of the job owner and high availability of the different participants. Due to this structure, there is no need for a more flexible handling of relationships. But the Grid community has started to think about more flexible relationships, where the availability of different parties is lower and more flexible and short to mid-term relationships have to be established and managed as for example addressed by the Diligent project [dc04]. Additional dynamics are introduced into Grids by an increasing integration of Web Services. In particular, there are currently efforts going on to apply Web Service technologies to Grid infrastructure [Glo05] implicitly introducing the concepts of loose coupling at least to the lower Grid layers. However, the increasing size of Grids and their stronger interrelations will increase the difficulties for a job owner to assign the resources efficiently guaranteeing good quality of service, thus an automated decentralized establishment of a job initiated by the job owner becomes more relevant.

A further example of a potential technology are Peer-to-Peer (P2P) systems. One definition of P2P considered suitable for this discussion is provided by the Intel P2P working group: "P2P is the sharing of computer resources and services by direct exchange between systems" [MKL+02]. In P2P environments every party (peer in P2P terminology) is considered to be independent. This means that a peer offers services or resources to a community, but at the same time, it can consume services/resources from others in the community. An important property of P2P systems is the lack of a central administration, the flexibility of the set of peers forming the community, and the decentralized organization of the community. As illustrated by Risse et al. [RKW04], P2P systems are on the move from familiar file sharing applications to large scale decentralized and reliable systems relying on decentrally coordinated and established multi-lateral collaborations.

All these technologies have in common that they provide a description of services/resources and the corresponding requests. Further, all of them have partitioned work into services, which might be based on a locally maintained state. As a consequence, these technologies are potential application areas for the decentralized establishment of multi-lateral collaborations presented in this thesis.

Conceptual

Conceptually, the presented approach can be applied to decentralized systems based on components/services maintained autonomously by different parties that have to be combined to reach a specific goal. Two examples are e-contracting and component based software engineering.

E-contracting means setting up a contract electronically, where a contract is "a binding agreement between two or more persons that is enforceable by law" [Wor04]. Thus a contract specifies legal aspects as well as technical ones like for example quality of service, duration, the agreement on the corresponding offer [MB03]. While deontic logic has been used to model legal and normative systems it turned out that only parts of a relevant normative system can be modeled. However, it is more likely to formally describe the technical aspects also known as Service Level Agreements (SLA) as for example discussed in [LKD+03]. In particular, the modeling of the conversation supported by the trading partners as a basis for bilateral and multi-lateral consistency checking during the establishment phase of a SLA can be used as a subset of the SLA, while additional constraints like for example quality of service and semantic aspects have to be added.

In the domain of software engineering component based architectures have been introduced to improve the re-use of code encapsulated in components. Different components are bundled in libraries and are provided to other people to reuse the code. Unfortunately, the description of the components is informally written down and to get familiar with a library takes quite a long time. In particular finding relevant components is quite difficult when starting with a new library. Bilateral consistency checking may be used in such a scenario to improve the re-use of components. This entails describing the behavior of components in more detail in terms of annotated Finite State Automata, that is, the required execution sequences of methods of a component guaranteeing exception free execution of the component. Further, dependencies between different components can be represented, thereby treating the usage of several components by a programmer as a multi-lateral collaboration, where consistency checking helps to improve the pre-selection of relevant components and provides static checking of their correct usage.

7.3 Future Research Topics

Several issues are raised within this thesis, but could not be addressed in detail. In the following some of these issues are discussed and directions for further research are described.

Message Equivalence

The comparison of message sequences is based on a notion of message equivalence that has been defined as equivalence of syntactical structure as well as intended semantics. However, this definition can be relaxed to a subsumption relation between messages. Applying this to the semantic aspect means that ontological knowledge can be used to propose an automatic mapping of messages. With regard to the modeling of workflows this can introduce bundling or aggregation of several messages into a single one. An example illustrating such an aggregation is for example provided in the MiniPay payment protocol, where several micro-payments are performed, collected by the clearing house, and after a certain threshold has been reached the customer is charged. Thus, several small payments are aggregated into a single bigger one, where the single payment subsumes several of the smaller ones. Another example of aggregated messages can be found in [AW01b], where a logic based workflow model has been proposed [ADDW03].

Time-based Parameter Constraints

Modeling business processes involves quite often a notion of time and in particular has specific constraints which are based on this notion of time, like for example *"the offer is valid within the next three weeks"*. In the current model presented in this thesis there is no notion of time, because the focus has been on decentralized consistency checking rather then a complete modeling approach for business models. However, to extend the aFSA model a notion of time as for example used in Timed Petri Nets [Jen92] could be added. The difficulties which may arise are due to the complexity of modeling time. As a consequence, the complexity for a normalized aFSA model is expected to be much higher than without a time extension.

Similarity based Service Discovery

Bilateral service discovery as introduced in Section 6.2 requires a non-empty intersection of the local workflows resulting in a list of service providers. Based on this definition, two extreme cases can be observed: the list is empty or the list contains too many service providers.

If the list does not contain any service providers at all the query seems to be too restrictive. Thus, it could be helpful to be able to relax the query by allowing not only exactly matching message sequences, but also accepting similar message sequences. A similarity measure of message sequences has not been discussed in this thesis. A potential starting point for such an investigation could be similarity measures on strings such as Levenshtein's edit distance [Lev66].

However, if the list contains too many service providers, it would be convenient for the user to have a ranking of the retrieved service providers. Again, a similarity measure of automata is needed serving as a ranking value, such as the overall length of shared message sequences.

Dynamic in Workflows

Multi-lateral collaborations in a Web Services or Peer-to-Peer environment have to face a certain dynamic with regard to the local workflows of a service as well as the availability of a service itself. These issues become more critical when a multi-lateral collaboration represents a long running business relationship increasing the probability of such changes.

The first issue is known from classical workflow management theory by the term dynamic workflow management, that is, change of a workflow model during its run-time. A dynamic change requires a special treatment only when the change is applied to a running process itself. Issues addressed within this area are which changes to the local workflow are allowed without affecting the running process and in which cases the running process gets corrupted requiring for example a manual compensation of the process. With regard to multi-lateral collaborations the effects of a change on the consistency of the running collaboration have to be addressed explicitly, because this might cause an unexpected termination of the collaboration.

The second issue of an unavailable service might also result in an unexpected termination of a collaboration. A multi-lateral collaboration is only allowed to terminate when a finite state in the multi-lateral/global workflow has been reached. In the case of a termination in a non final state a notion of roll-back or compensation to the nearest final state of the global workflow is required. These issues are addressed by the decentralized systems community in the area of consensus making and are also related to the distributed data management community in the area of transactions. An alternative approach instead of compensation might be to replace individual parties to guarantee a proper execution of the multi-lateral collaboration, although synchronization of the decentrally stored state information with the newly assigned party is considered to be challenging.

Bibliography

[Aal99] W.M.P. van der Aalst. Interorganizational workflows: An approach based on message sequence charts and petri nets. *Systems Analysis - Modelling - Simulation*, 34(3):335–367, 1999.

[Aal00] W.M.P. van der Aalst. Inheritance of Interorganizational Workflows: How to agree to disagree without loosing control? Technical Report, CU-CS-899-00, University of Colorado, Department of Computer Science, Boulder, USA, 2000.

[Aal02] W.M.P. van der Aalst. Inheritance of Interorganizational Workflows to Enable Business-to-Business E-commerce. *Electronic Commerce Research*, 2(3):195–231, 2002.

[Aal03] W.M.P. van der Aalst. Don't go with the flow: Web services composition standards exposed. *IEEE Intelligent Systems*, pages 72–76, Jan/Feb 2003.

[ABH+02] DAML-S Coalition: A. Ankolekar, M. Burstein, J. R. Hobbs, O. Lassila, D. McDermott, D. Martin, S. A. McIlraith, S. Narayanan, M. Paolucci, T. Payne, and K. Sycara. DAML-S: Web service description for the semantic web, 2002. http://citeseer.nj.nec.com/ankolekar02damls.html.

[ACD+03] Tony Andrews, Francisco Curbera, Hitesh Dholakia, Yaron Goland, Johannes Klein, Frank Leymann, Kevin Liu, Dieter Roller, Doug Smith, Satish Thatte, Ivana Trickovic, and Sanjiva Weerawarana. Business process execution language for web services. version 1.1. http://msdn.microsoft.com/library/default.asp?url=/library/en-us/dnbiz2k2/html/BPEL1-1.asp, May 2003.

[ADDW03] Karl Aberer, Anwitaman Datta, Zoran Despotovic, and Andreas Wombacher. Separating business process from user interaction in web-based information. *Electronic Commerce Research: Special Issue on Business Process Integration and E-Commerce Infrastructure*, 3(1-2):83–111, January - April 2003.

[AH02] W.M.P. van der Aalst and Kees van Hee. *Workflow Management - Models, Methods, and Systems*. MIT Press, 2002.

[APY+02] M. Aiello, M. Papazoglou, J. Yang, M. Pistore, M. Carman, L. Serafini, and P. Traverso. A request language for web services based on planning and constraint satisfaction. In *Proceedings of 3rd International Workshop on Technologies for E-Services (TES)*, LNCS 2444, pages 76–85. Springer, 2002.

[ARAAW03] A. Shaikh Ali, O. F. Rana, R. Al-Ali, and D. W. Walker. UDDIe: An extended registry for web services. In *Proceedings of the 2003 Symposium on Applications and the Internet Workshops (SAINT-w)*. IEEE Computer Society, 2003.

[ASW98] N. Asokan, V. Shoup, and M. Waidner. Asynchronous protocols for optimistic fair exchange. In *Proceedings of the IEEE Symposium on Research in Security and Privacy*, pages 86–99, Oakland, California, 1998.

[Aus65] J. L. Austin. *How to do things with words*. Oxford University Press, 1965.

[AW01a] W.M.P. van der Aalst and M. Weske. The P2P approach to interorganizational workflows. In *Proceedings of 13. International Conference on Advanced Information Systems Engeneering (CAISE)*, Interlaken, Switzerland, 2001.

[AW01b] K. Aberer and A. Wombacher. A language for information commerce processes. In *Proceedings of the Third International Workshop on Advanced Issues of E-Commerce and Web-based Information Systems*, San Jose, California, USA, June 2001.

[BA99] T. Basten and W.M.P. van der Aalst. Inheritance of Behavior. Computing Science Report 99/17, Eindhoven University of Technology, Eindhoven, 1999.

[Ban96] M. Banville. SONIA: an adaptation of linda for coordination of activities in organizations. In P. Ciancarini and C. Hankin, editors, *Coordination Languages and Models*, volume 1061 of *LNCS*, pages 57–74. Springer-Verlag, Berlin, Germany, 1996.

[BBB+02] A. Banerji, C. Bartolini, D. Beringer, V. Chopella, K. Govindarajan, A. Karp, H. Kuno, M. Lemon, G. Pogossiants, S. Sharma, and S. Williams. Web services conversation language (WSCL) 1.0 W3C note, March 2002. http://www.w3.org/TR/wscl10/.

[BBM+01] K. Ballinger, P. Brittenham, A. Malhotra, W. A. Nagy, and S. Pharies. Specification: Web services inspection language (ws-inspection) 1.0, November 2001. http://www.ibm.com/developerworks/library/ws-wsilspec.html.

[BCM+03] Franz Baader, Diego Calvanese, Deborah McGuinness, Daniele Nardi, and Peter Patel-Schneider, editors. *The Description Logic Handbook - Theory, Implementation and Applications*. Cambridge University Press, 2003.

[Bea87] J.E. Beasley. An algorithm for set covering problem. *European Journal of Operational Research*, 31:85–93, 1987.

[BH79] Kent Bach and Robert M. Harnish. *Linguistic Communication and Speech Acts*. The MIT Press, Cambridge, Massachusetts, 1979.

[BH91] F. Baader and P. Hanschke. A scheme for integrating concrete domains into concept languages. In *Proceedings of the 12th International Joint Conference on Artificial Intelligence (IJCAI)*, pages 452–457, Sydney (Australia), 1991.

[BK02] Abraham Bernstein and Mark Klein. Discovering services: Towards high-precision service retrieval. In *Proceedings of CAiSE International Workshop, Web Services, E-Business, and the Semantic Web (WES)*, LNCS 2512, pages 260–275. Springer, 2002.

[BLHL01] T. Berbers-Lee, J. Hendler, and O. Lassila. The semantic web. *Scientific America*, 284(5):34–43, 2001.

[BMMZ03] Nadia Busi, Cristian Manfreedini, Alberto Montresor, and Gianluigi Zavattaro. Peerspaces: Data-driven coordination in peer-topeer networks. In *Proceedings of the 2003 ACM symposium on Applied computing*, pages 380–386. ACM Press, 2003.

[BRM04] BRML. BRML: Business rules markup language. http://xml.coverpages.org/brml.html, Sept 2004.

[BS86] G. Berry and R. Sethi. From regular expressions to deterministic automata. *Theoretical Computer Science*, 48(1):117–126, 1986.

[Bur00] D. Burdett. Internet open trading protocol - IOTP - version 1.0. http://www.ietf.org/rfc/rfc2801.txt, 2000.

[Bus03] Christoph Bussler. *B2B Integration - Concepts and Architecture*. Springer, 2003.

[CD01] F. Casati and A. Discenza. Modeling and managing interactions among business processes. *Journal of Systems Integration - Special Issue: Coordination as a Paradigm for Systems Integration*, 10(2):145–168, April 2001.

[CDK01] George Coulouris, Jean Dollimore, and Tim Kindberg. *Distributed Systems - Concepts and Design*. Addison-Wesley, 3 edition, 2001.

[CHTY96] J. Camp, M. Harkavy, J.D. Tygar, and B. Yee. Anonymous atomic transactions. In *Proceedings of the 2nd USENIX Workshop on Electronic Commerce*, pages 123–133, 1996.

[CIJ+00a] Fabio Casati, Ski Ilnicki, Li-Jie Jin, Vasudev Krishnamoorthy, and Ming-Chien Shan. Adaptive and dynamic service composition in eFlow. Technical Report HPL-2000-39, HP Labs, 2000.

[CIJ+00b] Fabio Casati, Ski Ilnicki, Li-Jie Jin, Vasudev Krishnamoorthy, and Ming-Chien Shan. eFlow: a platform for developing and managing composite e-services. Technical Report HPL-2000-36, HP Labs, 2000.

[Coa99] Workflow Management Coalition. Workflow standard - interoperability abstract specification. http://www.wfmc.org/standards/docs/TC-1012_Nov_99.pdf, Nov 1999.

[Coa01] Workflow Management Coalition. Workflow standard - interoperability Wf-XML binding version 1.1. http://www.wfmc.org/standards/docs/Wf-XML-11.pdf, Nov 2001.

[Coa04] OWL Service Coalition. OWL-S: Semantic markup for web services. http://www.daml.org/services/owl-s/1.0/owl-s.pdf, 2004.

[com04] commonRules. IBM commonRules. http://www.research.ibm.com/rules/home.html, Sept 2004.

[Cox96] B. Cox. *Superdistribution*. Addison-Wesley, 1996.

[Cro04] CrossFlow. CrossFlow home page. http://www.crossflow.org/, 2004.

[CS98] Jan Chomicki and Gunter Saake, editors. *Logics for Database and Information Systems*. Kluwer, 1998.

[CTS95] Benjamin Cox, J. D. Tygar, and Marvin Sirbu. NetBill security and transaction protocol. In *Proceedings of the First USENIX Workshop on Electronic Commerce*, pages 77–88, July 1995.

[CTZ02] Paolo Ciancarini, Robert Tolksdorf, and Franco Zambonelli. Coordination middleware for XML-centric applications. In *Proceedings of the 2002 ACM Symposium on Applied Computing (ACM-SAC)*, pages 336–343. ACM Press, 2002.

[dc04] diligent consortium. A digital library infrastructure on grid enabled technology. http://diligentproject.org/, 2004.

[DGLA00] H.-P. Dommel and J. J. Garcia-Luna-Aceves. A coordination architecture for internet groupwork. In *Proceedings 26th EUROMICRO Conference - Informatics:*, Maastricht, Netherlands, Sep 2000. IEEE. http://citeseer.nj.nec.com/dommel00coordination.html.

[DW95] F. Dignum and H. Weigand. Communication and deontic logic. In R. Wieringa and R. Feenstra, editors, *Information Systems, Correctness and Reusability*, pages 242–260. World Scientific, 1995.

[DWV96] Frank Dignum, Hans Weigand, and Egon Verharen. Meeting the deadline: On the formal specification of temporal deontic constraints. In Zbigniew W. Ras and Maciej Michalewicz, editors, *Proceedings of the 9th International Symposium of Foundations of Intelligent Systems (ISMIS)*, volume 1079 of *Lecture Notes in Computer Science*. Springer, June 1996.

[ebX04] ebXML. ebXML home page. http://www.ebxml.org/, 2004.

[EN94] J. Esparza and M. Nielsen. Decibility issues for Petri nets - a survey. *Journal of Informatik Processing and Cybernetics*, 30(3):143–160, 1994.

[EP99] J. Eder and E. Panagos. Towards distributed workflow process management. In *Proceedings of the Workshop on Cross-Organisational Workflow Management and Co-ordination*, San Francisco, USA, Feb 1999.

[ESAA04] Fatih Emekci, Ozgur D. Sahin, Divyakant Agrawal, and Amr El Abbadi. A peer-topeer framework for web service discovery with ranking. In *Proceedings IEEE International Conference on Web Services (ICWS)*, pages 192–199. IEEE Computer Society, 2004.

[FBS04] Xiang Fu, Telfik Bultan, and Jianwen Su. Realizability of conversation protocols with message contents. In *Proceedings IEEE International Conference on Web Services (ICWS)*, pages 96–103. IEEE Computer Society, 2004.

[FFH+03] C. Facciorusso, S. Field, R. Hauser, Y. Hoffner, R. Humbel, R. Pawlitzek, W. Rjaibi, and C. Siminitz. A web services matchmaking engine for web services. In *Proceedings of the 5nd International Conference on Electronic Commerce and Web Technologies (EC-WEB)*, pages 37–49. Springer, Sept 2003.

[FFMM94] T. W. Finin, R. Fritzson, D. McKay, and R. McEntire. KQML as an agent communication language. In *Proceedings of International Conference on Information and Knowledge Management (CIKM)*, pages 456–463, 1994.

[FH03] S. Field and Y. Hoffner. Web services and matchmaking. *International Journal of Networking and Virtual Organisations (IJNVO)*, 1(3):16–32, 2003.

[Fie00] Roy Thomas Fielding. *Architectural Styles and the Design of Network-based Software Architectures*. PhD thesis, University of Calivornia, Irvine, 2000.

[FIP04] FIPA. Foundation for intelligent pysical agents. FIPA spefcifications. http://www.fipa.org, 2004.

[Fis04] Layna Fischer, editor. *The Workflow Handbook 2004*. Future Strategies Inc., 2004.

[FK03] E. Folmer and D. Krukkert. openXchange as ebXML implementation and validation; the first results. In *Proceeding of XML Europe 2003 Conference & Exposition*, May 2003.

[FK04] CCA Forum and Kate Keahey. CCA terms and definitions. http://www.cca-forum.org/glossary.shtml, 2004.

[FKT01] Ian Foster, Carl Kesselman, and Steven Tuecke. The anatomy of the Grid: Enabling scalable virtual organization. *The International Journal of High Performance Computing Applications*, 15(3):200–222, Fall 2001.

[FLM97] Tim Finin, Yannis Labrou, and James Mayfield. KQML as an agent communication language. In Jeffrey M. Bradshaw, editor, *Software Agents*, chapter 14, pages 291–316. AAAI Press / The MIT Press, 1997.

[Fu04] Xiang Fu. *Formal Specification and Verification of Asynchronously Communicating Web Services*. PhD thesis, University of California Santa Barbara, Sept 2004.

[FUMK03] Howard Foster, Sebastian Uchitel, Jeff Magee, and Jeff Krame. Model-based verification of web service compositions. In *Proceedings of 18th IEEE International Conference Automated Software Engineering (ASE)*, pages 152–161, 2003.

[GAHL00] P. Grefen, K. Aberer, Y. Hoffner, and H. Ludwig. CrossFlow: Cross-organizational workflow management in dynamic virtual enterprises. *International Journal of Computer Systems Science & Engineering*, 15(5):277–290, Sep. 2000.

[Gel85] D. Gelernter. Generative communication in linda. *ACM Transactions on Programming Languages und Systems*, 7(1):80–112, 1985.

[Gen87] Hartmann J. Genrich. Predicate/Transition Nets. In W. Brauer, W. Reisig, and G. Rozenberg, editors, *Petri Nets: Central Models and Their Properties, Advances in Petri Nets 1986 Part I*, volume 254 of *Lecture Notes in Computer Science*, pages 207–247. Springer-Verlag, Berlin, Germany, 1987.

[GHS95] D. Georgakopoulos, M. Hornick, and A. Sheth. An Overview of Workflow Management: From Process Modelling to Workflow Automation Infrastructure. *Distributed and Parallel Databases*, 3(2):119–153, April 1995.

[GJ79] M. R. Garey and D. S. Johnson. *Computers and Intractability : A Guide to the Theory of NP-Completeness*. W.H. Freeman, New York, 1979.

[GL00] Benjamin N. Grosof and Yannis Labrou. An approach to using XML and a rule-based content language with an agent communication language. In Frank Dignum and Mark Greaves, editors, *Issues in Agent Communication*, pages 96–117. Springer-Verlag: Heidelberg, Germany, 2000.

[GLC+95] Benjamin N. Grosof, David W. Levine, Hoi Y. Chan, Colin J. Parris, and Joshua S. Auerbach. Reusable architecture for embedding rule-based intelligence in information agents. In Tim Finin and James Mayfield, editors, *Proceedings of the CIKM Workshop on Intelligent Information Agents*, Baltimore, MD, USA, 1995.

[GLC99] Benjamin N. Grosof, Yannis Labrou, and Hoi Y. Chan. A declarative approach to business rules in contracts: courteous logic programs in XML. In *Proceedings of the 1st ACM Conference on Electronic Commerce*, pages 68–77. ACM Press, 1999.

[Glo05] Globus. Open grid services architecture. http://www.globus.org/ogsa/, 2005.

[Gra78] Jim Gray. Notes on data base operating systems. In Michael J. Flynn, Jim Gray, Anita K. Jones, Klaus Lagally, Holger Opderbeck, Gerald J. Popek, Brian Randell, Jerome H. Saltzer, and Hans-Rüdiger Wiehle, editors, *Operating Systems, An Advanced Course*, volume 60 of *Lecture Notes in Computer Science*, pages 393–481. Springer, 1978.

[GSCB99] Dimitrios Georgakopoulos, Hans Schuster, Andrzej Chichocki, and Donald Baker. Managing process and service fusion in virtual enterprises. *Information Systems*, 24(6):429–456, Sept 1999.

[GWW01] C. Gunter, S. Weeks, and A. Wright. Models and languages for digital rights. In *Proceedings of the 34th Hawaii International Conference on System Sciences (HICSS)*, page 9076. IEEE Computer Society, 2001.

[Hac76] M.H.T. Hack. The equality problem for vector addition systems is undeciadable. *Theoretical Computer Science*, 2:77–95, 1976.

[Han] J. E. Hanson. cpXML: Conversation policy XML version 1.0. http://www.research.ibm.com/convsupport/papers/index.html.

[Har87] D. Harel. Statecharts: A visual formalism for complex systems. *Science of Computer Programming*, 8(3):231–274, June 1987.

[HB04] Hugo Haas and Allen Brown. Web services gloassary. http://www.w3.org/TR/2004/NOTE-ws-gloss-20040211/, Feb 2004.

[HLGA01] Y. Hoffner, H. Ludwig, P. Grefen, and K. Aberer. CrossFlow: integrating workflow management and electronic commerce. *ACM SIGecom Exchanges*, 2(1):1–10, 2001.

[HMU01] J. E. Hopcroft, R. Motwani, and J. D. Ullman. *Introduction to Automata Theory, Languages, and Computation*. Addison Wesley, 2001.

[HN96] D. Harel and A. Naamad. The STATEMATE semantics of statecharts. *ACM Transactions on Software Engineering and Methodology*, 5(4):293–333, 1996.

[HNL02] James E. Hanson, Prabir Nandi, and David W. Levine. Conversation-enabled web services for agents and e-business. In *Proceedings of the International Conference on Internet Computing (IC)*, pages 791–796. CSREA Press, 2002.

[HPS+00] James G. Hayes, Effat Peyrogvian, Sunil Sarin, Marc-Thomas Schmidt, Keith D. Swenson, and Rainer Weber. Workflow interoperability standards for the internet. *IEEE Internet Computing*, 4(3):37–45, 2000.

[HS01] Ian Horrocks and Ulrike Sattler. Ontology reasoning for the SHOQ(D) description logic. In Bernhard Nebel, editor, *Proceedings of the seventeenth International Conference on Artificial Intelligence (IJCAI)*, pages 199–204, San Francisco, CA, Aug 2001. Morgan Kaufmann.

[HW01] W. Hasselbring and H. Weigand. Languages for electronic business communication: State of the art. *Industrial Management & Data Systems*, 101(5):217–227, 2001.

[HY97] Amir Herzberg and Hilik Yochai. MiniPay: charging per click on the web. In *Selected papers from the sixth international conference on World Wide Web*, pages 939–951. Elsevier Science Publishers Ltd., 1997.

[ICE04] ICE. Information and content exchange protocol home page. http://www.icestandard.org/, 2004.

[IET] IETF. Internet engineering task force. http://www.ietf.org/.

[IMH+02] IBM, Microsoft, HP, Oracle, Intel, and SAP. Universal description, discovery and integration, July 2002. http://www.uddi.org/.

[Int04] Intertrust. Intertrust home page. http://www.intertrust.com/, 2004.

[Jen92] K. Jensen. *Coloured Petri Nets*. Springer Verlag, Heidelberg, 1992.

[jud] juddi. jUDDI. http://ws.apache.org/juddi.

[Kay03] Doug Kaye. *Loosely Coupled - The Missing Pieces of Web Services*. RDS Press, 2003.

[KB01] Mark Klein and Abraham Bernstein. Searching for services on the semantic web using process ontologies. In *Proceedings of 1st Semantic Web Working Symposium (SWWS)*, Stanford, 2001.

[KH95] Daniel Kuokka and Larry Harada. On using KQML for matchmaking. In Victor Lesser, editor, *Proceedings of the First International Conference on Multi-Agent Systems (ICMAS)*, pages 239–245, San Francisco, CA, USA, 1995. The MIT Press: Cambridge, MA, USA.

[Kim98] S. Kimbrough. Formal language for business communication (FLBC): Sketch of a basic theory. *International Journal of Electronic Commerce*, 3(2):23ff, 1998.

[KM97] Steven O. Kimbrough and Scott A. Moore. On automated message processing in electronic commerce and work support systems: Speech act theory and expressive felicity. *ACM Transactions on Information Systems*, 15(4):321–367, 1997.

[KMR00] Ekkart Kindler, Axel Martens, and Wolfgang Reisig. Inter-operability of workflow applications: Local criteria for global soundness. In *Business Process Management, Models, Techniques, and Empirical Studies*, pages 235–253. Springer-Verlag, 2000.

[Kru03] Dennis Krukkert. Matchmaking of ebXML business processes. Technical Report IST-28584-OX_D2.3_v.2.0, openXchange Project, Oct 2003.

[KWA99] J. Klingemann, J. Wäsch, and K. Aberer. Adaptive outsourcing in cross-organizational workflows. In *Proceedings of the the 11th Conference on Advanced Information Systems Engineering (CAiSE)*, pages 417–421, Heidelberg, Germany, June 1999.

[Lev66] L. I. Levenshtein. Binary codes capable of correcting deletions, insertions, and reversals,. *Soviet Physics–Doklady*, 10(8):707–710, 1966.

[LF94] Y. Labrou and T. W. Finin:. A semantics approach for KQML - a general purpose communication language for software agents. In *Proceedings of International Conference on Information and Knowledge Management (CIKM)*, pages 447–455, 1994.

[LH03] Lei Li and Ian Horrocks. A software framework for matchmaking based on semantic web technology. In *Proceedings of the twelfth international conference on World Wide Web*, pages 331–339. ACM Press, 2003.

[LKD+03] Heiko Ludwig, Alexander Keller, Asit Dan, Richard King, and Richard Franck. A service level agreement language for dynamic electronic services. *Electronic Commerce Research*, 3(1-2):43–59, 2003.

[Lut02] Carsten Lutz. *The Complexity of Description Logics with Concrete Domains*. PhD thesis, Teaching and Research Area for Theoretical Computer Science, RWTH Aachen, 2002.

[Lut03] C. Lutz. Description logics with concrete domains—a survey. In *Advances in Modal Logics Volume 4*. King's College Publications, 2003.

[Lyn96] Nancy A. Lynch. *Distributed Algorithms*. Morgan Kaufmann, 1996.

[Mar02] Dan C. Marinescu. *Internet-Based Workflow Management - Towards a Semantic Web*. John Wiley, 2002.

[Mar04] Axel Martens. Analysis and re-engineering of web services. In *Proceedings of 6th International Conference on Enterprise Information Systems (ICEIS)*, pages 419–426, 2004.

[MB03] L. G. Meredith and Steve Bjorg. Contracts and types. *Communications of the ACM*, 46(10):41–47, 2003.

[MC94] Thomas W. Malone and Kevin Crowston. The interdisciplinary study of coordination. *ACM Computing Surveys (CSUR)*, 26(1):87–119, 1994.

[Mey88] J.-J. CH. Meyer. A different approach to deontic logic: Deontic logic viewed as a variant of dynamic logic. *Notre Dame Journal of Formal Logic*, 29(1):109–136, 1988.

[MGT+98] Michael Merz, Frank Griffel, M. T. Tu, Stefan Muller-Wilken, Harald Weinreich, Marko Boger, and Winfried Lamersdorf. Supporting electronic commerce transactions with contracting services. *International Journal of Cooperative Information Systems*, 7(4):249–274, 1998.

[Mic99] Thierry Michel. Common markup for micropayment per-fee-links. http://www.w3.org/TR/WD-Micropayment-Markup/, 1999.

[MJSSW03] Carlos Molina-Jimenez, Santosh Shrivastava, Ellis Solaiman, and John Warne. Contract representation for run-time monitoring and enforcement. In *Proceedings of Conference on Electronic Commerce (CEC)*, pages 103–110. IEEE, 2003.

[MKL+02] Dejan Milojičić, Vana Kalogeraki, Rajan Lukose, Kiran Nagaraja, Jim Pruyne, Bruno Richard, Sami Rollins, and Zhichen Xu. Peer-to-peer computing. Technical report, HP Labs Technical Report, HPL-2002-57, 2002.

[MMP+95] O. Matz, A. Miller, A. Podtthoff, W. Thomas, and E. Valkema. Report on the program AMoRE. Technical Report 9507, Christian-Albrechts Universtaet, 1995.

[Moh98] C. Mohan. Workflow management in the internet age. In Witold Litwin, Tadeusz Morzy, and Gottfried Vossen, editors, *Proceedings of the Second East European Symposium on Advances in Databases and Information Systems (ADBIS)*, pages 26–34. Springer LNCS 1475, Sept 1998.

[Moo00] Scott A. Moore. KQML and FLBC: Contrasting agent communication languages. *International Journal of Electronic Commerce*, 5(1):109ff, 2000.

[MPC01] M. Mecella, B. Pernici, and P. Craca. Compatibility of e-services in a cooperative multi-platform environment. In F. Casati, D. Georgakopoulos, and M. Shan, editors, *Proceedings of 2rd International Workshop on Technologies for E-Services (TES)*, pages 44–57. Springer LNCS 2193, 2001.

[MSZ01] S. McIlraith, T. Son, and H. Zeng. Semantic web services. *IEEE Intelligent Systems (Special Issue on the Semantic Web)*, April 2001.

[MWD98] J. Meyer, R. Wieringa, and F. Dignum. The role of deontic logic in the specification of information systems. In J. Chomicki and G. Saake, editors, *Logics for Databases and Information Systems*. Kluwer, 1998.

[OMG97] OMG. Omg business object domain task force BODTF-RFP 2 submission workflow management facility, jFlow - joint RFP submission. http://www.omg.org/docs/bom/97-08-05.pdf, Aug 1997.

[OMG04] OMG. Object management group. http://www.omg.org, 2004.

[OT02] S. Overhage and P. Thomas. Ws-specification: Specifying web services using UDDI improvements. In A.B. Chaudhri, M. Jeckle, E. Rahm, and R. Unland, editors, *Web, Web-Services, and Database Systems: NODe, Web- and Database-Related Workshops, Erfurt, Germany*, volume 2593, pages 100 – 119. Springer LNCS, 2002.

[OTA04] OTA. Open travel alliance (OTA). http://www.opentravel.org, 2004.

[ÖV99] M. Tamer Özsu and Patrick Valduriez. *Principles of Distributed Database Systems*. Prentice Hall, 2 edition, 1999.

[Pan98] Giovanni Panti. Multi-valued logics. In Dov Gabbay and Philippe Smets, editors, *Handbook of Defeasible Reasoning and Uncertainty Management Systems*, volume 1: Quantified Representation of Uncertainty and Imprecision, chapter 2, pages 25–74. Kluwer, Dordrecht, October 1998.

[PAPY02] Mike Papazoglou, Marco Aiello, Marco Pistore, and Jian Yang. Planning for requests against web services. *Bulletin of the Technical Commitee on Data Engineering*, 25(4):41–46, Dec 2002.

[Per95] A. Peron. Statecharts, transition structures and transformations. In *Proceedings International Conference Colloquium on Trees in Algebra and Programming (CAAP-TAPSOFT'95, Springer, LNCS 915)*, pages 454–468, 1995.

[Pet62] C. A. Petri. *Kommunikation mit Automaten.* Schriften des Institutes fur Instrumentelle Mathematik, Bonn, 1962.

[Pet81] James L. Peterson. *Petri Net Theory and the Modeling of Systems.* Prentice-Hall, 1981.

[PH02] Jeff Z. Pan and Ian Horrocks. Extending datatype support in Web ontology reasoning. In *International Conference on Ontologies, Databases and Applications of Semantics (ODBASE)*, volume 2519 of *LNCS*. Springer, 2002.

[php04] openXchange project home page. http://www.openxchange.org/, 2004.

[PKPS02] M. Paolucci, T. Kawmura, T. Payne, and K. Sycara. Semantic matching of web services capabilities. In *First International Semantic Web Conference*, volume 2342 of *LNCS*, pages 333–347. Springer, 2002.

[PL01] Randall Perrey and Mark Lycett. Workflow standards and XML. In *Americas Conference on Information Systems*, 2001.

[PN03] Sanjay Patil and Eric Newcomer. ebxml and web services. *IEEE Internet Computing*, 7(3):74–82, 2003.

[PRR97] C. Greg Plaxton, Rajmohan Rajaraman, and Andrea W. Richa. Accessing nearby copies of replicated objects in a distributed environment. In *ACM Symposium on Parallel Algorithms and Architectures*, pages 311–320, 1997.

[PSG02] Anna Perini, Angelo Susi, and Fausto Giunchiglia. Coordination specification in multi-agent systems. from requirements to architecture with tropos methodology. In *Proceedings of SEKE*. ACM, 2002.

[PSNS03] Massimo Paolucci, Katia Sycara, Takuya Nishimura, and Naveen Srinivasan. Using DAML-S for P2P discovery. In *Proceedings of the First International Conference on Web Services (ICWS)*, pages 203–207, 2003.

[RKW04] Thomas Risse, Predrag Knezevic, and Andreas Wombacher:. P2P evolution: From file-sharing to decentralized workflows. *it-Information Technology*, 4:193–199, 2004.

[Ros04] RosettaNet. RosettaNet home page. http://www.rosettanet.org, 2004.

[SBG$^+$00] Hans-Jorg Schek, Klemens Böhm, Torsten Grabs, Uwe Rohm, Heiko Schuldt, and Roger Weber. Hyperdatabases. In *Web Information Systems Engineering*, pages 14–25, 2000.

[SBW95] Olin Sibert, David Bernstein, and David Van Wie. The DigiBox: A self-protecting container for information commerce. In *Proceedings 1st USENIX workshop on Electronic Commerce*, pages 171–183, 1995.

[Sch04] Jens Schiedung. Analysing and modelling of IOTP business transactions using coloured petri nets and BPEL. Master's thesis, Technical University of Darmstadt, 2004.

[SGH00] Bernd Schopp, Markus Greunz, and Joachim Haes. Supporting market transactions through XML contracting container. In *Proceedings of the Sixth Americas Conference on Information Systems (AMCISS)*, Long Beach, CA,, Aug 2000.

[Sin03] Munindar P. Singh. Distributed enactment of multiagent workflows. In *Proceedings of the 2nd International Joint Conference on Autonomous Agents and MultiAgent Systems (AAMAS)*, pages 907–914. ACM Press, July 2003.

[SPS04] Naveen Srinivasan, Massimo Paolucci, and Katia Sycara. Adding OWL-S to UDDI, implementation and throughput. In *First International Workshop on Semantic Web Services and Web Process Composition (SWSWPC)*, 2004.

[SS96] Kjeld Schmidt and Carla Simone. Coordination mechanisms: Towards a conceptual foundation of CSCW systems design. *Computer Supported Cooperative Work - The Journal of Collaborating Computing*, 5(2/3):155–200, 1996.

[SSOH95] T. Stricker, J. Stichnoth, D. O'Hallaron, and S. Hinrichs. Decoupling synchronization and data transfer in message passing systems of parallel computers. In ACM, editor, *Proceedings of the 9th International Conference on Supercomputing*, pages 1–10. ACM Press, Jul 1995.

[SSSW02] H. Schek, H. Schuldt, C. Schuler, and R. Weber. Infrastructure for information spaces. In *Proceedings of the 6 th East-European Conference on Advances in Databases and Information Systems (ADBIS)*, pages 22–36, Bratislava, Slovakia, Sept 2002. Springer LNCS 2435.

[SWSS04] C. Schuler, R. Weber, H. Schuldt, and H.J. Schek. Scalable peer-to-peer process management - the OSIRIS approach. In *Proceedings of IEEE International Conference on Web Services (ICWS)*, pages 26–34. IEEE Computer Society, July 2004.

[Tea01] Business Process Team. Business process specification schema v1.01, May 2001.

[TG01] Robert Tolksdorf and Dirk Glaubitz. Coordinating Web-based systems with documents in XMLSpaces. *Lecture Notes in Computer Science*, 2172:356ff, 2001.

[Tol00a] R. Tolksdorf. Coordinating work on the web with workspaces. In *Proceedings 9th IEEE International Workshop on Enabling Technologies: Infrastructure for Collaborative Enterprises (WETICE)*. IEEE Computer Society, 2000.

[Tol00b] R. Tolksdorf. Coordination Technology for Workflows on the Web: Workspaces. In *Proceedings 4th International Conference on Coordination Models and Languages*, Lecture Notes in Computer Science, pages 36–50. Springer-Verlag, Berlin, 2000.

[Tyg98] J. D. Tygar. Atomicity versus anonymity: Distributed transactions for electronic commerce. In *Proceedings of International Conference on Very Large Databases (VLDB)*, pages 1–12, 1998.

[udd03] uddie. UDDIe homepage, 2003.

[Uni99] International Telecommunication Union. Message sequence charts. ITU-T Recommendation Z.120, Nov 1999.

[VSS$^+$04] K. Verma, K. Sivashanmugam, A. Sheth, A. Patil, S. Oundhakar, and J. Miller. METEOR-S WSDI: A scalable infrastructure of registries for semantic publication and discovery of web services. *Journal of Information Technology and Management*, 2004.

[W3C02] W3C. Web service choreography interface (WSCI) 1.0. http://www.w3.org/TR/wsci/, Aug 2002.

[W3C04a] W3C. Web services architecture - W3C working group note. http://www.w3.org/TR/2004/NOTE-ws-arch-20040211, Feb 2004.

[W3C04b] W3C. Web services choreography description language version 1.0. http://www.w3.org/TR/ws-cdl-10/, Oct 2004.

[WF86] T. Winograd and F. Flores. *Understanding Computers and Cognition*. Addison-Wesley, Boston, 1986.

[WfM04a] WfMC. WfMC workflow reference model. http://www.wfmc.org/standards/model.htm, 2004.

[WfM04b] WfMC. Workflow management coalition. http://www.wfmc.org, 2004.

[WFN04] A. Wombacher, P. Fankhauser, and E. Neuhold. Transforming BPEL into annotated deterministic finite state automata enabling process annotated service discovery. In

Proceedings of International Conference on Web Services (ICWS), pages 316–323, 2004.

[WH01] Hans Weigand and Wilhelm Hasselbring. An extensible business communication language. *International Journal of Cooperative Information Systems*, 10(4):423–441, 2001.

[WMN04] Andreas Wombacher, Bendick Mahleko, and Erich Neuhold. IPSI-PF: A business process matchmaking engine. In *Proceedings of Conference on Electronic Commerce (CEC)*, pages 137–145, 2004.

[WMR03] Andreas Wombacher, Bendick Mahleko, and Thomas Risse. Classification of ad hoc multi-lateral collaborations based on workflow models. In *Proceedings of Symposium on Applied Computing (ACM-SAC)*, pages 1185–1190, 2003.

[WMW89] R. Wieringa, J-J. Meyer, and H. Weigand. Specifying dynamic and deontic integrity constraints. *Data and Knowledge Engineering, N-H*, 4(2), 1989.

[WOH+98] Neil Webber, Conleth O'Connell, Bruce Hunt, Rick Levine, Laird Popkin, and Gord Larose. The information and content exchange (ICE) protocol. http://www.w3.org/TR/1998/NOTE-ice-19981026, 1998.

[Wom05a] Andreas Wombacher. Competition proposal for decentralized service composition. In *Proceedings of Conference on Electronic Commerce (CEC)*, 2005. submitted.

[Wom05b] Andreas Wombacher. Decentralized decision making protocol for service composition. In *Proceedings IEEE International Conference on Web Services (ICWS)*. IEEE Computer Society, 2005. submitted.

[Wor04] WordNet. a lexical database for the english language. http://wordnet.princeton.edu, 2004.

[WVD96] H. Weigand, E. Verharen, and F. Dignum. Integrated semantics for information and communication systems. In *Proceedings of the Sixth IFIP TC-2 Working Conference on Data Semantics*, pages 500–525. Chapman & Hall, Ltd., 1996.

[WvdH98] Hans Weigand and Willem-Jan van den Heuvel. Meta-patterns for electronic commerce based on FLBC. In *Proceedings of the 31nd Hawaii International Conference on System Sciences (HICSS)*, page 261ff. IEEE Press, 1998.

[WW97] Dirk Wodtke and Gerhard Weikum. A formal foundation for distributed workflow execution based on state charts. In Foto N. Afrati and Phokion Kolaitis, editors, *Proceedings of the 6th International Conference on Database Theory (ICDT)*, pages 230–246. Springer LNCS 1186, jan 1997.

[XML04] XMLSpaces. homepage. http://www.inf.fu-berlin.de/inst/ag-nbi/research/xmlspaces/, 2004.

[YK04] Xiaochuan Yi and Krys J. Kochut. Process composition of web services with complex conversation protocols: a colored petri nets based approach. In *Proceedings of the Design, Analysis, and Simulation of Distributed Systems Symposium at Adavanced Simulation Technology Conference*, pages 141–148, 2004.

[ZBNN01] L. Zeng, B. Benatallah, P. Nguyen, and A. H. H. Ngu. AGFlow: Agent-based cross-enterprise workflow management system. In P. M. G. Apers, P. Atzeni, S. Ceri, S. Paraboschi, K. Ramamohanarao, and R. T. Snodgrass, editors, *Proceedings of 27 International Conference on Very Large Databases (VLDB)*, pages 697–699, 2001.

[ZFCJ02] Liangzhao Zeng, David Flaxer, Henry Chang, and Jun-Jang Jeng. PLMflow - dynamic business process composition and execution by rule inference. In *Proceedings of 3rd International Workshop, Technologies for E-Services (TES)*, LNCS 2444, pages 141–150. Springer, 2002.

[ZNBO01] Liangzhao Zeng, Anne Ngu, Boualem Benatallah, and Milton O'Dell. An agent-based approach for supporting cross-enterprise workflows. In *Proceedings of the 12th Australasian conference on Database technologies*, pages 123–130. IEEE Computer Society, 2001.

Appendix A

Appendix

A.1 Example Requiring Unique Message Names

In the following, an example of a multi-lateral workflow is presented which is considered to be consistent if message names are not unique, although the multi-lateral collaboration is considered to be inconsistent if message names are not disambiguated. The representation of an automaton with disambiguated message names as a normalized automaton is discussed in Section 4.3.8. The reason for the wrong consistency decision is that history constraints are represented as sets, thus disregarding order and multiple occurrence of messages. To illustrate the effect, let's discuss the example depicted in Figure A.1.

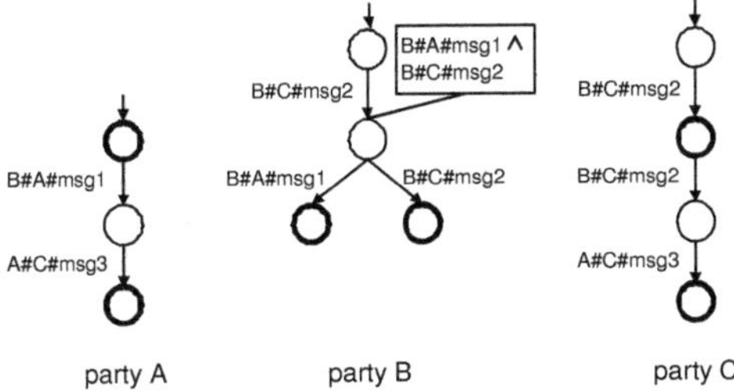

Figure A.1: Guarded aFSA Representation of Local Workflows

Three parties *A*, *B*, and *C* are involved in a multi-lateral collaboration. The workflow starts with *B* sending message *B#C#msg*2 to party *C*. Afterwards, party *B* has to decide to continue the process either by sending message *B#C#msg*2 to party *C* again, or sending message *B#A#msg*1 to party *A*. However, party *A* finally has to send message *A#C#msg*3 to party *C*. Constructing the multi-lateral workflow by the intersection of the extended local workflows results in the automaton depicted in Figure A.2. Since the multi-lateral workflow is empty, the multi-lateral collaboration is inconsistent.

Applying the parameter constraint propagation on the local workflows resulting in a fixed point as discussed in Section 4.3.9 and applying the occurrence graph constraint propagation the first time

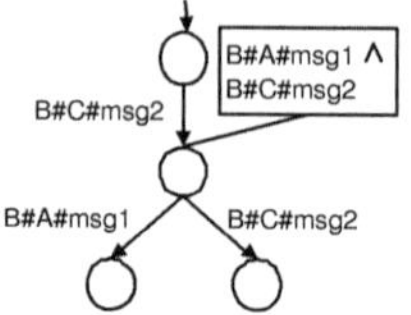

Figure A.2: Guarded aFSA Representation of Multi-lateral Workflow

as introduced in Section 4.3.10, while the identically labeled messages are not disambiguated results in the automata depicted in Figure A.3. This representation of the local workflows is already a fixed point.

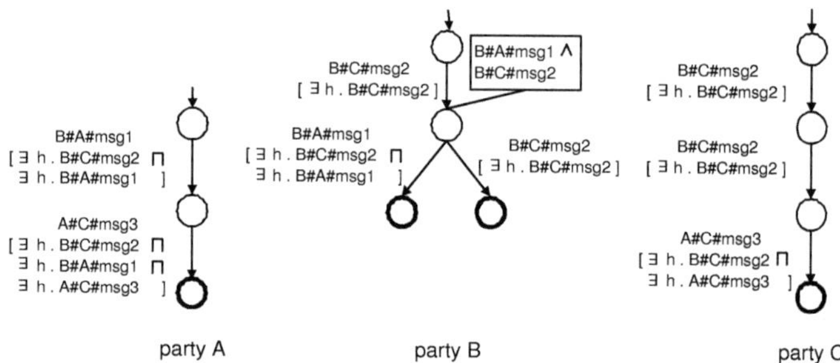

Figure A.3: Fixed Point Local Workflows Without Disambiguated Messages

Since each local workflow is consistent, the multi-lateral collaboration is considered to be consistent, although it is not. Wrong decision making is caused by the duplicate usage of message *B#C#msg*2. In particular, the history role cannot distinguish between the first and second occurrence of message *B#C#msg*2, thus, it seems to suffice if the message has been exchanged at least once. However, the number of a message that has been exchanged has to be equal in every path. As a consequence, different occurrences of identically labeled messages are annotated by a subscripted number of occurrence of this message in a path to reach the message. Applying parameter constraint propagation again, resulting in a fixed point, and applying the first occurrence graph constraint propagation results in the automata depicted in Figure A.4.

The last transition in party A's workflow is false $\bot$, because the subsumption

$$B\#A\#msg1_1 \sqcap B\#C\#msg2_1 \sqcap A\#C\#msg3_1 \subseteq B\#A\#msg1_1 \sqcap B\#C\#msg2_1 \sqcap B\#C\#msg2_2 \sqcap A\#C\#msg3_1$$

is not fulfilled, thus, the guard expression is set to $\bot$. This is similar for the last transition in party

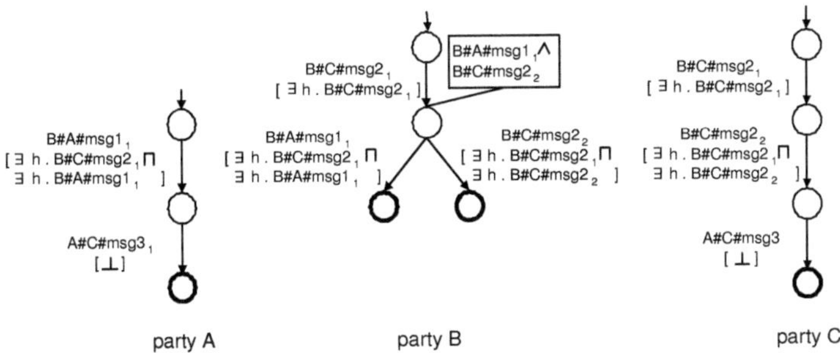

Figure A.4: Fixed Point Local Workflows With Disambiguated Messages

B's workflow, where

$$B\#C\#msg2_1 \sqcap B\#C\#msg2_2 \sqcap A\#C\#msg3_1 \subseteq B\#A\#msg1_1 \sqcap B\#C\#msg2_1 \sqcap B\#C\#msg2_2 \sqcap A\#C\#msg3_1$$

is not fulfilled.

As a consequence, party *A* and *C* are empty, therefore the multi-lateral collaboration is considered to be inconsistent.

A.2 Normalization Operation on Guarded Annotated Finite State Automata

In the following a procedure is specified, which allows the derivation of an acyclic normalized guarded aFSA in accordance with Definition 4.38 from a guarded aFSA.

Definition A.1
A guarded aFSA $A = (Q, \Sigma, \Delta, q_0, F, QA, G, P)$ can be transformed into a normalized acyclic guarded aFSA A' where $A' := \Theta(A, \emptyset, \top, q_0, q_0, \emptyset, \emptyset)$ which models a finite subset of the language of a guarded aFSA using the definition of Θ defined as follows:

$$\Theta\begin{pmatrix} A \\ path \\ e'_i \\ q_{cur} \\ q_{new} \\ t_{new} \\ \theta \end{pmatrix}^T := \begin{pmatrix} \{q_{new}\} \cup \bigcup_{(q_{cur},\alpha,q)\in\Delta,e''_i} Q'' \\ \{\alpha_{new}\} \cup \bigcup_{(q_{cur},\alpha,q)\in\Delta,e''_i} \Sigma'' \\ \{t_{new}\} \cup \bigcup_{(q_{cur},\alpha,q)\in\Delta,e''_i} \Delta'' \\ q_0 \\ \left(\bigcup_{(q_{cur},\alpha,q)\in\Delta,e''_i} F''\right) \cup \begin{cases} \{q_{new}\} & if\ q_{cur} \in F \\ \emptyset & otherwise \end{cases} \\ \{(q_{new}, \tau_a(\tilde{e}, \tilde{\theta}))\} \cup \bigcup_{(q_{cur},\alpha,q)\in\Delta,e''_i} QA'' \\ \{(t_{new}, \tau_g(e'_i, \theta))\} \cup \bigcup_{(q_{cur},\alpha,q)\in\Delta,e''_i} G'' \\ P \end{pmatrix}^T$$

where $path$ is the path of transitions already traversed to reach the current state q_{cur} of the original automaton A. Further, the state q_{new} represents the equivalent of q_{cur} within the result automaton, while transition $t_{new} = (q'_{new}, \alpha_{new}, q_{new})$ is the equivalent of the last transition contained in $path$. The last transition's guard expression e can be normalized in disjunctive normal form resulting in a disjunction of conjunctions $e' = e'_1 \sqcup \ldots \sqcup e'_n$, while each e'_i is treated explicitly. e''_i represents a conjunction of the disjunctive normal form of the guard expression e'' associated to transition $(q_{cur}, \alpha, q) \in \Delta$ being a transition reachable from the current state q_{cur}. The annotation of state q_{cur} is given by $\tilde{e}$, that is, $(q_{cur}, \tilde{e}) \in QA$. The automaton $A'' = (Q'', \Sigma'', \Delta'', q_0, F'', QA'', G'', P)$ is derived by the following recursion:

$$A'' := \begin{cases} \Theta(A, path.(q_{cur}, \alpha, q), e''_i, q, q', (q_{new}, \alpha_j, q'), \theta \cup \{\alpha \to \alpha_j\}) & if\ Occ((q_{cur}, \alpha, q), path) \leq N \\ (\emptyset, \emptyset, \emptyset, q_0, \emptyset, \emptyset, \emptyset, P) & otherwise \end{cases}$$

where q' is a new unique identifier of a new state in the result automaton corresponding to q of the original automaton and α_j is the j-th occurrence of α in $path$. The relevant substitutions $\tilde{\theta}$ for the annotations are constructed as follows:

$$\tilde{\theta} := \bigcup_{(q,\alpha,q')\in\Delta} \begin{cases} \{\alpha \to \alpha_j\} & if\ Occ((q, \alpha, q'), path) \leq N \\ \{\alpha \to intermediate\} & otherwise \end{cases}$$

where j in α_j represents the number of occurrences of α in $path$.

A.3 List of Figures

Printed by Books on Demand GmbH, Norderstedt / Germany